THE POETICS OF
YVES BONNEFOY

THE POETICS OF
YVES BONNEFOY

JOHN T. NAUGHTON

THE UNIVERSITY OF CHICAGO PRESS

CHICAGO AND LONDON

John T. Naughton is assistant professor of
Romance languages and literatures, Colgate
University. He has taught at the University
of Tours and the University of California at
Santa Cruz.

The University of Chicago Press, Chicago 60637
The University of Chicago Press, Ltd., London

93 92 91 90 89 88 87 86 85 84   54321

Library of Congress Cataloging in Publication Data

Naughton, John T.
  The poetics of Yves Bonnefoy.

  Bibliography: p.
  Includes index.
  1. Bonnefoy, Yves—Criticism and interpretation.
I. Title.
PQ2603.O533Z8   1984   841'.914   83-18075
ISBN 0-226-56947-0

For my mother, my wife, and my daughter

Contents

Preface

Yves Bonnefoy has long been considered the most important poet to have emerged in France since the Second World War. He is also a literary and art critic of the first rank, a celebrated translator of English poets, particularly of Shakespeare, and a specialist in the problem of the relation of poetry to the visual arts. His recent election to the Collège de France—to fill the seat vacated by the untimely death of Roland Barthes—is official recognition of his contributions to contemporary French intellectual life. As no full-length study of his work has yet appeared in English, I hope that the present book will provide a useful introduction not only for French scholars but also for a more general reading public.

My thinking about Yves Bonnefoy has been enriched by the contributions of a number of distinguished scholars: John E. Jackson and Jean Starobinski, Richard Vernier, Alex E. Gordon, Mary Ann Caws, and Richard Stamelman, among many others. I gratefully acknowledge my indebtedness to them.

The translations from the French in this book are, in all cases, my own, although I make no particular claim for them. We translate, Bonnefoy himself has said, in order to better understand a text, and it has been a joy for me to try in this way to know his work more intimately. I do hope, of course, that readers will go to the French text indicated at the end of every passage cited. I do not feel entirely comfortable including only the English translation of Bonnefoy's prose, but it did seem less awkward to present only the poems in both French and English. Readers will surely want to consult the other translations of his poetry, which are excellent and illuminating. Ohio University Press has published Galway Kinnell's translation of *Du mouvement et de l'immobilité de Douve* under the title *On the Motion and Immobility of Douve* (1968). Susanna Lang's translation of *Pierre écrite* (*Words in Stone*) was published by the University of Massachusetts Press in 1976. The publication of Bonnefoy's collected poems in English is planned by Random House, under the direction of John Galasi and Galway Kinnell. The University of Chicago Press will be bringing out a selection of Bonnefoy's prose, translated by Susanna Lang.

Since Bonnefoy is still an extremely active writer, and since new texts are regularly being published, the bibliography provided at the end of this work is, as might be expected, incomplete. My book was, for the most part, finished before the publication of the most recent texts. At least two of these should be mentioned here: the Bonnefoy interviews on poetry and poetics entitled *Entretiens sur la poésie*, published in Switzerland by the Éditions de la Baconnière, and the "Inaugural Lesson at the *Collège de France*," published in France by the Mercure de France, and in America, in an English translation, by the *New Literary History*.

The title *The Poetics of Yves Bonnefoy* points to the fact that this study seeks to define a general orientation, an *intention*, and does not pretend to deal exhaustively with all the poems. On many occasions I would have liked to have spent more time on individual poems, many of which merit prolonged analysis. My constant desire, however, was to respect a total effort, to strive for the comprehensive overview of an immensely complex and varied opus. I tried to keep in mind what Bonnefoy himself has said: "The more one seeks to analyze the subtleties, the ambiguities of expression, the more one risks forgetting an effort at salvation which is the only real concern of the poem" (*I*, 250). Bonnefoy's best translator, the American poet Galway Kinnell, has said much the same thing: "I distrust discussions of poetry which are heavily technical; the source of the poem, and all its worth, lie in what one knows and feels."

I would like to express my thanks to the University of California for fellowship support granted me for the academic year 1979–80. This support greatly facilitated the completion of a first version of the present study. In addition, I would like to acknowledge my deep gratitude to my friend Martin Kanes, of the State University of New York at Albany, who has been a careful reader of my work at every stage of its development. His wide knowledge and experience in literary matters, together with his meticulousness and good taste in questions of style, were of great help to me. Many weaknesses of this study were minimized through Martin Kanes's attentiveness and concern.

I would also like to thank Jean Alter of the University of Pennslvania and Robert W. Greene of the State University of New York for their interest in my work. Jean Alter was an unusually perceptive reader who helped me to see my own rhetorical emphases in clearer perspective. I was very lucky to have in Robert W. Greene the assistance and encouragement of an expert in the general field of my inquiry.

The comments of other readers and friends were also of great value to me. Priscilla Shaw and Harry Berger of the University of California at Santa Cruz were of particular assistance during the early stages of this work. Maureen McCarthy and Bett Miller gave me the advantage of their attentive readings and helpful suggestions. Kenneth Fields of Stanford

University and Richard Stamelman of Wesleyan University provided constant support and encouragement for this project, and I thank them for it here.

I owe a very special debt of gratitude to Helen T. Naughton of the College of Notre Dame in Belmont, California, not only for her unfailing patience and generosity in reading and commenting on this manuscript, but also, and especially, for her example.

Finally, I should say a word or two about Yves Bonnefoy himself. I first met him in the context of the "Distinguished French Visitor Program" organized by Martin Kanes for the Literature Board at the University of California at Santa Cruz. Bonnefoy was for me then, as now, an attentive and generous presence, quick to offer suggestions and advice about my work and to engage me in that kind of free and equal dialogue in which one is somehow made to feel not so much the superiority of the other as the interest and the support. When I was later encouraged by my colleagues at Santa Cruz to undertake a comprehensive study of his work, I wrote to Bonnefoy to ask him what he thought. His response was prompt and positive. His assistance in my work, whether in providing inaccessible texts or in answering questions, has been of an exemplary generosity. In his case, kindness and simplicity are not incompatible with literary greatness. I am not alone in this experience; many scholars both in America and in Europe have been touched by Bonnefoy's kindnesses. On the occasion of a reading at Wesleyan University in the fall of 1979, Richard Stamelman justly remarked in his introduction that Yves Bonnefoy is a poet "in the fullest and deepest meaning of that word, as much in his everyday life as in his poetry." To know the man, to study his work, is an occasion for gratitude: ". . . ad ora ad ora / m'insegnavate come l'uom s'etterna."

Abbreviations

P   *Poèmes* (Mercure de France, 1978)

I   *L'Improbable* suivi de *Un Rêve fait à Mantoue*
        (Mercure de France, 1980)

R   *Rimbaud, par lui-même* (Seuil, 1961)

AP   *L'Arrière-pays* (Skira, 1972)

NR   *Le Nuage rouge* (Mercure de France, 1977)

A QUESTION

Today sensible goods are accessible to all. The crudest man, even the savage, sees the sun and the sky, hears the song of the nightingale, breathes the odor of lilac and lily of the valley, etc. Spiritual goods, on the contrary, are the lot only of the elect. But what if the opposite were the case: what if spiritual goods were accessible to all, what if everyone could assimilate geometry, logic, and the lofty ideals of morality, while sight, hearing, sense of smell were the portion of some only? How then would we establish our hierarchy? Would we continue, as before, to consider spiritual goods beautiful and sublime and declare sensible goods vile and base? Or would the arbiter elegantium (you know, of course, who he is and where he is to be sought) be obliged to proceed to a transmutation of values?

Lev Shestov, *Potestas Clavium*

1　Collaborations

". . . in our lives which have reached a certain stage . . ."

In the spring of 1978, Mercure de France brought out Yves Bonnefoy's collected poems. Bonnefoy had said that he conceived of his poetical enterprise as involving at least four books,[1] and the publication in 1978 of *Poèmes* brought the four major works—*Du mouvement et de l'immobilité de Douve, Hier régnant désert, Pierre écrite,* and *Dans le leurre du seuil*—together in one volume while including the short works *Anti-Platon* and *Dévotion*. The volume represents the fruit of thirty years of serious poetry writing. Taken with the ever increasing body of critical texts—on poetics, on important literary figures, on the arts, on the problematics of the Image and the creative act—the volume of poems signaled that the moment had perhaps come to assess Bonnefoy's work to date, and to argue that he has emerged, since the Second World War, as the most consistently articulate, serious, and interesting spokesman for poetry in France, while slowly elaborating a poetic *opus* of the most impressive ambition and power.

It might be best, in fact, to begin with a poem. This one comes from the collection *Pierre écrite* (1965) and is called "La Lumière, changée."

> Nous ne nous voyons plus dans la même lumière,
> Nous n'avons plus les mêmes yeux, les mêmes mains.
> L'arbre est plus proche et la voix des sources plus vive,
> Nos pas sont plus profonds, parmi les morts.
>
> Dieu qui n'es pas, pose ta main sur notre épaule,
> Ébauche notre corps du poids de ton retour,
> Achève de mêler à nos âmes ces astres,
> Ces bois, ces cris d'oiseaux, ces ombres et ces jours.
>
> Renonce-toi en nous comme un fruit se déchire,
> Efface-nous en toi. Découvre-nous
> Le sens mystérieux de ce qui n'est que simple
> Et fût tombé sans feu dans des mots sans amour.　　　　(P, 211)

THE LIGHT, CHANGED
We no longer see each other in the same light,
We no longer have the same eyes or the same hands.
The tree is closer and the water's voice more lively,
Our steps go deeper now, among the dead.

1

God who are not, put your hand on our shoulder,
Rough-cast our body with the weight of your return,
Finish blending our souls with these stars,
These woods, these bird-cries, these shadows, and these days.

Give yourself up in us the way fruit falls apart,
Have us disappear in you. Reveal to us
The mysterious meaning in what is only simple
And would have fallen without fire in words without love.

Why, and how, has the light been "changed"? What are the components of this transformation? What has constituted the change in vision, in sensual perception? How has the tree become "closer"? What does "closer" have to do with perception, with a "poetics of space?" What is the role of nature, of the concrete real in this vision? Why does Bonnefoy repeatedly use definite articles to describe nature: i.e., *la lumière, l'arbre, la voix des sources*? Why are the trees not given their specific names? Similarly, who are the *nous* ("we" or "us") of this poem? Why has the poet asked that the category "soul" be mixed up entirely with the elements of the real, with woods, with stars, with bird cries? What is the relation of the living to the dead? Why is God an absent presence? Or, put another way, why is God most present when he "is not"? What are the conditions of his return? What is the relation between the "us" and God? With what difficulty has the poet established this "us"? How does God's "renunciation" of himself in "us" contribute to our identification with him? What are the conditions of "effacement?" Why is it necessary? What is the simple? Why is it mysterious, unknown? And what is the relation between language—the poetic act—and the celebration of this mysterious and immanent simple?

These are the key questions one raises reading the entire *œuvre* of Yves Bonnefoy. In this sense, the poem just cited may be seen as a central one, although to use the word "central" is to run the risk of falling into a kind of trap. For, in a way, all the poems are central, and each contributes its part to a giant tapestry. Bonnefoy is like a painter in words: the best way, finally, to appreciate any single poem is to see it in the context of all the other poems (and even all the other texts) Bonnefoy has written. The linear progression we associate with narrative has been effaced; the best way to understand the poems is to read them all "simultaneously," as it were—as one sees a Poussin painting, for instance, as the sum of all its components.

The poem I have cited here is by way of simple introduction. It seemed to me most appropriate to let the poetic text have the first say. My idea is to speak very generally, in the first two chapters of this study, about some of the questions I raise in connection with "La Lumière, changée." In this first chapter I attempt to place Bonnefoy in the context of those wide-ranging preoccupations which structure his poetic vision and define the nature of his poetic quest. In the second, I will focus on the lures which have endangered this quest but through which Bonnefoy has defined himself. The second chapter will look closely at the dangers of what the poet calls "excarnation," will examine Bonnefoy's early relationship with the surrealists, and will define his "poetics" through an assessment of his attitude toward the poetic "world" and prevalent poetic personae. The last four chapters concentrate on each of the four major books of poetry.

To study the work of Yves Bonnefoy is to become aware of an enormous "collaboration" of interests. To enter sensitively into his vision requires that we examine the astonishing range of these preoccupations and try to inform our own vision by what has deepened his. His poetic texts are the intersections of a familiarity with the great works of Western and Byzantine art, of a knowledge of the important metaphysical and existential philosophers as well as of contemporary trends in criticism; they are enriched by his devotion to "les mathématiques sévères," by his translations of Shakespeare, and by his concern for the differences between English and French literature and language; they are inspired by a love of "archaic" texts; they reflect, in his most recent work, an increasing interest in the poetry and philosophy of the Orient. Perhaps most of all, his poetry may be seen as the result of a long and patient contemplation of the concrete real, of the earth. The man who has equated poetry with voyaging[2] is himself an indefatigable traveler, and his vision has been matured and substantiated by the trains and boats which have carried him over the unity of earth in the variety of its seasons and moods. The earth *is*. Bonnefoy will never cease insisting upon it. The earth is our reality. The tree. The stone. Fire. Water. The poet gives speech to the most elementary, to the most intimate of our relationships.

> *Oui, je puis vivre ici. L'ange, qui est la terre,*
> *Va dans chaque buisson et paraître et brûler.*   (P, 226)

> Yes, I can live here. The angel, who is the earth,
> Will in every bush appear and burn.

Our experience of the sacred depends on an acceptance of this "what-is." A great part of the spiritual journey of Yves Bonnefoy will be devoted to mastering his thirst for an "elsewhere," his natural tendency toward *excarnation* and flight. He will strive to see the incarnation of the divine in the real, in the present and unmistakable moment.

> . . . *Et l'attente se change*
> *En ce proche destin, cette heure, ce séjour.*   (P, 224)

> . . . And may our waiting be changed
> Into this destiny close by, this hour, this place.

*   *   *

Bonnefoy has often maintained that the life of an artist is not important.

> It matters little, in fact, what a man's life was. It is not necessary to
> know about it in order to grasp the sense of what he has accom-
> plished. All the more so in that his life grows simpler the moment
> his work touches greatness. The vocation of creativity has very
> little need of the accidents of destiny. (*I*, 166)

These sentiments are consistent with Bonnefoy's general tendency to de-
value the particular differences that exist between people—and are often
explored by the artist, who fusses over what he thinks sets him apart, his
heart and mind "clutching at his difference"—in favor of universal experi-
ence and a poetics of pure ontology, in which words seek to elaborate "the
common speech": "No longer being concerned with anything separated,
closed off, they [words] dissipate the last enchantments of the mythical
self, they speak of the simplest of human desires in the presence of the sim-
plest of objects, which is being; they bring together the universal self"
(*NR*, 279–80). If poetry is for Bonnefoy what painting was for Degas,
that is, "an activity in the absolute, infinitely removed from the anecdote"
(*I*, 166), it is nevertheless true that certain details in his "biography" are
worth retaining and contemplating. I am referring to those details which
Bonnefoy finds useful in discrete biographies—in other words, to "that
part of the life which is related to the work" (*I*, 165).

Yves Bonnefoy was born in Tours, 24 June 1923. His father was a loco-
motive assembly worker and his mother a grade school teacher, as her own
father had been. This grandfather seems to have been a rather remarkable
man. It was at his home ("a large house near the Lot river")[3] that the sum-
mer vacations of Bonnefoy's youth were spent. The grandfather made fur-
nishings and, for his own amusement, wrote, copied, and bound a number
of books. The moments spent at Toirac, in the atemporality of an ever re-
peated summer, were decisive for the development of the young boy's nos-
talgia, but they also determined his deepest affinities.

> Yes, I found this country beautiful; it even formed me in my deep-
> est choices, with its great empty plateaus where the grey stone
> emerges and its rainstorms, sometimes several days long, above
> the closed-up châteaus. (*AP*, 103)

Although interested in poetry from his childhood (he had begun to
write at a very early age), Bonnefoy's studies at the Lycée Descartes in

Tours, and later at the University of Poitiers, were not in literature but rather in mathematics and philosophy. His interest in mathematics was a lasting one, and he abandoned its serious study with the liveliest regret. There is everywhere present in Bonnefoy's work, in fact, the sense of a careful ordering, although I do not mean to suggest that such close attention to matters of construction is a direct reflection of a "mathematical" consciousness. Certain elements of this attentiveness, although they may seem at first sight merely ornamental, are worthy of notice. Bonnefoy seems particularly sensitive, for instance, to the elaboration of numerical detail. He has published four major books of poetry, two of which are themselves divided into four sections. The four sections of *Hier régnant désert* and of *Pierre écrite*, however, contain 13, 19, 13, 11 and 17, 17, 19, 9 poems respectively—that is, are made up of uneven numerical units one might characterize as largely "nonsymbolic primes." Divisible (with the exception of 9) only by themselves and one, they evoke both Plotinus's notion of the One (about which I will say more in a moment) and the post–Nietzschean concept of a meaningless and unfounded multiplicity.

The first collection, *Du mouvement et de l'immobilité de Douve*, also plays with a dialectic between odd and even numbers: the five sections of *Douve* are made up first of 19 poems, then three sections of 14 poems, followed by a closing part of 7 poems. The number 7 (period of the finished and "perfect" creation of the world), which seems to be the decisive or key numerical figure, is "crippled" by the incomplete 19 poems of the first section, which requires two more poems to make it a multiple of 7.

Bonnefoy seems to have a special preference for the number 19. Three separate sections contain 19 poems, and the last book, *Dans le leurre du seuil*, made up of seven long sections, includes a series of intervening suspension points, placed at various intervals throughout the entire book (sometimes in a single, sometimes in a double line) each line of which contains exactly 19 points. These points are perhaps the most radical assertion of the forces of destruction and silence which Bonnefoy has always felt were on the verge of restraining the text: "One would have very little if one only had words," he wrote in his essay on *The Song of Roland*. "What we need are the presences which words leave in dotted lines in their mysterious intervals, and which words in themselves cannot restore to life" (*NR*, 175).

The care for meshing odd and even units is also seen in Bonnefoy's use of traditional French versification. Richard Vernier has counted 263 Alexandrine or twelve-syllable lines in Bonnefoy's *Douve*.[4] These vary, however, with lines of nine, eleven, and thirteen syllables.[5] The decasyllable lines, which traditionally break after four syllables to be completed by the regular Alexandrine hemistich, are reversed: the six-syllable hemistich is completed by the "incomplete" four syllables. As Vernier says of this kind of verse: "On peut donc le dire déchu par rapport à ce qu'il laissait attendre" ("One might therefore call it deficient with respect to what it gave us to expect").[6]

Although Bonnefoy tends to eschew the traditional sonnet form—two quatrains and two tercets—many of the earlier poems will create interesting variations and elaborate odd-even patterns. "Vrai Nom" of *Douve*, for instance, is made up of three four-line stanzas, while the sixth poem of the series entitled "Le Seul Témoin" is composed of four three-line stanzas. The three poems of "Rive d'une autre mort" in *Hier régnant désert* are composed in the following way: an incomplete sonnet (a quatrain and three tercets) is followed by a traditional and complete sonnet, and the series ends with a poem of three four-line stanzas. These examples could be greatly extended.

This concern for numerical detail is related to a general philosophical conviction. Bonnefoy is seeking to reconcile the ideal of formal perfection with the reality of movement and becoming. Static "perfection" is a threat to "being," in Bonnefoy's view: "The beauty of form is the dream on the borders of an ideal world" (*I*, 125). We are nevertheless drawn toward it, as to all forms of the absolute. The ideal of perfection draws or lures us; it calls us out toward effort and creation, but it can imprison and close us in. Therefore, as a famous poem will affirm, "Imperfection is the Summit," and destruction an imperative. Bonnefoy is consequently always on the frontier of silence; his poems will deliberately incorporate elements of emptiness and formal incompleteness. The silent vowel *e*, in particular, is for Yves Bonnefoy "that crack between the concepts, that intuition of substance" (*I*, 103). (In another place, Bonnefoy will further distinguish between vowels which evoke "the shadows of physical existence" and those, like the mute *e*, which are like "the light that comes from the One" [*I*, 261].)

The typical movement of Bonnefoy's poems is toward the reconciliation of dialectical elements. The lure of some dream, of some conceptual order, of the beautiful or the erotic, of the atemporality of images—illusions of all sorts which place the subject in an ideal and timeless realm—is opposed by the imposition of cruel realities, of death and decomposition, of inevitable change, of man's finitude and his inability to grasp his world directly. Bonnefoy's resolution is simply to accept, to *consent to*, the fundamental contradiction of the human situation and to reconcile himself to the eternal dialectic of ruin and reconstruction, to our ever defeated aspiration, which remains, nonetheless, boundless and indomitable. "We have being," he wrote in his book on Rimbaud, "only because of that desire in us which never obtains and which never gives up" (*R*, 130).

I mentioned Bonnefoy's studies in philosophy, and I would like to come back to this area of concern for a moment. In Paris, in the early fifties,

Bonnefoy worked at the *Académie de Paris* and studied philosophy with Bachelard, Jean Wahl, and Hyppolite (on Hegel). He wrote a thesis on Baudelaire and Kierkegaard which he subsequently destroyed. His studies in philosophy, however, and particularly his interest in the *Philosophie de l'Existence*, explain, in part, his predilection for a precise philosophical vocabulary. "Being-in-the-world," "presence," "plenitude," "immanence"—these are words he uses repeatedly, not only in his critical essays but even, in some cases, in the poems themselves. It is doubtless the insistence of such words ("They say it badly," he recently remarked, "but they do designate," *NR*, 347) that has led some to refer to Bonnefoy as a "philosophical" poet, or even as the "first Existential poet."[7]

The philosophers who seem most to have interested Bonnefoy and whose thought (and diction) can be felt in his own work are metaphysical philosophers, even if theirs is, like Heidegger's, a metaphysics of "nothingness"—Kierkegaard, Heidegger, Nietzsche, Plotinus. And one feels in Bonnefoy a certain struggle at work between Heidegger's (and Mallarmé's) "nothingness" and Plotinus's notion of "the One" as the ground of being. In Plotinus's thought, "the One" is the first Hypostasis of the Supreme Divine Triad; it is an ineffable Supra-Existence and Super-Act which transcends all the knowable; it transcends even the quality of Being. It exists in lonely majesty and is approached by what is most solitary in us. It is identified with absolute simplicity. Somehow it exists; somehow it implies act and generation. It is everywhere "in the sense that without its Supra-Existence, nothing could be; it is nowhere in that it is loftily alien from all else."[8] It is the goal of all our aspirations, but it cannot be spoken of in any terms of human thought.

It appears that Bonnefoy is sometimes haunted by the emergence of a kind of specter presence (what he calls *la mauvaise présence*, "under whose influence what is becomes absent at the very moment it appears before our eyes, shuts itself off from our reading of it"),[9] that the world may suddenly fall into silence and absurdity in spite of all his efforts to find meaning. At other times, however, these efforts will be rewarded by moments of insight and illumination during which meaning will take shape "in simple things, assuring a place to each, a reason for being, in the unity which is more than being, which is in itself the light" (ibid.).

It is clear that Bonnefoy is both profoundly aware of the principle of destruction of being, of emptiness and meaninglessness, of the void, and, at the same time, sensitive to an ineffable and luminous, a fracturable unity. And to say "fracturable unity" is immediately to raise the problem of Bonnefoy's "poetics of space." He is often at thresholds, at doors, on river banks or at crossroads. At the point of emergence: sometimes on the threshold of rediscovered presence; sometimes at the point of the intersection of worlds. Again and again he will raise the question of death's role, not only for our orientation towards existence, but also in its status as terminus, portal, or wall. It is important to stress, I think, that for Bonnefoy, on the level of existence, of our responsibility to our "ownmost self," to our "uttermost possibility," to speak in Heidegger's terms, the same orientation is required, regardless of what we might decide is the ultimate background of our being. Nevertheless, it is this tension between an invincible hope in the emergence of meanings that point to unity and the disillusionment and loss of sense that seem the proofs of nothingness which partly explains that, with the persistence of a notion such as "The One," Bonnefoy will also use, in his fashion, a number of theological categories, as I shall show in greater detail in a moment. The images of combat and struggle which mark the passage toward self-mastery and the journey toward presence—"in that true and not unsympathetic intimacy which is the joust"[10]—are the indications of an effort at a kind of "salvation." And Bonnefoy is often quick to locate his profoundest struggling on an inner battlefield.

> Against whom do we ever struggle if not against our own double? Against that *other* in us who seeks to have us feel that the world has no meaning; who wants us to turn, wounded and without hope, toward the stream where the blood of the dying day, of the battle lost, disappears. (*NR*, 171)

* * *

Heidegger, with Kierkegaard and Nietzsche, is a name Bonnefoy mentions in the early essay "Les Tombeaux de Ravenne." Bonnefoy is not without some reservations with respect to this thinker (see *I*, 12), but he must certainly have been touched by some primary convictions and, in particular, by Heidegger's belief that philosophical tradition had tended to shroud the manifestation and meaning of Being. "The ultimate business of philosophy," Heidegger wrote in *Being and Time*, "is to preserve the *power of the most elemental words* in which Dasein expresses itself, and to keep common understanding from levelling them off to that unintelligibility, which functions in turn as a source of pseudoproblems."[11] All readers of Bonnefoy's poetry are struck by his diction. His poetic vocabulary is made up of "elemental words": bread, water, stone, tree, earth, sky, blood. These are the words that recur, along with words designating movement and place: river, ravine, path. "I maintain," he once wrote, "that nothing is truer, and thus more reasonable, than wandering" (*I*, 128). Poetry and voyage are associated for Bonnefoy, and what poetry voyages toward is "presence" or the manifestation of being. Bonnefoy's use of both the most abstract, "philosophical" language and the most elementary, concrete words—"sur cette face de l'être où nous sommes exposés" ("on this slope of being where we are left exposed"), "jardin de présence" ("garden of presence"), "la bouche, la salive du rien" ("the mouth, the saliva of nothingness") are examples among many others—is one of the most singular and arresting aspects of his work.

If Bonnefoy shares Heidegger's concern for the preservation of the power of elementary words ("a few words in the end will glitter perhaps, which, though simple and transparent like the nothingness of language, will nevertheless be everything, and real," *AP*, 149), this concern will manifest itself not in a philosophical system, but rather in the poetic "endeavor," through the "approach" of words. "Poetic utterance can surely . . . celebrate presence, can sing of its being, can prepare us spiritually for encountering it, but it cannot in itself allow us to achieve it" (*I*, 123–24). The poetic word is "the means of an approach" (*I*, 124). And Bonnefoy's *choice* of words is significant. "In modern French poetry, there is a Grail procession passing by; the things that are most full of life on this earth— the tree, a face, a stone—and they must be named. All our hope rests in this" (*I*, 123).

These simple realities have at their basis the four elements themselves: earth, air, fire, and water are the stuff of Bonnefoy's poems. He has written of them in the following way:

> And it is true that in an authentic poetry nothing remains but these wanderers of the real, these categories of the possible, these elements without past or future, never entirely engaged in the present situation, always ahead of it and promising something else, which are the wind, fire, earth, the waters—everything that is undefined that the universe has to offer. Concrete, but universal elements. Here and now, but also everywhere beyond in the dome and on the parvis of our place and our moment. Omnipresent, animated. One could say that they are the very speech of being which poetry draws forth. (*I*, 125–26)

And poetry, for Bonnefoy, will be "a ceaseless battle, a theater where being and essence, form and formlessness will contend fiercely with one another" (*I*, 124).

The above passages, taken from his critical essays, may suggest that Bonnefoy is in fact a kind of "philospher" of poetry and of existence. He is quick to remark, however, that the essays cannot be taken as carrying the sense of the poems. He published two important essays—"Les Tombeaux de Ravenne" and "L'Acte et le lieu de la poésie"—with his poems *Du mouvement et de l'immobilité de Douve* and *Hier régnant désert*,[12] not for the elucidation they would bring to the poems, but rather "for the disparity they bring out, and which seems significant to me, between the domain of the image and that of the formulation" (ibid., 222). Nonetheless, most readers will be glad to have the vast ensemble of texts, which collaborate in an explicative act that the poems in themselves will not directly provide. And many readers will argue that Bonnefoy himself is the best commentator of his work.

*   *   *

Bonnefoy's interest in the elemental real is reflected by his early reading. He mentions,[13] as particularly formative and influential, readings not only of moderns such as Bataille and Jouve (as well as the greatest of all poets, Dante), but also of a number of "archaic" texts, such as the Finnish epic *Kalevala*, the Egyptian *Book of the Dead*, and the Guatemalan Book of Origins called the *Popol Vuh*. Originally written on the "bark of a certain tree" in the Quiche language, the *Popol Vuh* was translated into Spanish after the Conquest of 1524.[14] Variously known as the *Popol Vuh*, Book of the Council, Book of the Community, and the Sacred Book, the work "contains the cosmogonical concepts and ancient traditions of this aboriginal American people, the history of their origin, and the chronology of their kings down to the year 1550" (ibid., 5). Bonnefoy read the *Popol Vuh* in the French translation by Raynaud and was overwhelmed.[15] The book recounts how the world was begun, how dawn first appeared. The gods (the Creator and the Maker) of the *Popol Vuh* seek to be nourished and sustained by man. They ask the grandmother of the day, Xpiyacoc, and the grandmother of dawn, Xmucané, to enter into council. "Make light, make dawn, have us invoked, have us adored, have us remembered by Created man, by made man, by mortal man. Thus be it done."[16]

Bonnefoy once wrote that "the really *modern* act . . . is to want to establish a 'divine' life without God" (*R*, 114). His interest in "primitive" texts is related to his interest in the "elemental words," and his concern must be called a "religious" one. ("Why refuse the word," he has said recently.)[17] The *Popul Vuh* describes the punishment of "the arrogant ones," of those who exalt "their glory, their grandeur, and their power" (*R*, 104). For Bonnefoy, too, there are the traps of pride and the dependence on an illusory self, the artist's temptation to be "almost a god creating almost an earth" (*P*, 324), the danger of estrangement. His deepest desire is to join the real, to find the simple order of life, and to convert the nostalgia for a better world or a transcendent deity into a celebration of earthly, mortal presences: "I would like to bring together," he declared more than twenty years ago, "I would like almost to identify, poetry and hope" (*I*, 105). What Bonnefoy has written about Shakespeare could be applied to himself.

> In spite of the collapse of the "admirable edifice" which the Christian Middle Ages had built with heaven and earth around man

created by God, this poet of a harsher time felt that an order still remained in place, in nature and in us, a deep, universal order, the order of life, which, when understood, when recognized in its simple forms, when loved and accepted, can give new life through its unity and its sufficiency to our condition of exiles from the world of the Promise—just as grass springs up among the ruins.[18]

To found the "divine life." The persistent theological vocabulary in Bonnefoy is inescapable. Poetry "aims at salvation," and this *intention de salut* is, for Bonnefoy, "the only real concern of the poem" (*I*, 250). Bonnefoy will speak of "[s]on démon," of "l'ennemi." And repeatedly this demon's lure will be in the direction Bonnefoy calls *excarnation*—that call away from the situation at hand, the dream of another, better world, the refusal of time and death, enclosure in formal systems. Salvation will depend on the opposing principle of *incarnation*: the discovery and celebration—in spite of limitation and death—of the sacred in the *hic-et-nunc*.

Claudel once referred to Rimbaud as "a mystic at the primitive stage" ("un mystique à l'état sauvage").[19] The term also has a certain applicability to Bonnefoy, except that Bonnefoy arrives at the primitive state through, or in spite of, an immense culture and intellectual sophistication. Poetry, for Bonnefoy, is a kind of primitive or pretheological religion. Poetry strives to establish the sacred in the quotidian, to celebrate the sacredness of what is. The poet keeps the memory of a lost and fragmented unity; he seeks to reunite, as Claudel says, "those things that groan at being separated."[20] But this separation, for Bonnefoy, is based on a kind of forgetfulness encouraged by dream, credulity, and the veil of conceptual thinking.

Bonnefoy had been deeply impressed, from as early as 1944,[21] by the Russian theologian Lev Shestov, who wrote in his *Potestas Clavium*: "Among the hundreds of millions of men who have confessed God in words, only a few have truly felt his presence."[22] Our rationalism, which is linked to our desire for order, fixity, and permanence, has shaped a God of "Good," of "Law"—a false God. For "the tree of knowledge does not increase our powers but, on the contrary, diminishes them" (ibid., 157). We raise the qualities we think we admire—knowledge, power, and rest—to a superlative degree to obtain the notion of "the absolutely perfect being." And yet, Shestov will argue, "what could be more tiresome and more disgusting" (ibid., 131) than omniscience, omnipotence, and eternal rest? "One would not wish such a fate on one's worst enemy" (ibid., 132).

This thinker, who was a crucial influence in Bonnefoy's break with the surrealists (as I hope to show in the next chapter), emphasized the importance of human will and desire and was convinced of the contradictory, manifold, private, and often essentially incommunicable nature of truth. "Men willingly accept every explanation," he wrote, "even the most absurd, provided that the universe no longer have a mysterious aspect" (ibid., 177). Shestov places God precisely in the area of the unknown: "Abandon your calculations and generalizations," he exhorts, "and go daringly, without looking backward, toward the unknown where God will lead you" (ibid., 83). Life for Shestov is "so fantastic, so peculiar, so un-natural, that [it] does not permit itself to be enclosed either in the formulas of mathematics or in general concepts" (ibid., 190). "The general and the necessary are non-being *par excellence*. And it is only when it will recognize this that philosophy will redeem the sin of Adam and arrive at the . . . roots of life; at that . . . 'most important' of which men have dreamt for so many thousands of years" (ibid., 286).

There was an immediate appeal for Bonnefoy in these ideas, and he would take the notion of the *deus absconditus* to the point of absence, find-ing conducive, in his search for immediacy and presence, a radically "nega-tive" way. Nevertheless, through the repeated use of theological categories, Bonnefoy places his quest in a religious context. And, without basing the use of religious terminology on any specific theological credence or allow-ing this vocabulary to coagulate into dogma, Bonnefoy nonetheless, through the language of religious experience, sets his work in the tradition of religious poetry and cooperates in the collective efforts of modernist theology to "reinterpret" and salvage what is perennial and genuine in the religious experience. In this connection, Bonnefoy will concentrate on a number of the most important religious myths. He will focus, of course, on significant elements of the Christian myth, finding their truths in his experience, reshaping their expression. But his preoccupation with the re-ligious core of myth is in no way limited to the Christian myth, for special meditations on the myth of Kore or the story of the finding of Moses—to cite two obvious examples—also animate his work.

*   *   *

Another preoccupation deserves mention here: Bonnefoy's longtime de-votion to the visual arts. Twentieth-century French intellectual life is, in-deed, to a greater extent than is true in England and the United States, a collaboration between the arts. The relation between poetry and painting is particularly close. As Bonnefoy himself has said, "the more specifically poets have desired immediacy, the more they have shown an interest in the techniques of painting, which in their eyes, when all is said and done, seem miraculous" (*NR*, 320). Among contemporary French poets, not only Bonnefoy but also André du Bouchet, Francis Ponge, and Jacques Dupin have shown a deep interest in the arts and have felt with him that there is "a fundamental unity to everything related to the making of images"[23] and have tried, with him, to establish the nature of the relation between the visual image and the poetic word.

Bonnefoy's discovery of the perspectivists of the Italian Quattrocento—of Piero della Francesca and Masaccio—was like a kind of new birth for the poet (*AP*, 65). The irresistible luminosity of Piero dispersed "the old opacity of symbolic representations, with their colors frozen in their meanings" (*AP*, 67). Space, bathed in light, became like the morning of the first day; objects could be seen in their transcendance of all concepts and notions; yet the dispersed and scattered is gathered together in the "light and unity of the sacred" (*AP*, 64).[24]

Bonnefoy's inquiries widened to include the Roman Baroque, which came to seem to him "like the very theater of Presence" (*AP*, 154), as well as Byzantine art and a number of important painters of the Italian Renaissance. To date, Bonnefoy has done books on the Roman Baroque and on French Gothic mural painting, as well as monographs on Bellini and Mantegna. For artists of the contemporary period, Bonnefoy's interest is less in the direction of formal study and aesthetic appreciation and more in the nature of a true collaboration. Speaking of contemporary artist friends and their work, Bonnefoy wrote recently:

> Let me take care now not to raise the questions of the historian or the art critic, thus turning a work of art into an object of study, and soon of aesthetic appreciation, changing what is gathered together today into a summary of an era.
>   . . . I have gone regularly every evening to those I have learned to love through watching them at work, sometimes even through collaborating with them. (*NR*, 363).

This collaboration is in part manifested by the fact that several of Bonnefoy's books have appeared illustrated by contemporary artists. His *Anti-Platon* was illustrated by Joan Miró, for instance; *Pierre écrite* first appeared accompanied by Raoul Ubac's lithographs, and the chapters of the lost "novel" *L'Ordalie* were published by the Gallery Maeght with the etchings of Claude Garache. To each of these artists, Bonnefoy has devoted a study, as he has to Chagall, Balthus, Mondrian, Morandi, and the photographer Cartier-Bresson. His essay on Giacometti first appeared in *L'Éphémère*, the journal of contemporary art and literature of which Bonnefoy was an editor, in its first number, in 1967. He is presently at work on a longer piece on this artist.

For his own poetical works, Bonnefoy has repeatedly shown a concern for their visual aspect. I have already mentioned the suspension points in *Dans le leurre du seuil*. In *Pierre écrite*, as well, in the section which is also called "Pierre écrite," Bonnefoy will center his poems on the page in such a way as to suggest that the page is like a tombstone on which the words of the poem have been carved.

Bonnefoy's ongoing interest in the visual arts and his examination of their relation to poetry is associated with his constant struggle with the problematics of the image. The paradoxical reality of images is that they give us our world (without them, Bonnefoy seems to feel, we would have no world); but, though providing us with an approach to the world, images do not, in themselves, have any being. And Bonnefoy will constantly propose the image as the *expression* of desires, of truths, only to destroy or put into question the pretended ontological status of the image. Thus, it is "the ontological evaluation and not the reproduction of appearances" (*AP*, 77) that Bonnefoy admires in the art of the Italians until the end of the Baroque period.

The image, both in poetry and in the visual arts, must be seen as a means and not as an end. Seen as a means, the image may have an educatory, anticipatory possibility. "One can love images, even if, in each image, one recognizes the nonbeing: so much is it true that all these works taken together do not so much cancel each other out as provide for a potential deepening of oneself and a way of completing one's destiny" (*AP*, 80).

Stated another way, Bonnefoy is both *for* and *against* images. And he is not uncomfortable with the theological implications of this paradoxical position, for although one cannot adore images in themselves, without risking idolatry and blasphemy in the worship of "strange gods," one must acknowledge that images serve as our approach to the sacred. Neither an idolator nor an iconoclast, Bonnefoy will recognize that if the "presence" he seeks is normally abolished by the images of most kinds of writing, poetry, in striving to simplify and universalize its images, attempts to reconcile what are usually the mutually exclusive categories of *presence* and *image*. And this reconciliation is based on what one might call the "healing" of the image from the sickness of the imaginary by nourishing it by what is proposed to it directly from life and lived experience. Thus Bonnefoy, drawing inspiration from his reading of Shakespeare's *The Winter's Tale*, will speak of his admiration for those artists who "have tried, as inventors of images—and how aware of their excesses—to heal the image, to dissolve the imaginary, to bring back to life in these mediations what one might call origin, which then takes shape as a kind of simple sacred order, diffused throughout the larger perspectives of what everyone can experience" (*NR*, 356).

To mention the word "healing" is to hit upon yet another of the central concerns in this work. *Blessure* and *guérison*; "wound" and "recovery": the two terms recur throughout the entire opus. Existing as the recompense for trial and suffering, the healing process is our sign that we are struggling *for* something. In one of the most moving lines he ever wrote, Bonnefoy will speak of this with certainty.

Tu sais que c'est l'obscur dans ton cœur qui se guérit.

You know that it is the darkness in your heart that is healing.
(*P*, 201)

Process of simplification and acceptance, the course of healing is not without pain and crisis. The trial by ordeal of which Bonnefoy so often speaks, and the suffering it entails, are the proof of the poet's right to exist among men; they are also purifying. And to borrow Virgil's words to the pilgrim Dante, hesitating before the purgatorial wall of flames: "qui può esser tormento, ma non morte." [25]

*   *   *

I spoke a moment ago of the problematics of the image for Bonnefoy. The same problematics exists when Bonnefoy considers language. Again and again, Bonnefoy will insist that language is "la faute," the great sin which drove us from the garden, in that the ensemble of relations which exists between words tends to become autonomous, just as our representations tend to "abolish" the real world of choice, time, and lived experience. The extreme form of alienation through language is the *concept*. Language as concept draws from Bonnefoy a strong moral resistance. "Because we die in this world, and in an effort to deny our destiny, man has built with concepts this logical dwelling where the only principles considered important are those of permanence and identity. A dwelling made of words, but eternal (*I*, 12). Or again: "The slightest concept is the craftsman of flight" (*I*, 12).

If the dwelling made of words and logic is viewed as escapist, the desire for habitation, for centrality, for place is nevertheless a permanent one which Bonnefoy experiences intensely and never seeks to deny. In his vision, however, this desire is forever frustrated, and protective structures prove illusory or ephemeral in order to assure movement and becoming. Bonnefoy's battle is against those who, as he says in *Anti-Platon*, "traffic in the eternal" (*P*, 11). They propose to define categories so that even death becomes incorruptible in the realm of eternal ideas where nothing in fact dies. Concepts are "like opium" (*I*, 12). "I hope that one can feel through this image [of opium] the kind of criticism—which is above all moral—that I wish to apply to the concept."

This opposition to conceptual language and to the Myth of Order perpetuated by perfected forms is amplified by Bonnefoy's study of the English language. To date, he has translated eight works of Shakespeare—*Henry IV Part One*, *Julius Caesar*, *Hamlet*, *King Lear*, *The Winter's Tale*, *Romeo and Juliet*, *The Rape of Lucrece*, *Venus and Adonis*—as well as an impressive number of poems by W. B. Yeats. Characteristically, the recurrent verse line Bonnefoy chooses to translate Shakespeare is a "fractured" or "crippled" Alexandrine—an imperfect, incomplete line of eleven syllables. He has described this line in the following way. "Beginning like an alexandrine—that is, with these six syllables which lead in the alexandrine to

15

their symmetrical image in the second hemistich—it ends with only five syllables and thus breaks the arrogant symmetry of the great verse of Racine and Mallarmé, with its refusal of time, of everyday life, of death."[26]

More important, perhaps, is the fundamental difference between the two languages he has come to sense in the process of studying and translating English. English is more "concrete" than French, more concerned with the external world. French is a "Platonic," closed language: it has an entirely different metaphysical orientation from that of the more "Aristotelian" English. The physical, sensible world gets replaced, in French, by a world of intelligible essences, a world in which "the bewildering diversity of the real can be forgotten, and also the very existence of time, everyday life and death."[27] English is in surfaces; French in depths; English is rich in possibilities; French is reduced and ordered. Finally, "English poetry is like a mirror, French poetry like a crystal sphere" (ibid., 42). The exercise of translation becomes, for Bonnefoy, the struggle of a language with its own nature; it is a "metaphysical and moral experience" (ibid., 43). In his essay on "Shakespeare and the French Poet," Bonnefoy writes: "In general terms, we may have reached that point in Western history when the major languages have to emerge from their naiveté and break with their instinctive assumptions, so as to establish themselves in a different kind of truth with all its contradictions and difficulties" (ibid.). And "it is at the level of their deepest intuitions that the realism of Shakespeare and recent French poetry's denial of idealism may henceforth communicate" (ibid.). As Graham Dunstan Martin has said: "Poets sometimes soak themselves in other poets so as to be more themselves."[28] For Bonnefoy, the experience of translating Shakespeare will be to have raised his conception of language "to a new level of awareness,"[29] and, more particularly, to have encouraged the "pursuit of otherness, of absolute exteriority," which he sees as "not so far from Shakespeare" (ibid.).

Yves Bonnefoy has also raised the question of the difference between French and Anglo-American criticism. In the July 1958 issue of *Encounter* (58:39–45), Bonnefoy published an interesting discussion of the problem entitled "Critics—English and French / and the Distance between Them." In general, Anglo-American criticism, following English poetry itself, tends to search for "meanings." This criticism (and Bonnefoy is here thinking of such critics as I. A. Richards and William Empson) tends to "reduc[e] the work to the sum of the meanings which it can be found to imply, so as to reassimilate these into ordinary language" (Critics, 41). But this "scientific" approach also tends to lead to the "degradation of the poem by a scientific conception of truth" (ibid., 42). Bonnefoy is moved, in his discussion of Anglo-American criticism, to some very interesting remarks about poetry. The English and American critics tend to regard the poem as a thing, rather than as an *activity*.

16

What is poetry in reality? The rejection of that part of the object which expresses itself conceptually (or in any kind of logical meaning); the feeling that the concrete reality is lost when the discursive concept is formed; the grudge against having itself to suffer the travail of conceptualising which (from its own exacting angle) is just that very disjunction I have mentioned [the disjunction between signifier and thing signified]; and finally the will to rescue what has been lost, a realism of the depths, which can only come to birth obliquely and through struggle. (Ibid.)

Contrary to Anglo-American criticism, French criticism "would range itself against the analysis of meaning" (ibid., 43). French critics resist the notion that "a poem can be reduced to what it explicitly or implicitly asserts" (ibid.). Bachelard, for one, will see poetical "intuition" in the image, "the absolute and impersonal image" (ibid.). For Poulet and Richard, poetry is "an experience of the depths where first of all the poet is submerged and then retrieves himself, where he lets language go only to reform it the other side of a kind of silence" (ibid.). Bonnefoy concludes in the following way.

Generally speaking, what these critics are trying to do is to re-live the poet's unanalysable experience, that which words are deemed never to express but which can be felt in those very words just in so far as they are not its explicit expression. (Ibid., 45)

But the French critic tends to neglect "formal values." And these values—rhythms, texture, etc.—"are really decisive even when the poem transcends them" (ibid.).

The poem is the struggle between the conceptual meaning, which tends to establish itself in precise sign-language and to find support in the sign's most objective characteristics, and an intuition which transcends all signification and forces the sign to stop short of precise definition. French and Anglo-Saxon criticism each support one side of this profound struggle which is in itself a creative act. (Ibid.)

Perhaps, Bonnefoy concludes, we will one day see a "dialogue" between the two approaches.

Though somewhat dated, these distinctions are particularly interesting, not alone for the light they shed on Bonnefoy's conception of poetry, but also for the possible approach to his work which is recommended, albeit obliquely, by his remarks. For his work is precisely this struggle between conceptual meanings and the intuitions which unsettle those meanings: "so much evidence through so much enigma" (P, 233). And Bonnefoy is clearly right in suggesting that a reader of modern French poetry in general (and of his own work more specifically) would do well to find some course between a desire to find meaning in formal values or in "precise sign-language," on the one hand, and the intuition, on the other hand, that one can only recreate an essentially unanalyzable experience.

*   *   *

These preoccupations—the interest in philosophy, theology, and mathematics, the love of the archaic text, of the visual arts, the interrogation of the image and of language, the work as translator and critic—are all kinds of collaborations in the poetic enterprise. We will feel these forces intersecting in the poem, which is itself a kind of "theater" of vision and questioning, a battleground for aspirations and disillusionments.

To hear Yves Bonnefoy speak about poetry, to read his remarks on the subject, is to recognize his unmistakable integrity and high seriousness. Poetry aims at salvation. "It conceives of the Thing, the real object, in its separation from ourselves, its infinite otherness, as something which can give us an instantaneous glimpse of essential being, and thus be our salvation, if indeed we are able to tear the veil of universals, of the conceptual, to attain to it."[30] This is another way of saying that poetry strives to celebrate "presences," and I think that this is perhaps *the* key term in Bonnefoy's vision and quest. His earliest essays already give a sense of the way in which he conceives of this term. At first, in an attempt to situate the experience of "presence" at the furthest possible remove from the "veil of the conceptual," Bonnefoy will insist that "l'objet sensible est présence" (*I*, 123). The phrase means, on one level, that "the physical object is a presence." The idea, however, is still more complex. It might be said that a presence makes it appeal to the senses, although here, too, one would want to imagine a general "sensibility" or intuition; a presence is not apprehended by the intellect; it is "what heart heard of, ghost guessed." The French word *sensible* should not, therefore, be restricted to the "concrete" or the "tangible"; similarly, the word *objet* should not be limited to physical objects alone, since the category may be extended to include experiential "spaces," moments of a kind of "vaulted" or "arched" intensity.

In its most general sense, then, a "presence" is precisely what is beyond, or outside of, conceptual categories or a conditioned perception. And in this, Bonnefoy's idea of presence has some affinity with Roland Barthes's *punctum*, that wound which unsettles the culturally acquired, that wordless illumination which cuts through governing codes, that "seismical" experience which jars all our knowledge. The moment of presence might be compared to the Zen man's *satori* experience about which I will say more in my last chapter, that moment of empty illumination during which, as Barthes says, "words fail."[31]

For Bonnefoy, of course, the physical world is involved in the emergence of presence. It is so that the earth might appear, might exist, at specific moments and in specific places, that the poet refuses the image-world proposed by writing. The simplest, most common dimension of our earthly experience may be a "presence." And in this sense, the physical object itself may be a presence. It is here and it is now. As such, it may suddenly emerge from behind the veil of "everyday" or of "conceptual" thinking as a resplendent revelation. In this epiphanous moment, it has the savor of the eternal. "Whoever attempts the crossing of physical space rejoins a sacred water which flows through all things. And if he makes even the slightest contact with it, he feels himself immortal. . . . That this world exists, I am certain: it is, in the ivy and everywhere, the substantial immortality" (*I*, 26).

Indestructible and eternal, "presences" are yet no cure for death. In fact, what allows the world to emerge as a presence is precisely the menace of death. The "presence" of which Bonnefoy speaks is often, in his work, an epiphany of finitude. And he has often stressed that it is in absence, and because of death, that "presence" comes to full realization.

> O presence, strengthened by what is already its bursting apart on all sides! To the extent that it is present, the object ceaselessly disappears. To the extent that it disappears, it imposes, it cries out its presence. If it remained present, an order would be established, an alliance beyond causes, an agreement beyond the word set up between it and us. If it dies, it opens into that union in absence which is its spiritual promise, in absence it comes to full realization. . . . The physical world [*le sensible*] is a presence—notion almost entirely devoid of meaning, notion forever tainted according to the conceptual mind: but this is where salvation lies. (*I*, 23–24)

One senses, in this passage, why Bonnefoy should have written in the *Anti-Platon* of 1947 the following short prose poem:

> *Captif d'une salle, du bruit, un homme mêle des cartes. Sur l'une: "Éternité, je te hais!" Sur une autre: "Que cet instant me délivre!"*
> *Et sur une troisième encore l'homme écrit: "Indispensable mort." Ainsi sur la faille du temps marche-t-il, éclairé par sa blessure.* (*P*, 15)

> Prisoner of a room, of the noise, a man shuffles cards. On one: "Eternity, I abhor you!" On another: "May this moment deliver me!"
> And on still a third the man writes: "Indispensable death." Thus does he go forward along the fault of time, in the light of his wound.

The lure of eternal Forms and Ideas is the intoxicant which numbs us to our real situation in finitude and peril and robs us of what is mysterious and holy in the simple and the evident. For it is only because things vanish that they can speak to us as presences. Poetry allows them to speak, although this effort is the most difficult imaginable. For the "being" of things, "their metaphysical *thereness*, their presence before us, most remote from verbalisation," their "pure existence, their stubborn atomicity, and their opaque silence"[32] resist language. Writing and presence are mutually exclusive realities. Writing tends to describe things by transposing them into preexisting categories, thus failing to join the freedom and intimacy of specific "moments" of experience. Furthermore, writing prevents participation in lived situations which demand choice in the difficulty of urgency or chance. "There is a great difference between really suffering in mortal time and simply evoking it in one's work. And any inclination toward the precision of language in fact resembles the temptation to hide oneself from that night outside, which is nevertheless the only reality."[33]

There is a fundamental difference, for Bonnefoy, between poetry and other forms of writing, in that true poets try to surmount the conflict between language and presence by meditating its dangers, by placing it at the center of their consciousness and making it the very fiber of their work. Poetry, then, for Bonnefoy, is "this judgment that art makes of itself" (*NR*, 265). To denounce the loss of presence through language, as Baudelaire did, is to make of poetry a dialectical search for truthfulness, for "the authentic word" (*la probante parole*) and "the voice that will not lie" (*la voix qui ne veut pas mentir*) of which the poems speak.

Poetry can never "create" by itself what Bonnefoy calls "la présence." What poetry can do is "tell of it, 'cry out its name,' thus helping the reader to rediscover the memory of it, and making of the confinements in which we are all caught, and of which one's writing is only one example, the occasion, at last fully apprehended and grasped, for a superior form of lucidity."[34]

In this sense, poetry is exchange: it is the desire to communicate about existence. It is unlike either literature or philosophy in that, unlike the former, it does not seek to make or produce the work of art, and, unlike the latter, it does not attempt to reduce texts to systems. Poetry, for Yves Bonnefoy, is concerned with searching, with struggling for value and meaning. The desire to exchange is not without its risks. As I have tried to show, Bonnefoy knows that all expression in language tends to separate the writer from real experience. And the desire to communicate can lead a writer to modify (and falsify) his text in order to make it more susceptible to exchange. The poet will always need to move beyond his texts; he will renounce them in his effort to refuse the domination of language. Writing will exclude the idea of presence "if one overvalues what is written, freezing it in its acquired form, and deciding, through a sort of option, that its production is the only real task, so that the author, deprived of other goals, turns away from his possibilities, reifies himself, and thus all the more easily allows his human presence to become dissipated in his work" (*NR*, 280). The poet, therefore, will denounce the "primacy of the poem" (*NR*, 280); he will commit himself to a kind of perpetual revolution, waging war on the crystallization and systematization of *la langue* through the existential searching of *la parole*: for if language is our great sin, speech can be our deliverance ("autant la langue est la faute, autant la parole est la délivrance") (*NR*, 251). The poems will have their own way of expressing this conviction.

> *Plus tard j'ai entendu l'autre chant qui s'eveille*
> *Au fond morne du chant de l'oiseau qui s'est tu.*   (*P*, 130)

> Later I heard the other song that stirs
> In the mournful depths of the hushed bird's song.

In this way, "writing could reveal itself as the crucible in which, through a dialectic of our life and our book—action and dream reconciled!—presence will not only come to pass, but deepen its relationship to us" (*NR*, 280).

A complex verbal organization, more open and polyvalent than any other, poetry strives for knowledge of limits, for understanding of finitude, for a just appreciation of our "being-in-the-world." In short, it battles for a painful and highly complex idea of truth. And if it is capable of showing a world suddenly lit up, if it can affirm a miraculous and improbable state of "being-there," of *presence*, this possibility is not achieved without struggle and temptation. For powerful adversaries must be overthrown and perpetual "lures" resisted in order for the poet to enter into and celebrate the real.

Claudel once wrote to the critic Jacques Rivière: "Every artist comes into the world to say a single thing, a single little thing; it is this that you must find, and then organize all the rest around it."[35] Yves Bonnefoy's quest is a journey toward what he himself calls "incarnation"—that is, toward "presence," toward the "sacred heart of the moment" (*I*, 122). For, as he says, "it is in the depths of the moment that man will rediscover this immanent divinity" (*R*, 152). Poetry is like a kind of spiritual exercise which prepares one for the world of presence—"only sketching out intelligible worlds, personal languages, in order to simplify them to the point of seeing born in them, as it were, on its humble bed of straw, an absolute form, this time that of life itself" (*NR*, 280). In his long poem *Dans le leurre du seuil*, Bonnefoy will evoke the figure of "the child who carries the world," of "the child who is the sign," of "God the child and still to be born."

In Bonnefoy's vision, *incarnation* is "a richness close by" (*un bien proche*), is the "dream turned inside out" (*NR*, 279). But just as the "incarnation" of the Christ figure is authenticated through the trials in the wilderness, so Bonnefoy's project has been clarified and more sharply defined through resistance to three principal lures, and the poet has heard his demon propose a variation on the three great temptations of the desert.

2 The Three Temptations

Then Jesus was led up by the Spirit into the wilderness to be tempted by the devil. And he fasted forty days and forty nights, and afterward he was hungry. And the tempter came and said to him, "If you are the Son of God, command these stones to become loaves of bread." But he answered, "It is written, 'Man shall not live by bread alone, but by every word that proceeds from the mouth of God.'" Then the devil took him to the holy city, and set him on the pinnacle of the temple, and said to him, "If you are the Son of God, throw yourself down; for it is written, 'He will give his angels charge of you,' and 'On their hands they will bear you up, lest you strike your foot against a stone.'" Jesus said to him, "Again it is written, 'You shall not tempt the Lord your God.'" Again the devil took him to a very high mountain, and showed him all the kingdoms of the world and the glory of them; and he said to him, "All these I will give you, if you will fall down and worship me." Then Jesus said to him, "Begone, Satan! for it is written, 'You shall worship the Lord your God and him only shall you serve.'" Then the devil left him, and behold, angels came and ministered to him.

Matthew 4:1–12

For Dostoevsky's Grand Inquisitor, the three temptations of Jesus in the wilderness constitute a "real stupendous miracle."[1] Speaking of them to the Christ who has returned to earth, the Inquisitor says:

The statement of those three questions was itself the miracle. If it were possible to imagine simply for the sake of argument that those three questions of the dread spirit had perished utterly from the books, and that we had to restore them and invent them anew, in order to restore them to the books, and to do so had gathered together all the wise men of the earth—rulers, chief priests, learned men, philosophers, poets—and had set them the task of inventing three questions, such as would not only fit the occasion, but express in three words, three human phrases, the whole future history of the world and of humanity—dost Thou believe that all the combined wisdom of the earth could have invented anything in depth and force equal to the three questions which were actually put to Thee then by the wise and mighty spirit in the wilderness? From those questions alone, from the miracle of their statement, we can see that we have here to do not with the fleeting human intelligence, but with the absolute and eternal. For in those three questions the whole subsequent history of mankind is, as it were, brought together into one whole, and foretold, and in them are united all the unsolved historical contradictions of human nature. (Ibid., 265–66)

This passage from *The Brothers Karamazov* emphasizes the breadth of applicability inherent in the Gospel temptations. In fact, Dostoevsky will give them a well-known nineteenth-century reading: the temptations are the lures of the totalitarian spirit, its raison d'être. The temptations seduce the weak; they make life tolerable for those anguished by the idea of freedom. The Antichrist, because of his love for a feeble humanity, destroys Christ through systematic wielding of the powers of "*miracle, mystery,* and *authority*" (ibid., 269).

The "devil" or "tempter" has been conceived of as "a personal will actively hostile to God."[2] The *Diabolos* is a "slanderer." Dostoevsky's Inquisitor calls him "the spirit of self-destruction and non-existence."[3] Jesus is exposed to three categories of temptation by the devil, each of which has to do with the extension of personal power. My purpose here will be simply to use these categories as a paradigm for spiritual alienation. In applying them to a contemporary poet, I would not want to seem to be either wrenching these temptations from their spiritual specificity or inserting Yves Bonnefoy into some exclusively "Christian" context. Rather, I would suggest that there is, in the realm of the human spirit and in the problems it faces, a certain undeniable universality of application in these categories—that one can agree with Dostoevsky that they partake of "the absolute and eternal."

Bonnefoy himself has spoken explicitly to the question of the applicability of mythic structures to contemporary consciousness. We must, he has said, put them to the test of our condition as it really is, remake them with our very substance, "if not they quickly become merely beautiful images that speak of our nostalgia, but not at all of our truth" (*NR*, 102).

Jesus is led *by the Spirit* into the wilderness to be tempted by the devil. His temptation is therefore seen as "willed by God."[4] Jesus defines and perfects himself through the trial of temptation,[5] refusing both an exploitative, irresponsible use of "divine" power and the facile manipulation of worldly authority and prestige. For the purposes of discussing the particular lures Yves Bonnefoy has resisted, I would reduce the three temptations in the desert to the following categories: excarnation, magic, the world.

*   *   *

Incarnation, of which I spoke in the first chapter, works in two directions for Bonnefoy. In a general way, it follows the direction in which the term is commonly conceived: incarnation refers to the manifestation of the divine or sacred in the material and existential real. It is the "word" made flesh. But, in the other direction, it is the meaning which is allowed to emerge from the material situation. It is the "flesh" made word. ("Meaning is prefigured in materiality," Bonnefoy has said. "Through the image that comes into being is made known the absolute which bears witness against the image." *NR*, 361.) It is in this sense that Bonnefoy will often refer to "the few words," to those "patient, saving words," to "the few words saved / For a child's mouth." These words, like the hands in the psalm, "hold up the world." They are related to "the mysterious meaning in what is only simple / And would have fallen without fire in words without love" (*P*, 211).

Excarnation follows just the opposite orientation. (Bonnefoy has called the tendency toward excarnation "du religieux de travers,"[6] that is, "wrong-headed religion" or "religious spirit gone astray.") The divine or sacred is situated outside the *hic-et-nunc*. The term *excarnation* is distantly connected to the heretical ideas promulgated by the so-called Gnostics in the early history of the Church. Some Gnostics sought to attenuate the human or natural side of the Christ and his involvement in human history by denying the reality of his earthly body. They located salvation not in faith or in cooperation with the will of God but, rather, in the assimilation of an esoteric knowledge destined for only a limited elite. They stressed the complete "otherness" of God and emphasized his separation from the world of men—from which notions devolved the ontological dualisms which characterize the Gnostic tendency: God and the universe, mind and matter, soul and body are in opposition. The early Church fathers were quick to condemn the Gnostic or Docetic idea of a redeemer who only "seems" to become incarnate, insisting upon the doctrine of complete God and complete man. History and humanity, in the orthodox view of the Church, as well as the body and the material universe, are dignified and redeemed through the incarnation of the God-man.[7]

For Bonnefoy, through a dynamic analogous to the one operative for incarnation, the process of excarnation deprives the material real of its word. And for this poet, the moment of excarnation is "always possible in language as its innate failing" (*NR*, 344) and "the earth always betrayed by the image" (*NR*, 357). The languages of men separate; they detach themselves from the realities they are supposed to evoke and become autonomous. Things, then, are apt to fall silent and take on the ominous and arbitrary—the absurd—quality of "being-there" which Bonnefoy has named *la mauvaise présence*. Or, in the proliferation of special languages, the simple presence of things may be "brutalized" or forgotten.

> We have had, in this unlucky Western world of ours, so many artists, so many inventors, so many creators of structures, of private languages, of universes lacking simplicity, so much nostalgia

about existence from those who are above all infatuated with themselves and who brutalize what does exist, searching for truth, they sometimes think, but reifying it as well as forcing it, and spreading out far and wide around us the desert. (*NR*, 302)

Repeatedly, Bonnefoy will indict "pride" as the moving force behind ex-carnation. Pride and the difficulty of "the simple acceptance of oneself" are what "freeze" the given, as Hermione is frozen in *The Winter's Tale*; things, quite simply, die.

Of the stone, Bonnefoy has written that for him it is the exemplary form of the real. "I cannot contemplate the stone without seeing it as un-fathomable, and this abyss of plenitude, this night covered by an eternal light, is for me the exemplary form of the real" (*I*, 16). And in another place, Bonnefoy has referred to the stone as "a metaphor for being." "In a world already reduced to its most essential expression, it suggests an even tighter restriction, a silence, the light or the darkness of night according to the disposition of our hearts" (*I*, 59).

It is clear that for Yves Bonnefoy the stone is fundamentally a source of illumination. The biblical model opposes the "transformed" stone and the "word" of God, according to which one should live. Bonnefoy maintains, as I have said, that the sacred is only in the real, here represented by the stone. But the real exists under a heavy bark or veil of representation. A false word has prevented its emergence as a presence. For the stone is per-haps the most resistant, the most opaque example of "the vast unutterable matter" of which a poem in *Douve* will speak. To approach the stone with-out intermediary, without methods of analysis, ideation, or conceptualiza-tion is to be and to work according to the matter and the movement of a total becoming, nonrestrictive, forever open to the unknown, and to re-establish those roots of relatedness—those sources of "communion"—which have atrophied and died, but which establish a meaning that creates freedom and that opens us to what surrounds us—at once evident and in-explicable. The artist will tend, therefore, to think nothing, to say nothing, but in the hope that his silence will allow sense to emerge—the sense of the most elementary hierarchies. In a poem called "L'Éternité du feu," from his book *Hier régnant désert*, Bonnefoy speaks of the poetical fire which may visit the poet in the following terms:

> *Il regarde le feu. Comment il vient,*
> *Comment il s'établit dans l'âme obscure*
> *Et quand l'aube paraît à des vitres, comment*
> *Le feu se tait, et va dormir plus bas que feu.*
>
> *Il le nourrit de silence. Il espère*
> *Que chaque pli d'un silence éternel,*
> *En se posant sur lui comme le sable,*
> *Aggravera son immortalité.* (*P*, 140)

He watches the fire. How it comes,
How it finds a place in the darkened soul
And when dawn appears on the windowpanes, how
The fire falls silent, and goes to sleep deeper than fire.

He feeds it with silence. He hopes
That each layer of an eternal silence,
Falling upon it like the sand,
Will only aggravate its immortality.

The poetic word will be ruder and more fluid than the formula, and the poet will try to follow the *workings* of nature and not her effects, her *procedures* rather than her appearances. The reflex reference, the easy access to signification, discourse and rhetoric are all movements toward excarnation, for these reflexes soon become autonomous and cease to attach themselves to any real object; they function in a void. The universe we have built of logical structures must be dislocated; language must explode in a kind of "cry of anguish" before we can approach the transparency of reality, before we can set foot upon ordinary earth, before we can hope to enter into relationship with the intangible and bottomless foundation in and around us. And even when we are "lost" there—without the proper key or the proper map—we can recognize that we are in a state of proximity, that we have "gone astray" in what is indomitable and imponderable. The earth, Bonnefoy will never cease reminding us, "is the only true structure" (*NR*, 200). And it is perhaps above all toward a confidence in his participation in nature's regenerative powers that the poet will strive.

Bonnefoy's poetry struggles to affirm that the "communion bread" is in the stone if one stays with the stone long enough. There is the quick transformation or "abolition" of excarnation, and there is the patient acceptance of incarnation. It is perhaps one of the richest paradoxes in Bonnefoy's work that the accepted real (the stone) can assume the sustaining and sacramental quality associated with the bread refused in the temptation of excarnation. Many passages in Bonnefoy's work affirm this idea. I have selected a number from *Hier régnant désert*:

> *Tu ne dénieras pas les pierres du séjour*　　　　　　(*P*, 134)
>
> You will not deny the stones of your stay here
>
> *C'est ici en pierrailles qu'est le port*　　　　　　(*P*, 139)
>
> The home-coming is here in the bits of stone
>
> *Et j'ai rompu ce pain où l'eau lointaine coule*　　　　　　(*P*, 116)
>
> And I broke this bread in which the distant water flows
>
> *Ici l'inquiète voix consent d'aimer*
> *La pierre simple*　　　　　　(*P*, 149)

Here the troubled voice agrees to love
The simple stone

The "divine" or "sacramental" word to be drawn forth from the material real by the poetic endeavor is expressed by *la même voix, toujours* ("the same voice, always"):

Je suis comme le pain que tu rompras,
Comme le feu que tu feras, comme l'eau pure
Qui t'accompagnera sur la terre des morts.   (*P*, 152)

I am like the bread you will break,
Like the fire you will make, like the pure water
Which will be your companion on the earth of the dead.

But if Bonnefoy's conviction is that the accepted stone is the sacramental stuff of existence, if he will seek to build his lasting convictions on that "rock," and if he can recognize in the unfathomable stone "the word of God" struggling for expression in poetry, he will nevertheless be strongly and lastingly tempted by the lure of excarnation.

In 1972, Bonnefoy published an important prose work entitled *L'Arrière-pays* which provides the reader with both a general analysis of the principle of excarnation and a kind of specific assessment by Bonnefoy of his own literary productions to that date. The book traces Bonnefoy's effort to master what he calls his "gnostic" side; it describes a lifetime struggle toward the opposing center, incarnation. The words *effort* and *struggle* suggest that the movement toward incarnation is an ever renewed one, that it is never acquired once and for all. The poet describes his "approach" as "dark, hampered, where I have lost my way several times, still unfinished today, unfinishable perhaps: I mean for one who hasn't simple acceptance of oneself (powers as much as limitations) for a natural resource" (*AP*, 127). Thus the lure of excarnation is perennial and ineluctable; it is apt to be an especially dangerous trap for those who turn away from what is given and immediate, for those who are complicated.

The term *l'arrière-pays* may be thought of, on one level, as corresponding to that "background" in paintings which depicts (and this is often the case in Poussin and Piero), faraway and inaccessible to the scene or events represented in the foreground, some ideal and seemingly unattainable landscape.[8] Paradoxically, however, the "other place" one dreams of in the given will never be other, for Bonnefoy, than this world we know, will never possess other components than those of earth. "I would dream, as I was saying, of another world. But I wanted it to be made of flesh and time, like our world, and such that one could live there and grow old there and die there" (*AP*, 62). The place "over there" is like what we know of this place immediately before us, but mysteriously transformed, beautified, rendered more intense and complete. It is the "dream" of earth, and it is this dream accepted and controlled—*simplified*, to use Bonnefoy's own term—which will contribute to the return to a *terre seconde*. For it is toward a reconciliation, an "alliance" of *l'ici et l'ailleurs*—the "here" and the "there"—that Bonnefoy will strive: the simple evidence before us, seen anew in the light of dream.

Bonnefoy has often maintained that he considers himself as following in the tradition of Baudelaire and Rimbaud. At first sight, the comparison might seem far-fetched. Both poets were capable of self-destruction in debauchery and flight. Now nothing indicates that Yves Bonnefoy knows an inferno comparable to Rimbaud's stormy and defeating relationship with Verlaine or Baudelaire's refined and decadent sensuality. The lofty, essentialized diction which has bothered some readers, the simple, highly restrained landscape of much of the poetry seem, at first sight, at a rather significant remove from the violently scatological or abruptly cynical and "colloquial" intrusions which are sometimes characteristic of Rimbaud. Speaking of what distinguishes him from Rimbaud, Bonnefoy himself has written: "I don't have his ability to change suddenly, his rhythm, with its dazzling departures; it's not for me; I prefer to go back to things, to take them up again" (*NR*, 217). The sense of affinity comes rather from the coexistence in these poets of longing and awareness of limitation, of nostalgia and self-criticism. Speaking of the experience of reading the last pages of *Une Saison en enfer*, for instance, when Rimbaud "having verified the impossible, still decides that one can go beyond," Bonnefoy writes:

> Reading these pages which are so unadorned and yet so full of light, I have felt that "God is dead"—with all due respect for the ambiguity in Nietzsche—is a naive idea, which really has to do with the slough left behind by the mind, with yesterday's insufficiencies, and which does nothing so much as acknowledge—between the primordial sacred order and the future, that is, between the earth and the earth—the end, simply, of an emptiness; whereas the truth is that God, in substance, and collectively, is to be born, and little by little or all at once could come to birth, it is not out of the question, in the deletion of the unnecessary reference, this very name of God, already absence. (*NR*, 217–18)

"The glory of man," T. S. Eliot has said, "is his capacity for salvation."[9] Bonnefoy's project of salvation will, like Baudelaire's, do battle in the tension of "two postulations." His demon, as he will often call him, lures him toward a kind of aery evasion in formal idealism, toward a refusal to participate in the lives of others and to accept limitation: "this would have been to choose, to devote oneself to incarnation, to death" (*AP*, 126). Under the influence of this "sin," he will prefer to abolish the particular existence before him, with its inescapable contradictions and limitations (which are also his own) in order to recompose it in its eternal essence outside the fatalities of time and chance, as Hamlet will abolish the autonomous being of Ophelia in order that she become, as Mallarmé has said, the image of the "virginal childhood of the pitiful royal heir."[10] Yielding to this "temptation," the poet betrays even the "dream" of which I spoke a moment ago. But this temptation is the "sin"—the "gnostic attitude"—from which writing (and especially perhaps French writing) will never manage to completely extricate itself.

> The gnostic attitude, in other words, is the tendency to substitute for everything, and for other people in particular, an image, which one takes as the only reality: so that there is gnosis, in my view, or in any case, the risk of gnosis, the minute there is writing, since the writer clings to facts, to objects, to beings that he loves, that he therefore invests with his desire, that he therefore abolishes in their own being, that he deifies, in short, according to the laws of his own heaven, when they are in fact of this world.[11]

Baudelaire, whose "cult of images" (and whose critique of this cult) establishes an important affinity with Bonnefoy, may be thought of as providing one of the famous prototypes of the notion of an *arrière-pays* or back country with his well-known sonnet "La Vie antérieure." Although the poem obviously contributes most of its energy to the idea of a *là-bas* of order, beauty, luxury, calm, and delight, the last lines allow a sense of personal limitation and sorrow to invade the otherwise seemingly "ideal" and nonsplenetic atmosphere.

LA VIE ANTÉRIEURE
J'ai longtemps habité sous de vastes portiques
Que les soleils marins teignaient de mille feux,
Et que leurs grands piliers, droits et majestueux,
Rendaient pareils, le soir, aux grottes basaltiques.

Les houles, en roulant les images des cieux,
Mêlaient d'une façon solennelle et mystique
Les tout-puissants accords de leur riche musique
Aux couleurs du couchant reflété par mes yeux.

C'est là que j'ai vécu dans les voluptés calmes,
Au milieu de l'azur, des vagues, des splendeurs
Et des esclaves nus, tout imprégnés d'odeurs

Qui me rafraîchissaient le front avec des palmes,
Et dont l'unique soin était d'approfondir
Le secret douloureux qui me faisait languir.

THE PREVIOUS LIFE
For a long time I lived among vast porticoes
Which the suns of the sea tinged with a thousand fires,

And whose huge columns, noble and majestic,
Made them seem, at evening, like basaltic grottoes.

The sea swell, rolling in the images of the heavens,
Mingled solemnly and mystically
The all-powerful strains of their rich music
With the colors of the sunset mirrored in my eyes.

And there I lived in calm and bounteous pleasure,
Amid the azur, the waves, the splendors
And the naked slaves, all drenched with perfumes,

Who refreshed my brow with waving palms,
And whose only care was to deepen
The sorrowful secret that made me languish.

What is this "sorrowful secret" which comes to invade the ideal world of calm delight and splendor and which marks Baudelaire's departure from the governing codes of the idealistic and escapist literature of his time, his break with the stereotypes and conventions of other representations of the oneiric (Gautier's *Mademoiselle de Maupin*, for instance), and makes of the poem not so much a simple evocation of a previous and imaginary existence as a kind of oneirocriticism, a form of resistance to the heavy perfumes of nostalgic intoxication? Speaking of a certain category of woman in the paintings of Delacroix—a category he calls *des femmes d'intimité* (as opposed to a richer, healthier, and fleshier group) and in whose number he lists Ophelia and Desdemona—Baudelaire says that they "carry in their eyes a *sorrowful secret*, impossible to repress in the depths of dissimulation." "Their paleness," he goes on to say, "is like the revelation of inner battles."[12] As "characters" or "subjects," Desdemona and Ophelia obviously represent "types" who carry the fierceness of a projected image; beyond this obvious consideration, however, exists a subtler one: the "sorrowful secret" is the ontological precariousness of the image itself in the presence of finitude, the artist or dreamer's intuition that he is proliferating categories of nonbeing, that the realities he strives to evoke are dead in the sepulcher of the image, and that his own existence in real time and space, his participation in the *hic-et-nunc* may be throttled or drowned through the preference accorded to the imaginary.

One might call this the "moral" side of Baudelaire—his determination to counterbalance the invincible and ever recurrent motif of evasion and flight in his work with an equally obsessive and controlling theme: the intuition of limitation, opacity, and finitude—the remembrance of the fate of what Bonnefoy calls our "wounded body" (*I*, 34). Like Bonnefoy, Baudelaire chooses to have the recognition of death grow in him "like a conscience," knowing (and this is what particularly unites the two poets) that "nothing is except through death" (*I*, 32–33).

And yet, Bonnefoy knows that the desire for transcendence is highly complex, that the dream of another place cannot be condemned too hastily. The "faraway land" involves, for Bonnefoy, not only pride, "but also dissatisfaction, hope, credulity, departure, the ever imminent restlessness" (*AP*, 50). It is not wisdom, he says, "but, who knows, perhaps something even better" (*AP*, 50). When pride is at the root of this dynamic, the results are inadmissible evasion. The dissatisfaction with the immediate, however, is also seen as a possibly valuable mechanism in the transformation of vision. It can become a *felix culpa*, as I hope to show more fully in another place.

What is "the land of loftier essence" off in the direction not taken at a crossroad? Certainly it is not essentially other. "It is not my fancy to dream of unknown colors or forms, or of passing beyond the beauty of this world" (*AP*, 10). But some key is missing; we are dispersed in the midst of a dimly perceived unity. Here, we only know how to exist on the surface of things. Over there, forms are purer; perhaps, too, a language exists which translates a more immediate experience of the unity of things and a people, whose feelings for the realities of earth are unknown to us, to speak it. And yet, one must not imagine a people radically different from us. No, perhaps only the simplicity of their gestures marks their closer and clearer approach to what is. What is most evident seems to escape us here; over there, the evident is accepted and fully lived.

But, by a mechanism analogous to the one analyzed so searchingly by Proust, the object of our desire only becomes such through being "over there." Once possessed, however, like the other side of Capraia, and immediately its alluring appeal fades: "You belong to the 'here' of the world, like us. You suffer from finitude, you are dispossessed of the secret; withdraw then, fade into the falling night" (*AP*, 17).

The danger of the lure of some ideal and elusive other place is, as I have said, that it renders the place where one is a desert, as one sees in Poussin's "Landscape with a Man Killed by a Snake" a "background" of limpid majesty and order and a "foreground" of horror and strangulation. On the other hand, however, the dream of the other place can enrich the here and now. Bonnefoy will explain, for instance, an experience he had as a schoolboy playing with a short-wave radio. Turning the needle, he found, by accident, what he imagines are the chants of some primitive people living "high up in the solitude of the stones" and who exist, in the ecstatic projection of the listener, as if in "a kind of pole in the absolute" (*AP*, 25). But it is from this experience of the *arrière-pays* that the author dates his interest in and sensitivity to music: "One of the richnesses, one of the alchemies from over-there had come to influence our experiences here, to add to my limited powers" (*AP*, 29). And it is in this way that the world which one should love is abandoned for a time, to be returned to "as a presence en-

Nicolas Poussin, *Landscape with a Man Killed by a Snake*. Courtesy of the National Gallery, London.

countered for the second time, restructured by the unknown, but full of life and experienced at a greater depth" (*AP*, 29–30). The arts, and poetry in particular ("techniques of negation, intensification, memory"), are cultivated in our relation to the other place.

The other place can also be our "dream" of the future *hic-et-nunc*. And thus, the world we lose in dream is recovered and redeemed by dream. Yves Bonnefoy will insist that his hesitation between the hidden god and the principle of incarnation is a permanently evolving dialectic. His desire to understand it better, to denounce it if necessary, is the movement toward the reconciliation of its two poles.

L'Arrière-pays can be seen, in fact, to trace not only the threat posed to incarnation by the principle of excarnation, but also the struggle toward their reconciliation. The narrator recalls an experience at Amber, for instance, near a massive fortress. His first impression there is that place and evidence have been identified, that the "here" and the "there" are no longer in opposition. The ramparts of the fortress do not enclose what one might have thought to defend; they coincide with the horizon, with the visible. Here, it is "the presence, the fact of the undulating earth which has produced the locality" (*AP*, 53). But a sudden revelation comes to shatter this first impression: tiny separations of the walls from the horizon; glimpses of a world beyond. "The idea of another world was 'abolished' at first, but lucidity followed and allowed the depths which remained undestroyed to break through the power of enclosure" (*AP*, 54). And the narrator feels a sense of deeper reality: both affirmation and doubt are expressed here; impatience is liberated with nostalgia; desire with the realization of finitude. And what are these breaks in the walls but a tangible form of those ruptures in the process of duration which deliver a certain *saveur d'éternel* (*AP*, 55)?

Beauty is augmented in this reconciliation, for if the pride that shuns the earth has been mastered, the thirst for the place beyond, for transcendence, has not been renounced but incorporated in an alliance. "Why this need of an 'elsewhere,' which nothing can fill, but why, too, this union we sometimes establish with the perishable 'here' by opening it up to the road for the painfulness of departure, and for the joy, and more than the joy, of returning?" (*AP*, 59). "Union." "Marriage." By such terms, Bonnefoy emphasizes the mutual interdependence of the categories of excarnation and incarnation, the dream and the real, the place beyond and the here and now, and the love and patience that would bind them together. His collections *Pierre écrite* and *Dans le leurre du seuil* will show how the world is transfigured through the marriage of these oppositions.

Consciousness is in search of *centrality*—"And I, concerned about transcendence, but also about a place where it might be rooted" (*AP*, 45)—

and will discover that the central is everywhere to the extent that the simple and the evident are everywhere.

The prototype of the "*arrière-pays*" is the summer place at Toirac where the poet passed the vacations of his youth with his grandparents. Two places set in opposition: the city of Tours, where he spent his school years, and the summer residence which provided his escape. For Tours is remembered through its asphalt streets, washed by the "municipal watering trucks" (*AP*, 101). His mother's house, with its forbidden furnishings and its half-closed blinds, is recalled as an isolating and imprisoning enclosure, whereas the grounds of his grandfather's house at Toirac provided a world of plenitude and ever-ripened fruit. Always beheld in unchanging summer, the "garden" at Toirac belonged to the atemporal and the ideal; it offered a unity, a music of essences which structured all future nostalgia for another, better place.

The idea of enclosure is, of course, an important one for Bonnefoy. It is part of his quest for centrality, for the *true place*. Churches, houses, temples, even paintings, and the "book one dreams of" are special lures, as is the greater *compactness* of an ancient language. Latin, for instance, seems to condense and enclose the dispersiveness of French. Paradoxically, however, the search for center leads to a process of decentering. The great discovery of the painters of the Quattrocento, for example, who gather together what is scattered and diffuse and bring to experience "the light and unity of a sacred order" (*AP*, 64), who represent an art of affirmation, "a civilization of place" (*AP*, 65)—this discovery lends itself to the dream of another, more perfect locale and encourages the poet's dissatisfaction, sends him off in search of unknown works, hidden in unlikely places: "so that passing from work to work I would be capable of progressing toward the distant plenitude" (*AP*, 73). And this thirst for the "far off" is the mechanism by which one is deprived of precisely what one would love in the here and now; it is because of this nostalgia that one learns to depreciate that of which beloved works of art tell the value. And this abandonment is one dimension at least of the world "destroyed" told of in *The Winter's Tale*.

In this way, the poet dreams of traveling through thresholds of art and experience toward the absolute center, toward some place of origin where feelings, now unknown to us, are expressed in essential gestures and the relation of the human being to his situation is purer and more intense, being unfettered by unessential differences and conceptual orders.

It is the recognition of the essential paradox inherent in the very nature of this search—that in striving for some absolute world, one loses the world at hand, that in seeking the "all" of a timeless ideal, one lives in solitude and nothingness (the "everything and nothing" which will become the epigraph of Bonnefoy's "darkest" book *Hier régnant désert*)—that encourages a resolution through *dispersion* of the dream in the real. To clarify this new paradox, Bonnefoy uses two key examples.

The first example is the figure of the "Sphinx des Naxiens" whose eyes appear to be wide open. With the passage of time, however, the upper eyelid has all but disappeared, with the result that one can also be led to think that the eyes are closed. Are the eyes open to the infinite metamorphoses of time or closed in contemplation of some inner and changeless form? Bonnefoy feels that the figure of the Sphinx represents the joining or merging of the two orientations in a kind of new vision. And this project was consciously conceived by the artist, in Bonnefoy's view, for the artist knew what time would do to the eyelid and, in calculating its work, he not only meditated the ambiguous figure which would result but also recognized his own ontological status. The dream of a timeless ideal; the recognition of its impossibility in finitude. This is perhaps *the* essential contradiction for Bonnefoy, and its *fatality* and the acceptance of its fatality are what I would call the heart of his work. "Contradiction is the fatality of what is real," he would write in his book on Rimbaud.

Bonnefoy will come to take the dream seriously, to *live* it and to shape it. He will no longer situate the eternal and the absolute in the "elsewhere," but diffuse them in the here-and-now. One must recognize and accept the dream for what it is; that is, a dream.

> The earth *is*, the word *presence* has a meaning. And the dream is as well, but not to devastate earth and presence, to destroy them, as I sometimes think in my hours of doubt or pride: provided of course that I dispel it as dream, having not so much written it as lived it. For then, recognizing itself as dream, it grows simpler, and the earth comes slowly back into focus. (*AP*, 149)

The center is everywhere. The sacred resides in the simple things we find before us. And it is the other example—of the Roman Baroque—which teaches that "*the existence of place*, which is everything for us, is forged from nothing, thanks to an act of faith which is like a dream one has lived so intensely, and so simply, that it becomes as if incarnate" (*AP*, 154). Bernini creates life from the acceptance of this dream. And Poussin will pick up a handful of earth and say that this is Rome. Poussin, who labors for reconciliation of essential conflicts, will decide to paint his great pictures on "The Finding of Moses" after having seen a washerwoman bathe and then lift her child from the waters of the river. These pictures, so important for the long poem *Dans le leurre du seuil*, have, in Bonnefoy's view, dissipated a kind of charcoal of dream half-crushed in the fatality of the grass through a vision at once irrational and inspired.

It is not difficult to discern a corrective stance in Bonnefoy's insistence on the priority of the concrete real. That the "ideal" or the "essential" is a special lure for him may be felt in his very manner of exhorting a return to the real and to the *hic-et-nunc*. And the real will never be spoken for in a more abstract diction. One might go so far as to say that abstract writing (and the "gnostic" substitution it automatically implies) which nevertheless affirms the simple evidence of earth or "these two unpretentious rooms, for the preservation of the gods *among us*" (*P*, 159), is another manifestation—and this one at the very paradoxical core of Bonnefoy's work—of that principle of dispersion and dissipation of which I have been speaking. For Bonnefoy will overcome the first of the major temptations of the desert world—the desire for something other and better—by incorporating this desire into the real itself, thereby simplifying and mastering it as dream. And the stone, which would have been lost through excarnation, is redeemed through acceptance. It is the sacramental bread, the exemplary real, for a vision which has measured and consented.

*   *   *

To speak of the status of the "dream"—even in the very different context elaborated above—is to raise the problematics of the unconscious in Bonnefoy's work and to consider the second of the major temptations through which he has defined himself, and which I have designated by the term *magic*.

Yves Bonnefoy began his career under the influence of the surrealist movement which he has called "the only genuine poetic movement this century has had."[13] The surrealists offered the young provincial "the first step toward the first true light."[14] In a short piece he contributed to an issue of *Yale French Studies* devoted to the surrealists, Bonnefoy wrote: "The greatness of this movement . . . was its effort to reanimate in secular times, and necessarily outside the perimeter of religion because of the times that are ours, the feeling of transcendency."[15]

Breton had written, in his *Manifeste*, of the reconciliation of dream and reality. "I believe," he wrote, "in the future resolution of these two apparently so contradictory states which are dream and reality in a kind of absolute reality, of *surreality*, if one might so put it."[16] What Bonnefoy could appreciate in certain surrealists was the image which gives "renewed life . . . to the profound unity of the world."[17] The "surreal" is then "nothing other than the real seen in the perspective of the One" (ibid.). But there is an ambiguity, for Bonnefoy, in the Surrealist movement which lies in its ability to be "simultaneously hopeful and pessimistic; to act and to refuse to act" (ibid., 136). "Proudly it recognized hope—our cardinal virtue and our inkling of the *real life*—only to let it drift and become degraded between suicide and commerce" (ibid.).

The *passivity* of Breton's method of "automatic writing"—"we who avoided all effort to filter, who made ourselves in our work the hollow receptacles of so many echoes, the unobtrusive recording apparatus not the least interested in the pattern it traces"[18]—is apt to elicit apparitions, the specters of *la mauvaise présence*. For Bonnefoy would come to judge that the surrealists lacked faith. Their "error . . . was, all things considered, not having faith in the simple forms of life, preferring the parade of the imaginary to the restrictions of evidence, the peacock's tail to the stones of the threshold."[19] It is Bonnefoy's conviction that

> there cannot be true presence unless sympathy, which is knowing in action, has been able to pass like a thread not only through those few aspects of the object or of the world which lend themselves to our reveries, but through all their dimensions, taking them upon oneself and reintegrating them in the context of a unity which I feel is guaranteed to us by the earth in its evidence before us—the earth which is life. (Ibid.)

One has only to remember how fascinated an André Breton was by the outer sign—by billboards and monuments—how unwilling he was to have his Nadja assume her *own* truths, to get a sense of the limitations of some of the aspects of the movement and to feel why the surrealists never managed to keep Bonnefoy's allegiance. What he speaks for in the passage above is an idea of Unity as the basis of all being and which allows things to participate in being rather than falling into fragmentation and absurdity. Of this Unity he has said:

> It is what asks us to put our faith in finitude, since totality only exists through the mutual recognition of each part, which has limitation as its essence: but this is what grants us, in the very assumption of our nothingness, access to the universal. And here is what I would call the religious act, here is the potential sacred order—and enough to break with surrealism. (Ibid.)

The influence of the theologian Lev Shestov was crucial in the process of Bonnefoy's break with the surrealists. What Shestov gave to the young poet (who discovered Boris de Schloezer's translation of *Potestas Clavium* in 1944) was a certain faith in that *puissance libre*, that free power in us which demands in the name of love and righteousness to have an impact not only on the present and the future, but even on the past: "If some event seems horrible to us, let us learn to see in that horror only the proof that the event cannot truly be real" (*I, 274*). Shestov is obsessed with the idea of resurrection, with the overthrow of the irreversibility of history (which can be rewritten by our authentic desires). Shestov views man, as Bonnefoy has said, as having "doubted in God who had guaranteed him liberty and glory, and he therefore cut himself off at once from his own power as it were" (*I*, 275). In short, Shestov, "by laying claim to eternity" ("à coups d'éternité réclamée"), by insisting on the superior power of love, opened Bonnefoy to what was missing for him in surrealism, namely, a vigilant hope. Bonnefoy's resistance to the surrealists' passivity was supported by this passionate affirmation of freedom and desire. And if the Bonnefoy of today recognizes the limits of Shestov's essential orientation, the younger poet found inspiration in the Russian's unrelenting insistence on the power of the individual's spiritual obstination.

At some point in the forties, Bonnefoy seems to have come to assume fuller responsibility for his own voice, to have taken up seriously the notion of his own answerableness, the idea that he had the right and even the obligation to enter into contact with the power of the unconscious by responding to it, by trying to understand it. If the "I" is another, as Rimbaud maintained, if we are written, if our voice is always the echo of other voices, it is nonetheless true, Bonnefoy seems to feel, that the "I" seeks to impose its desire, its "idea of meaning" (*P*, 306) on the chaos of phenomena, that the "I" is in *relation* to otherness and not merely in a position of passive reception. As he matured, took on his first practical responsibilities—marriage, work—Bonnefoy seems to have found the surrealist "leap" into the realms of dream and unconsciousness—certain at all times that "angels would bear them up"—increasingly insufficient. But this is not to say, of course, that he valued less his relation to the unconscious. In his book *Rue traversière* (1977), Bonnefoy speaks of trying to cooperate or collaborate with the messages and needs of the depths, of helping such a signal "to grow, to breathe better, through the cautious exercise of crossing out which is only one more way of serving its needs." [20] To the surrealists' idea of "automatic writing" he would oppose a notion of *rature*, that is "erasure" or "crossing out."

> To cross out, on the other hand, to choose while letting the other choose as well, this is what allows for economy, what encourages a deposit to form—who knows? perhaps incites the thought from below to profit more fully from the first construction through that increase in composition by means of which, in certain works of poetry or art, meaning becomes appeasement, and music. (Ibid., 64)

Furthermore, the automatic writing of the surrealists is not without providing glimpses of "the deep personality of its author . . . his obsessions, needs, quirks, sometimes even neurotic traits . . . the reality of this world, all the same." [21] What is denied or censored by surrealist writing returns "as the sum of these imaginings, of these sketches of dreams. One even ends up noticing at work from one book of Breton's to the next—to mention again the most important example—that finitude which one can perhaps refuse but which one cannot but undergo" (ibid.).

It is impossible to evade "the laws, the values, the bondages of our world, refused but nevertheless in effect" (ibid.). And an attitude of patient attention to what is given from the unconscious seems the most loyal and conscientious way of entering into genuine relationship with it. For if man is *ce rêveur définitif*, the permanent and ultimate dreamer Breton claimed he was, why not take the dream seriously? One should "remain of course in the dream which writing opens up for us, but also watch it live and 'criticize' it . . . , which will mean to work on oneself, and therefore on the dream as well, which will grow simpler at being thus elucidated, which will render the writing more transparent" (ibid.). There is, therefore, for Bonnefoy, a relationship in the poetic act between consciousness and unconsciousness, between the critical faculties and creative inspiration. What is asked of consciousness is to sort out and shape what imposes itself from the depths in order to better understand and care for what is struggling there for expression. Bonnefoy will come to recognize that it is a *responsibility* of an ethical and moral nature, and on which one's "salvation" depends (not to mention whatever incalculable and generally unverifiable impact such salvation is apt to engender through poetry), to shape the imaginary as though it were the real. The "dream"—and under this category I would include not only literal dreams and the workings of the unconscious and inspiration, but also all the other forms of the atemporal and the imaginary (writing, as well as the visual arts, the nostalgia for another place, as well as the hope of "other," more elementary gestures, feelings, and speech)—the dream and the real in the here and now should merge and marry, should be treated with equal respect and seriousness. Interplay, interconnection, mutual simplification: these are the extensions of what Bonnefoy could see as valid in the surrealist idea of *les vases communicants*. But here the reconciliation is taken on the highest level of seriousness. The conscious mind is in a posture of openness and attentiveness, but the imaginary, the message from the depths, is not deified; "the phrases that knock at the window" are not granted an immediate and "automatic" entrance, but rather are interrogated with patience and concern. The *irréel*, then, is approached with the same respect, is structured and shaped with the same care that one would devote to one's existence in time and in situations of choice.

What Bonnefoy came to resist in the surrealist movement—and he refused to sign the *Rupture inaugurale* of 1947—were precisely the *rêveries de magie*, that faith in magic, that "subversion of the principles of our understanding of the world" which deprive us of *la musique du lieu*, (ibid.) the music of our mortal place on earth. The *occultisme* of the movement, its trust in a kind of providence, in "hidden powers" (ibid.)—what is nicely symbolized by the temptation to throw oneself into the all-providing depths, blithely trusting in aery spirits to sustain one—eventually alienated the young poet, who became convinced that his poetic orientation must "exclude belief systems" (ibid.)—which is simply another way, it seems to me, of refusing to "tempt" God. And if some surrealist images could give "renewed life . . . to the profound unity of the world," others would conjure up "la mauvaise présence." And the eventual "taste for the unheard of," the "surrender to the night" came to seem to the young Bonnefoy "a world inhabited by nothingness alone."[22]

*   *   *

To speak of what kind of lure "all the kingdoms of the world" could have for a man of Yves Bonnefoy's integrity and commitment to "the god urgent in me" (P, 176) may seem at first sight a futile enterprise. Nevertheless, he has clearly taken position against—and hence defined himself in the face of—the "peacocks" of the world.[23] In a poem in *Pierre écrite*, he wrote,

> *Là-haut, dans les jardins de l'émail, il est vrai*
> *Qu'un paon impie s'accroît des lumières mortelles.*   (P, 177)

> Up there, in the enamel gardens, it is true
> That an impious peacock is strutting in the lights of men.

The lines contrast a world of depths, where desire, which brings forth the poetic images, is internalized toward the universal, with a world "up there," where desire is hypnotized and distracted by "objects which are too private and particular and in which [desire] becomes alienated."[24] The "enamel gardens" contrast, in their artificiality, with the Edenic garden of eternal life—with the "god"—the poet strives to recapture in the instant and in the presence of ephemeral realities. If the peacock is "impious" it is precisely because he has grown rich in an alluring, but meritricious glory. Perhaps he is one who has sought to make himself appear "in the guise of his own particular individuality, which is considered the standard for truthfulness" (ibid.), one who has eschewed the simple. To the peacock of *Pierre écrite*, one might oppose the salamander of *Douve*, "allegory / Of all that is pure" (P, 89).

> *Son regard n'était qu'une pierre,*
> *Mais je voyais son cœur battre éternel.*
> . . . .
> *Que j'aime qui s'accorde aux astres par l'inerte*
> *Masse de tout son corps,*
> *Que j'aime qui attend l'heure de sa victoire,*
> *Et qui retient son souffle et tient au sol.*   (P, 89)

41

Its look had turned to stone,
But I saw its heart beating eternal.

. . . .

How I love what is in harmony with the stars through the inert
Mass of its whole body,
How I love what awaits the hour of its victory,
And holds its breath and clings to the ground.

This poem, which is called "Lieu de la salamandre" ("Place of the Sala-mander"), is an extremely important one, and I will discuss it in some de-tail in the next chapter.

The issue of a "world" is a central one in Bonnefoy's work, as Jean Sta-robinski has recently pointed out.[25] Two books of poems will have as epi-graph a citation involving the notion of a "world": *Hier régnant désert* ("'Tu veux un monde,' dit Diotima. 'C'est pourquoi tu as tout, et tu n'as rien'"—"'You want a world,' said Diotima. 'This is why you have every-thing, and you have nothing'") and *Dans le leurre du seuil* ("They look'd as they had heard of a world ransom'd, or one destroyed"). And it is at once the discovery and elaboration of a world which Bonnefoy's work has at its deepest aspiration.

> If one dedicates oneself to the words that say hearth, tree, path, wandering, returning, no, it won't necessarily be a deliverance, since even in a world which makes sacred these simple things, the spirit of possessiveness can reemerge, turning presence into an ob-ject once more, and living knowledge into yet another science, and thus impoverished: but at least he who so wishes would be able to work, without any inner contradiction, at reassembling what avarice scatters, and then that co-presence could take shape again in which the earth becomes speech and in which the heart grows peaceful since at last it can listen to it and mingle its voice with others. The world of these words, it is true, is only structured through us who have built it with the sand and the lime gathered from without. (*NR*, 342–43)

Bonnefoy has often contrasted, in a general way, the *metonymic* quality of modern Anglo-American poetry—its tendency to present us with a kind of "mininovel" in which some "personality" is shown in the specificity of some situation in the unraveling of which he experiences a kind of illu-mination[26]—with the *metaphoric* orientation of modern French poetry, which has a tendency to efface the specificity of experience in the depths of universal imagery. For Bonnefoy, the metaphoric tendency will not be a Mallarméan "abolition" where Mallarmé "amazed and disappointed by the empirical self, transferred his hope to the possibilities of language," as if "the things of this world . . . [were] stale, 'sickly'" (*NR*, 185), but rather a resistance to poetic *personae*, to facile access to the representations of the world such *personae* often elaborate, to a poetry whose "story" would be a series of *coups de théâtre* or sensational events. Poetry, for Bonnefoy as for Eliot, is "not the expression of personality, but an escape from personality."[27]

Bonnefoy has himself started three novels—*Le Voyageur*, *Rapport d'un agent secret*, *L'Ordalie*[28]—only to reject their incompleteness. (Of *L'Ordalie*, for instance, he has said: "Those bifurcations, those prismatic splittings were certainly irreducible to any form of psychology, to any verisimilitude, withdrawing from finished writing like water" [*AP*, 98].) He has therefore felt himself, as he has sometimes said in conversation, "toujours chassé vers la poésie" ("always driven off toward poetry") of which he has written that for him it is "more deeply rooted, more demanding" than the prose which yields to it. The poetry is "the highest, the most intense part of the current,"[29] and the novels gradually gave way to the poems of *Douve*.

> This writing took up the more or less mythic events I had conceived of for the narrative, wanting them for its altogether different space, seeking to free them from their gangue of fiction and psychology in order to establish a resonance at once less strictly determined and at a deeper level of my own personal expression (or construction). Bits of poetry were already coming to birth in the doubtless rather emblematic descriptions I had made of two or three situations and of certain strange feelings which remained unclear. And this to such a degree that *L'Ordalie* had scarcely been "torn up" when certain passages managed, thanks to words which continued to seek their meaning and their place, to rearrange themselves in the other book—*Du mouvement et de l'immobilité de Douve*—especially in its fourth part, *L'Orangerie*. (Ibid., 40–41)

Bonnefoy summarizes, in the passage which follows, the nature of his poetic orientation—an orientation he found for himself early and which he has pursued with steadfastness and perseverance.

> By the end of my surrealist phase, I had a premonition of a poetry which would not seek to formulate our existential problems—this is the business of conceptual thinking—nor to have me appear in the guise of my own particular individuality, which is considered the standard for truthfulness. . . . in spite of how it seems this would merely be a presence viewed from without, a kind of rhetoric—but rather would carry consciousness in action directly into the field of the forces in play, those that determine as much as those that desire, the forces of the unconscious but also those of being, and would compose these forces by withdrawing, the self thereby expanding, deconditioning itself of its name, of its psychological past, by examining the effect of the finitude of fact on the infiniteness of language.[30]

In Bonnefoy's view, then, "images, in their sustained irrationality, propose themselves to the act of poetry" (ibid.).

For Yves Bonnefoy, psychological determinants—and more specifically the Freudian view of these determinants—must be considered as part of a general category of chance and fatality to which one opposes his understanding and freedom, as well as the moral resolve to acknowledge, love, and thus integrate these determinants. Pierre-Jean Jouve, in his "Inconscient, spiritualité et catastrope," had spoken of "the possibility of relationship and fundamental harmony between the superego, archaic restraining power, and the more universal erotic depths which constitute the nonself: so that, on the level of the unconscious, the war waged by the superego against the erotic self no longer results, as for so many, in sickness or accident, but produces on all sides an unlimited deepening."[31] Jouve aspired after a kind of reintegration, a mending of the divided self. In "the most privileged natures," he felt, "the lowest suddenly reconnects with the highest" (ibid.). Bonnefoy will refuse Jouve's dualistic orientation, preferring to maintain that "what one feels as unconscious in fact is only what is misunderstood in our existence, or to put it better, *unloved*, what is simply observed (and from the outside) by that cold, judgmental eye, by that lifeless eye that Jouve and Bataille . . . had as a common obsession, the one eye too many that Oedipus was left with" (*NR*, 242–43).

For Bonnefoy, "one gets the Oedipus one wishes, according to whether one approaches him as language (*langue*) or as speech (*parole*), with suspicion or with trust."[32] An important poem in the collection *Hier régnant désert* will speak of an *Oedipe sauvé*, an Oedipus delivered—the "misunderstood," the "unloved" redeemed by the poetic word whose mission is not separation but integration: "One might say of any god who comes to bring things together that he is the speech of poetry [*la parole*]" (*NR*, 251).

Resistant, then, to "psychological" poetry, to poetry as "mininovel," to a poetry celebrating the plight of an illusory and limited conception of the self, to a poetry of division, Bonnefoy has systematically sought "simply an ontology, and the pure act of poetry."[33] But this is not to say that a curious *remnant* of narrative is not dimly present in the aftermath of poetic "effacement." One can sense a sort of hidden narrative line, an absent story, which, though burned away—

> *l'espace d'un sol nu sous le feu paraîtra*　　　　　　　　　(*P*, 135)

The space of a barren soil beneath the fire will appear—

though invisible, is felt, imprecisely, unexplicitly under the higher, more violent, more universalized poetic current which remains. By diminishing the specificity of personal experience, the poet opens his poem to the deep experience of the reader—anonymous now as the writer.[34] For the "story" elaborated by the four books of poems is itself, in its way, timeless and universal, in the sense that it does not recount events as *coups de théâtre* but rather narrates what is always the same for everyone: birth, death, solitude, the meeting of the other, new birth. It is the structure or intelligible form of our relation to the world. Still, a particularly subtle complication emerges in the resistance to "worldliness." If the poet rejects "difference," if he is opposed to the elaboration of novel and *persona*, he nonetheless must struggle with the question of just how much of his own rather specific experience to include in the poetic text, for this question is related to the general problematics of "incarnation" I have been raising. Each volume will deal with this question in a different way, although it seems to me that one can trace an increasing acceptance of the "metonymic" detail, as the "story" Bonnefoy wants to tell becomes clearer to him, as he accepts more fully the passage of time, as the sense of "the other" and of place become concrete realities for him.

*   *   *

Yves Bonnefoy has spoken on many occasions of "the desert origin of artistic creation" (*NR*, 261). His resistance to the principal temptations of this desert, however, may be viewed as the effort to master exile and aridity, as the desire to reestablish himself in the "garden of presence." He has struggled against the lure of excarnation, the easy reliance on a miraculous providence (as well as its other face: the complacency in nihilism), and the false prestige of exhibitionism to concentrate on the true nature of his experience in real time and space and to define his being in the context not only of his desires but also of his limits. In short, he has sought to establish his yearning for transcendence in the very heart of finitude and in the midst of a reality which, while ever changing, yet remains ever the same. And it is this ideal of "incarnation" which he has served with the devotion of "the whole heart, the whole soul, and the whole mind."

3   The Baptism in Death

> . . . that decisive death which gives vibrancy to time, orientation to being. . . .

The publication in 1953 of Bonnefoy's first major collection of poems—*Du mouvement et de l'immobilité de Douve (On the Motion and Immobility of Douve)*—was greeted by a virtually unanimous critical approval. Here was a voice, as even the resistant Jean Grosjean admitted, to listen to with *la plus sévère attention.*[1] Inevitably, the question was raised: Who or what is Douve? A mysterious feminine category, her death, physical decomposition, and resurrection put one in mind of the romantic notion enunciated by E. A. Poe that "the death . . . of a beautiful woman is, unquestionably, the most poetical topic in the world."[2] And her relationship to the poetic narrator would seem also to support Poe's conviction that "the lips best suited for such topic are those of a bereaved lover" (ibid.).

On the other hand, she seems intimately related to the poetic process itself, to the nature of inspiration and to the impact on inspiration of death. Now death is a category in this poem which involves not only inevitable physical decomposition but also the inertia and lifelessness of established representation, the paralysis of *la langue* and the ever renewed struggle of *la parole* to pass beyond, to resurrect from the ashes of a spiritless "letter."[3] Bonnefoy has spoken of this principle in a number of his most important essays. In his piece on Jouve, for instance, he speaks of poetry as "a place where a voice, like the Phoenix, dies as language [*langue*], but in order to resurrect as speech [*parole*]" (*NR*, 265).[4] The "immortality" of which he writes in the early essay "Les Tombeaux de Ravenne" "has the freshness and echo of a dwelling only for those who are passing by" (*I*, 26). And "for those who would seek to possess, it will be a lie, a disappointment, a darkness" (*I*, 26). Furthermore, as Bonnefoy has remarked in a more recent essay (on Rimbaud), "Any work that would have itself considered a text, or that one would seek to interpret simply as a text, no longer touches anything but an already acquired reality, only retains relations between essences, records a state of the relation of consciousness to the world, and therefore places itself, irremediably, in the *past*, even if its words contribute to the development of language" (*NR*, 215).

The constant resurrections of Douve, her almost Ovidian metamorphoses, are the poetic expression of the recurrent but ephemeral moment of epiphanous vision. The fourth poem of the collection already announces this mysterious and paradoxical dimension of Douve's reality:

> . . . *à chaque instant,*
> *je te vois naître, Douve,*
>
> > *À chaque instant mourir.* (P, 26)

> . . . every moment
> I see you being born, Douve,
>
> > Every moment dying.

In this sense, Douve seems to be related to Joyce's now famous notion of the *epiphany*—that sudden "'revelation of the whatness of a thing,'" the moment in which "the soul of the commonest object . . . seems to us radiant."[5] Consciousness, or what Bonnefoy calls the "witness," is developed and matured through these isolated and unpredictable moments of insight and illumination. The "space" of these illuminations seems, in turn, to be related to Bonnefoy's notion of the "true place": "the true place is a fragment of duration consumed by the eternal, in the true place time comes apart in us" (*I*, 128). The "true place" is here before us: "Here (the true place is always a 'here'), here the mute or distant reality and my own existence reunite with one another, turn into one another, and rejoice in the sufficiency of being" (*I*, 20).

Many passages from *Douve* seem to confirm this idea of an intermittent illumination.

> *Le bras que tu soulèves, soudain, sur une porte,*
> *m'illumine à travers les âges.* (P, 26)

> The arm that you raise, suddenly, at a doorway, enlightens me
> across the ages.

A word such as *braises* (i.e. "burning coals" or "glowing embers") will often serve to suggest the moment of sudden revelation: ". . . Or, ce grand jour en / Toi des braises m'aveuglait" ("Now this bright day in / You of the burning coals was blinding me") (*P*, 75). There is, furthermore, a nice ambiguity in the use of the French conjunction *or* ("now"), since the word is also a substantive meaning "gold." Much of the energy of the book is directed at tearing the veils of artistic mediation, at "burning up" the bark of conceptual protection, at transforming the base material of "everyday" thinking into the gold of illumination and pure in-sight. I will return to the alchemical implications of Bonnefoy's project in my last chapter.

Above all, it is revelation of death that imposes itself with the greatest insistence in the pages of *Douve*. Among other things, Douve's death and the awesome realities it imposes on the consciousness of the narrator will have an impact on the viability of established poetic conventions and images. The thirteenth poem of "Théâtre," for instance, calls its own somewhat "surreal" images into question.

> *La mer intérieure éclairée d'aigles tournants,*
> *Ceci est une image.*
> *Je te détiens froide à une profondeur où les images ne*
>   *prennent plus.* (*P*, 35)

> The inner sea lit up by whirling eagles,
> This is an image.
> I am keeping you coldly mine at a depth where images no
>   longer take.

The name "Douve" is a marvelous polysignifier. On one level the word denotes a "moat"—the water-filled ditch surrounding a castle—or the ditches used to mark off fields and to allow for the flow of water. A poem from the section "The Orangery" will read:

> *Douve sera ton nom au loin parmi les pierres,*
> *Douve profonde et noire,*
> *Eau basse irréductible où l'effort se perdra.* (*P*, 82)

> Douve shall be your name far off among the stones,
> Douve deep and dark,
> Irreducible low water where all effort shall die out.

Moat of separation and limit, Douve evokes the impasse blocking off the voyager from the castle. If poetry is present as a reality, it is absent from the word which would try to possess it explicatively. Since illuminations are, by definition, privileged and fleeting moments, they resist permanence and expression. And one of the insistent ideas which emerges from the experience of reading *Douve* is that poetic expression is itself unequal to reality, that what it touches dies from its touch—only to resurrect as an unreached domain which retreats with inevitable encroachment—inexhaustible and eternally elusive, the empty square in the game of letters. "There is no immediacy," Bonnefoy has said, "there is only this desire for the immediate which so many feel. . . . Speaking, one looses the unity which is the only real place to live; . . . drawing, painting, writing, one forces being—power thereafter misunderstood—to hobble along even more on the crutches of the sign" (*NR*, 323).

The poetry of a dark time, for which belief in the transcendent deity and specific systems of sacred order has died out, will have to build its fires in the midst of "vast unutterable matter." Its refusal to accept the disappearance of meaning, its determination to reconstruct even amid the ruins are the indication, however, that "Douve" is associated with human spirit, with those spiritual aspirations suggested by the English word "Dove"—the traditional symbol of the Holy Spirit. The impossibility of ever understanding why such a spirit—who, while leading us toward inevitable failure and disillusionment, yet encourages us to keep up a futile struggle—should visit man, why there should be, as Proust has said, these "in-

visible laws" written on the human heart, is nicely conveyed by the sylla-
bles themselves: Douve, *D'où vient?* (i.e. "whence"?) or even *D'ouverture*,
for Douve is that effort at "opening"—"undertaken in the thickness of the
world" (*P*, 41).

Most readers of the poem, of course, will begin with the feeling that the
work treats of death by first focusing on the loss of a "beautiful woman."
And Bonnefoy has spoken of woman as "l'*autre*, par excellence" (*NR*, 262).

A theater of voices announces and develops the problem: a feminine
"you" is established by an "I" who will be called "the only witness." Even-
tually, the "you," named Douve, will speak, will become the "I" and desig-
nate the masculine witness as a "you."[6] On occasion, an "us" is constituted,
seemingly through the "assimilation" of the dead Douve by the speaking
witness. And repeatedly a dramatic structure will isolate a "he" or a "she"
through the murmurings of strange, unidentified "voices" who speak out
as though part of a kind of chorus, commenting on the essential drama of
the piece:

> *Tu fus sage d'ouvrir, il vint à la nuit,*
> *Il posa près de toi la lampe de pierre.*
> *Il te coucha nouvelle en ta place ordinaire,*
> *De ton regard vivant faisant étrange nuit.* (*P*, 68)

> You were wise to open, he came in the night,
> He placed close beside you the lamp of stone.
> He laid you down in a new form in your usual place,
> Turning your living gaze into strange night.

A mysterious stag and a salamander frozen on a wall play emblematic roles
in the drama, as do the figures of Cassandra and the "Knight of Mourn-
ing." The abstract notion of "place" is made more concrete through the
use of the Orangery—symbol of seventeenth-century French classicism.
The most strikingly metonymic detail of the piece is provided by the lovely
poem to the Chapel Brancacci—the idea of place suddenly illuminated by
a specific locale.

It might be said, therefore—and this is characteristic of Bonnefoy's
work—that several poetic lines run throughout the book. What one might
call the principal thematics of loss, and struggle against loss, is presented in
a number of poetic registers—sometimes mythic, sometimes "novelistic,"
sometimes lyric, sometimes dramatic—which reappear throughout the
book as a system of motifs illuminating a common set of concerns.

That the poem is a kind of drama is borne out not only by the presence
of the major "characters" and the chorus of voices but also by the use of
such words as *théâtre, gestes, comédie, parler, simuler, jouer, personnage*. This
vocabulary contributes to the sense that the poet knows that a poem can
only "act out" the realities it strives to evoke, or worse, may delight in its

own posturing and extravagance. The metamorphoses of Douve in part reflect the transformations in poetic expression, the succession of provisional masks, of *personae* assumed by the spirit of poetry. The poem, in fact, summarizes, in its way, through the use both of emblematic devices and intertextual echoing, a great deal of French poetic history and convention. But if the poem is a drama, what is it about?

Alex L. Gordon has compared *Douve* to a "classical tragedy with a downward curve through the first three movements and an upward sweep to resolution in the last two."

> The heroine's death [in "Théâtre"] is an event which overtakes her body and dissolves its unity in the shapeless multiplicity of grass and foliage or the nonform of earth, wind, and snow. . . . In "Théâtre" the world has been directed primarily by unconscious matter and almost speechless flesh. In "Derniers Gestes" consciousness proclaims its right to bear witness to Douve's death and to pass articulate commentary. The narrator thus proceeds to identify bodily with his dead beloved. . . . Section III, "Douve Parle," constitutes to some degree at least, a reply to the bold assertions of the narrator in section II. . . . What Douve really fears is that the word of poetry will fail to keep pace with her funeral descent. . . . The last two movements of *Douve* represent a slow struggle upward from the nadir of total death. . . . Douve halts, but does not stay in the "Orangerie." She is well aware of the dangers of an ideal light which floods the opaque realities of existence and robs them of their true character. . . . In "Vrai Lieu" the salamander which had appeared parenthetically in the "Orangerie" now emerges as the adequate emblem. . . . It can merge with the dense otherness of the stone and it can also live unscathed in the fire of the spirit.[7]

The movement isolated by Gordon—in one sense linear or diachronic—is not wholly incompatible with a radically different way of seeing the construction of the poem: that is, as composed metaphorically with the emphasis on a synchronic arrangement of its elements.

The narrator of the first poem says,

Je te voyais courir sur des terrasses.

I saw you running on the terraces.

In the fourth poem, he will say,

Je suis sur une terrasse. (emphasis mine)

I *am* on a terrace.

It is raining in this early poem, as it is in the last poem of "L'Orangerie." The fifth poem of the series "Le Seul Témoin" ("The Only Witness") from the section "Derniers Gestes" ("Last Acts") will evoke a *cerf pourchassé aux lisières* ("stag tracked to the outskirts") who will reappear in the penultimate poem of the book. An unidentified voice in the fourth poem of "Douve Parle" ("Douve Speaks") will speak of *les mots enfin de l'aube et de la pluie* ("the words of dawn and rain at last"), thus anticipating the *aube difficile* ("arduous dawn") of the last section, "Vrai Lieu" ("True Place"). The "events" of the third poem of "La Salamandre" seem to substantiate and precede the "memories" of the first poem of the book. There is everywhere the sense of "the way things once were," of loss. This sense is developed, however, not so much through a strict sequential or diachronic ordering as through the orchestration of poetic motifs. It is, of course, only natural to approach the poem as though its "drama" were working out a "story"—perhaps because some of the poem was "born from" a failed novel. Bonnefoy seems also to be suggesting, however, a general and inescapable condition. Paradoxically, this timeless drama celebrates the ravages of time within the context of the eternal death and rebirth cycle—which is to say that the poem allows for the coexistence of both the sense of movement in time, the "story" of the apprehension of personal finitude, and the intuition of an endless process of collapse and reconstruction.

In the first edition of *Anti-Platon*, Bonnefoy imagines a Plato "calcareous, stratified, horizontal . . . who is put together in space and knows nothing of time."[8] His Douve, on the other hand, is caught *dans le filet vertical de la mort* ("in the vertical net of death") (*P*, 38). Verticality, nevertheless, does seem an appropriate spatial representation of the *metaphoric*, as horizontality does for a *metonymic* or narrative mode. And Douve, in death, is characteristically imagined stretched out—*étendue*—suggesting that while the poem will not hesitate to acknowledge the horrible realities brought to beings by time, it will do so through an art which sets out to deemphasize the idea of the narrative of some one person in order to stress an ever reenacted drama—what the narrator calls the "fontaine de ma mort *presente* insoutenable" ("fountain of my death, *present* and unbearable") (*P*, 33; italics mine). I shall try to discuss the poem both in terms of its development and "movement" and in terms of its "simultaneity," its cyclical "immobility," its capacity to evoke an immemorial and ever recurring process.

* * *

Philippe Jaccottet has characterized the volumes of poetry before *Dans le leurre du seuil* as "véritables recueils" ("true collections"),[9] implying an absence of unifying structure or identifiable continuity among the parts. All the volumes, and *Douve* in particular, however, seem to elaborate their dynamics along a barely perceptible narrative line. Douve dies; her lover assimilates the idea of loss; Douve and other voices speak of death; a scene in an orangery evokes an erotic moment in its futility and points out the vanity of protecting structures, while the final section imagines consciousness in search of proper orientation or "true place"—the disillusioned contact with simple, mortal presences.

Bonnefoy has spoken of himself at the end of his surrealist period as "caught between a kind of spontaneous materialism which has remained natural to me, and an innate concern for transcendence, a profound inclination toward the categories and even toward the myths which give expression to it"[10] Part of the search recorded in the pages of *Douve* is for "an acceptable compromise" (ibid.).

The first two sections of the poem look with unblinking honesty at the processes of the natural order, at the fate of flesh, at the devastating triumph of matter over the illusory aspirations of mind and spirit. For Bonnefoy, death founds the "true discourse" (*I*, 34). The "play acting" of Douve is tempered and clarified through death. Like Baudelaire before him, Bonnefoy will replace the theater of ruses and posturing with "another theater, the theater of evidence, the human body" (*I*, 34). Like Baudelaire's, his poetic word will seek to establish itself where death has "its chosen place"—the "wounded body" (*I*, 34). Few poems in the French language will treat of physical decomposition with equal power. Douve is "couverte de l'humus silencieux du monde" ("covered by the world's silent humus") (*P*, 33); "elle rayonne une joie stridente d'insectes" ("she radiates a strident insect joy") (*P*, 34); her hands are "condamnées à l'herbe luxuriante qui l'envahit de toutes parts" ("condemned to the lush grasses which invade her on every side") (*P*, 36); the specificity of her profile is effaced by the workings of the earth (*P*, 37); and "des yeux à facettes, des thorax pelucheux, des têtes froides à becs, à mandibules, l'inondent" ("faceted eyes, shaggy thoraxes, cold heads with beaks, with jaws, flood over her") (P, 36).

Death, of course, had been treated with terrible frankness before Bonnefoy. In this sense, Villon is a precursor. And Baudelaire wrote of *une charogne* ("carrion"):

> *Les mouches bourdonnaient sur ce ventre putride,*
> *D'où sortaient de noirs bataillons*
> *De larves, qui coulaient comme un épais liquide*
> *Le long de ces vivants haillons.*

> The flies were humming on that rotting belly
> Out of which black battalions of larvae
> Were streaming, oozing like some thick fluid
> Down the length of those living rags of flesh.

Like Bonnefoy—and this is only one example among many of the intertex-
tual echoing in *Douve*—Baudelaire will also speak of the "weird music" of
decomposition. Valéry wrote of "les mort cachés . . . dans cette terre / Qui
les rechauffe et sèche leur mystère" ("the dead hidden . . . in the earth /
Which warms them and dries out their mystery"). One of the most arrest-
ing passages in "Le Cimetière marin" will evoke "un peuple vague aux
racines des arbres" ("a vague people at the roots of the trees"):

> *Ils ont fondu dans une absence épaisse,*
> *L'argile rouge a bu la blanche espèce,*
> *Le don de vivre a passé dans les fleurs!*
> *Où sont des morts les phrases familières,*
> *L'art personnel, les âmes singulières?*
> *La larve file où se formaient des pleurs.*

> The personal style, the unique soul?
> The larva winds where once tears would form.
> The gift of life has passed into the flowers!
> Where are the common phrases of the dead,
> The personal style, the unique soul?
> The larva winds where once tears would form.

And Cébès in the first act of Claudel's *Tête d'Or* knows that "toutes les mal-
adies veillent sur nous" ("every illness lies in wait for us"):

> *. . . Il y a des gens dont les yeux*
>   *Fondent comme des nèfles fendues qui laissent*
> *couler leur pépins.*
> *. . . . .*
>   *La phtisie fait son feu; les parties honteuses*
> *moisissent comme du raisin; et le sac du ventre*
>   *Crève et vide dehors les entrailles et les*
> *excréments!*

> . . . there are people whose eyes
>   Fall apart like split medlars spilling
> out their seeds.
> . . . .
>   Consumption rages; the body's private parts
> turn moldy like rotting grapes; and the sack of the belly
>   Bursts, pouring out intestines and excrement!

Bonnefoy's "body" is also the *theater* of a tremendous battle between
form and formlessness. In fact, an astonishingly complete physical body
emerges in the pages of *Douve*. To the word *corps* ("body") repeated eleven
times come the following to render more specific and hence to define the
physical topography: *arm, heart, lips, teeth, hands, fingers, head, hair,*

breasts, throat, leg, flanks, face, mouth, knees, shoulder, eyes—even *bones* and *flesh, blood* and *arteries* to structure and fill. Feeling, nurturing, receiving organs; the instruments of locomotion, construction, mastication, articulation. And this is not to mention the activities ordinarily associated with specific organs and which the poem distinctly mentions: i.e., *regard* ("look"), *voix* ("voice"), *boire* ("drink"), *sourire* ("smile").

If at first Douve reigns "absent from [the] head" (*P*, 25) of the narrator in a kind of eroticism in death—"toute / En quête de la mort sur les tambours exultants de [s]es / gestes" ("all / Bent on death on the exulting drums of [her] gestures") (*P*, 25)—if at first her reality on a "day of [her] breasts" (*P*, 25) is stronger than all purely mental constructions, the poem as a whole will dramatize the way in which her physical death finishes the process of what Gordon calls "the humbling of the head." [11]

> *La musique saugrenue commence dans les mains, dans*
> *les genoux, puis c'est la tête qui craque . . .*   (*P*, 30)

> The weird music begins in the hands, in
> the knees, then it is the head that cracks . . .

And,

> *Le ravin pénètre dans la bouche maintenant,*
> *Les cinq doigts se dispersent en hazards de forêt*
>   *maintenant,*
> *La tête première coule entre les herbes maintenant,*
> *La gorge se farde de neige et de loups maintenant.*   (*P*, 39)

> The ravine breaks into the mouth now,
> The five fingers are scattered in forest changes
>   now,
> The all-important head flows among the grasses now,
> The throat is painted up with snow and wolves now.

The repeated use of the word *maintenant* ("now") underscores the fact that the action of destruction and decay is ever at work, that death is always "present." The notion of the primacy of the mental functions is deflated in the evocation of an equal and indifferent reduction of the entire body.

Bonnefoy will raise the question of the relationship between physical realities and the poetic act, for he knows of "ce / sang qui renaît et s'accroît où se déchire le poème" ("this / blood which revives and flourishes there where the poem is torn apart") (*P*, 40). The short poem "Art Poétique" seems to speak of a loss of orientation in the poetic spirit.

> *Visage séparé de ses branches premières,*
> *Beauté toute d'alarme par ciel bas,*
>
> *En quel âtre dresser le feu de ton visage*
> *O Ménade saisie jetée la tête en bas?*   (*P*, 56)

Face cut off from its first branchings,
Beauty all in alarm beneath a gloomy sky,

In what hearth can the fire of your face be built
O Maenad seized and thrown down head first?

(A later poem—the "Vérité" of "L'Orangerie"—will speak of "visages ré-
unis" ("faces reunited"), and of "gestes gauches du cœur sur le corps retro-
uvé, / Et sur lequel tu meurs, absolue vérité" ("awkward gestures of the
heart on the rediscovered body, / And on which you perish, absolute
truth") [P, 83].) In "Art Poétique" the emphasis is on a poetic situation
which has become separated from its idealistic traditions, from its convic-
tion that it is the expression of some absolute truth, that it is a divine reve-
lation. It especially insists that the "head"—with its productions (whether
of intellectual categories or lyrical beauty)—is defeated in the new poetics.
The Maenad is thrown head downward in a posture reminiscent of the
burial of those treacherous Simoniac popes of Dante's *Inferno*—those who
more literally "traffic in the eternal"—those "who are held upside down
. . . planted like a post," [12] or even of his Satan "upside down" ("his legs
held upwards") and Judas in Satan's mouth "who has his head inside and
plies his legs without." [13] If part of the movement of the *Inferno* will be to
restore Dante to an upright position, to allow him at last to say, "fui
dritto" ("I had risen"), [14] the movement of *Douve* is just the reverse. "Celui
qui brulait *debout*" ("he who was burning *upright*") (P, 63; italics mine) is
thrown from his peak to illuminate vast and unutterable matter. The head
is "repudiated" (P, 41), and is "livré(e) . . . aux basses flammes / De la
mer" ("turned over . . . to the low flames / Of the sea") (P, 45).

The recognition of finitude obliterates the earlier pretensions of poetry.
If the narrator holds Douve at "a depth where images no / longer take," her
death encourages a "deep knowledge which burns to ashes / The old besti-
ary of the mind" (P, 37).

As I have already mentioned, Bonnefoy cites Dante, Jouve, and Bataille
as key influences during the period of his studies in Paris during the for-
ties. Like Bonnefoy, Jouve insisted on locating the sacred "sur la chair
même de la vie" ("on the very flesh of life"). [15] And Bonnefoy seems to
have felt immediately drawn to the work of Bataille, whose wide-ranging
interests are marked by a particular fascination for those extreme states,
those paroxysms of joy, pain, sacrifice, torture, pleasure which uncover ul-
timate truths about being, the menace of destruction and death being for
him, as for Bonnefoy, a source of affirmation. The erotic experience, which
in *Douve* provides both disillusionment and knowledge, is for Bataille "the
approbation of life even unto death." [16] The intensity of the erotic experi-
ence is "at its greatest when destruction, when the death of being are al-

lowed to show through" (ibid., 175). In his *L'Erotisme*, which would appear a few years after *Douve*, Bataille writes:

> The movement toward the continuity of life, the intoxication of this continuity override the thought of death. To begin with, the first turbulent surge of erotic experience gives us a feeling which overwhelms all else, so that the gloomy thought of our own personal discontinuity is forgotten. Then, beyond these youthful transports, we are given the power to look death in the face, and to see in it at last the pathway into the incomprehensible and unknowable continuity of life, which is the secret gift of eroticism and which eroticism alone can provide.[17]

(Bonnefoy himself, in a particularly moving passage from his piece on *The Song of Roland*, will speak of death in a somewhat similar fashion: "'Dying,' Roland destroys that boundary which shuts in the created being: the enclosure of the self, vain rival of being. . . . He comes into contact with the stuff of life and makes it well up once again, a fountain in which every existence can find itself in every other—and it is true that there is a synthetical function in the gift of the self; Jesus, who prefigures Roland, taught him this, Jesus who, through his death, founded a communion" [*NR*, 179].)

In *Douve*, death becomes "ce destin *éclairant* dans la terre du verbe" ("this destiny *shining* in the earth of words") (*P*, 55; italics mine) and an incentive to a menaced poetry. "Ne suis-je pas," a voice will say, "ta vie aux profondes alarmes, / Qui n'a de monument que Phénix au bûcher?" ("Am I not your life in its deepest alarms / Whose only monument is the Phoenix on its pyre?") (*P*, 65). And Douve will ask that "le froid par [s]a mort se lève et prenne un sens" ("the cold through [her] death rise up and take on meaning") (*P*, 63).

If the narrator must come to the awesome recognition that "tout se défait . . . tout s'éloigne" ("everything dies . . . everything vanishes") (*P*, 50), he will also understand that Douve is an "être défait que l'être invincible rassemble" (a "decomposed being that invincible being recomposes") (*P*, 31). The horrible language of decomposition also designates the stuff, the material of earth's regenerative power. Death is thus a force which contributes its weight to the question of the self. Already the *Anti-Platon* of 1947 had established the dialectic between a kind of life force and a specific conscious self facing extinction, disintegration, and recombination within this unthinking and tenacious power.

> *Nous sommes d'un même pays sur la bouche de la terre,*
> *Toi d'un seul jet de fonte avec la complicité des*
> *feuillages*

Et celui qu'on appelle moi quand le jour baisse
Et que les portes s'ouvrent et qu'on parle de mort.   (*P*, 16)

We are from the same country on the mouth of the earth,
You in one molten flow with the complicity of the
     leaves

And the one they call me when day grows dim
And the doors open and they start talking about death.

Douve, on one level, charts the progress of illumination in death. In this
sense, it is less Douve's book than that of the *je* or witness whose principal
stance in "Théâtre" is the act of looking. This act will have as its conse-
quence an impact on the act of speaking, on the poetic orientation. By the
seventeenth poem of "Théâtre," the narrator will have so assimilated the
process of death as to be able to exclaim: "c'est / *nous* dans ce vent dans
cette eau dans ce froid / maintenant" ("*we* are / the ones in this wind in this
water in this cold / now") (*P*, 39; italics mine). The *nous* or "us" consti-
tuted in the eternal present of this vision is not simply the identification of
the lover with the dead beloved; the *nous* points to the greater relationship
between the living and the dead, between the conscious self and the un-
conscious procedures of a continuous natural unity.

Poem XVIII of "Théâtre" will insist

Il fallait qu'ainsi tu parusses aux limites sourdes,
et d'un site funèbre où ta lumière empire, que tu
subisses l'épreuve.

O plus belle et la mort infuse dans ton rire! J'ose à
présent te rencontrer, je soutiens l'éclat de tes gestes.   (*P*, 40)

It was necessary for you to appear, thus, at the hollow limits,
and to undergo the ordeal of a land of death where your light
is threatened.

O more beautiful still and your laughter steeped with death!
Now at last I dare to meet you, I can bear the radiance of your
gestures.

This movement may be said to reach its moment of culmination in the ex-
tremely beautiful poem "Vrai Corps" ("True Body").

Close la bouche et lavé le visage,
Purifié le corps, enseveli
Ce destin éclairant dans la terre du verbe,
Et le mariage le plus bas s'est accompli.

Tue cette voix qui criait à ma face
Que nous étions hagards et séparés,

Murés ces yeux: et je tiens Douve morte
Dans l'âpreté de soi avec moi refermée.

Et si grand soit le froid qui monte de ton être,
Si brûlant soit le gel de notre intimité,
Douve, je parle en toi; et je t'enserre
Dans l'acte de connaître et de nommer.

(*P*, 55)

The mouth has been closed and the face washed,
The body cleansed, this destiny
Full of light buried in the earth of words,
And the humblest marriage is fulfilled.

Silenced that voice which would cry in my face
That we were wild and apart,
Walled up those eyes: and I hold Douve dead
In the pure bitterness of being, shut in with me.

And however terrible the coldness rising from you,
However searing the frost of our intimacy,
Douve, I will speak in you; and I will hold you close
In the act of knowing and of naming.

The destiny of death is clarifying for the poet. Although a humbling recognition for the proud head, for the intellectual constructions of men, elaborated outside the fatalities of time and mortality, the awareness of death is espoused here in an act of intimacy, of marriage with consciousness which will have for consequence that the subjectivity will henceforth speak from the context of a new vision, a new orientation. The verbs *tenir* ("to hold"), *refermer* ("to shut in"), and *enserrer* ("to clasp," "to embrace," "to hold close") all emphasize a voluntary adhesion to the principle of death seen as a necessary component of both a just appreciation of one's being-in-the-world and the poetic act which would take honest stock of this situation—that is, of knowing and naming.

In this sense, a true recognition of death is the proper baptismal experience for poetic consciousness. It is Claudel's notion of "knowing" that Bonnefoy is echoing here: the idea that the poet comes to birth with (*co-naître*) what he knows (*connaître*) through naming it. The dead Douve becomes the apparition of the living Dove who is discovered to an awakened consciousness—at once an illumination of finality and a call to authentic poetic orientation. A strange voice will speak of this impersonally and with a kind of incantatory conviction on more than one occasion in *Douve*.

Que saisir sinon qui s'échappe,
Que voir sinon qui s'obscurcit,
Que désirer sinon qui meurt,
Sinon qui parle et se déchire?

(*P*, 44)

What can be seized except what escapes,
What can be seen except what grows dark,
What can be desired except what dies,
Except what speaks and is torn asunder?

And later,

> La lumière profonde a besoin pour paraître
> D'une terre rouée et craquante de nuit.
> C'est d'un bois ténébreux que la flamme s'exalte.
> Il faut à la parole même une matière,
> Un inerte rivage au-delà de tout chant.
>
> Il te faudra franchir la mort pour que tu vives,
> La plus pure présence est un sang répandu.   (P, 52)

> If it is to appear, the deep light needs
> An earth broken and cracked with night.
> It is a somber wood that gives life to the flame.
> Speech itself needs such substance,
> A listless shore beyond all song.

> You will have to pass through death in order to live,
> The purest presence is blood which is shed.

The first passage emphasizes the paradoxical relationship between mental operations (and the poetical function, in particular) which are capable of fixing and the elusive material on which they place their attentions. The second passage insists upon the *necessity* of this paradox. To exist truly, the poetical word must attach itself to matter, to the processes of nature, which if they inevitably involve death and decomposition, also elaborate resurrections and assure new forms. In addition, the second passage develops, in spatial terms, the idea of a passage toward greater awareness and clarification. Recognition and acceptance of death must be passed through as one crosses a river; on "the other side" is life—that is, a vision "purified" of illusion and a poetics beyond mere lyricism or formal beauty.

The idea of a passage across a river to some other bank is a recurrent one in Bonnefoy; here, the emphasis on purification puts one in mind of Dante's crossing of the river Lethe in Purgatory. In fact, in a general way, the two poems have a number of striking parallels. A poetic consciousness is deeply marked by the death of a beloved woman. In both cases, the poets seek to communicate with and to be guided by the lost presence. Dante crosses a "sacred river" to arrive at *la beata riva*, "the blessed shore."[18]

> Quando fui presso alla beata riva,
> "Asperges me" si dolcemente udissi,
> che nol so rimembrar, non ch'io lo scriva.   (ibid., 97–99)

When I was close to the blessed shore,
I heard "Asperges me" sung so sweetly,
That I cannot recall, far less write it.

The passage in *Douve*, of course, is toward a far less reassuring shore, but it does suggest a similar, though infinitely less confident, reassessment of the status of poetic discourse. Beatrice would have Dante learn the lesson of her "buried flesh"; since all physical beauty is scattered to dust (*so' 'n terra sparte*), the poet must learn to *levar suso*, to "rise up." The mortal pleasures of life should not, Beatrice warns her pilgrim, "weigh down" his wings (ibid., 48–60). A characteristic movement after recognition of death in *Douve*, on the other hand, is downward into the silences of matter and the realities of the natural process. And the movement of inspiration "upward" seems evasion in the modern poem; Douve's arrow "retombe / Et brise sur le sol les palmes de sa tête" ("falls back down / And breaks its crown of palms against the ground") (*P*, 41).

If the "true body" is conceived of as participating in nature's cycles, as being fundamentally a collection of material doomed to collapse and recombination, if its fate once embraced leads to a disillusioned "knowing," the "true name" will inevitably designate desert, night, absence, and nothingness (*P*, 51). And the *je* will both name in death and be named: "A peine si je sens ce souffle qui me nomme" ("I scarcely feel this breath that names me") (*P*, 57).

The poem strives to work out poetically the truth of the epigraph from Hegel that the life of the spirit does not flee from death but, rather, maintains itself in death, and it does so along the lines evoked by the title of the poem. Like the epigraph, the title sets up a fundamental contradiction: movement and immobility. Characteristically, the "I" will regard Douve in postures of movement: "Je te voyais courir sur des terrasses, / Je te voyais lutter contre le vent. . . . Je t'ai vue te rompre et jouir d'être morte" ("I saw you running on the terraces, / I saw you fighting against the wind. . . . / And I have seen you break apart and know the ecstacy of being dead") (*P*, 23). In death, Douve becomes that "purest form of presence" which is in absence and disappearance, in "blood that is shed." But if Douve is presented in the context of verbs of movement (*courir*, "to run"; *lutter*, "to struggle or fight"; *se mouvoir*, "to move or stir"), if the realities the "I" encounters are conceived of in their elusiveness (*s'échapper*, "to escape"; *se déchirer*, "to tear apart"; *se rompre*, "to break"), the desire for stability, for habitation, for place will remain a constant one. Modern consciousness is like the "personnage ayant froid et privé de maison" ("figure who is cold and homeless") (*P*, 85) evoked in the first poem of "Vrai Lieu" ("True Place").

The voices of "Douve Parle" ("Douve Speaks") know, however, that all lodgings are necessarily impermanent. Our movement, our openness to the shocks of the exterior and the other, our willingness to risk our security in order to brave the cold winds of finitude are all forms of threat to the warmth of permanence and stability. The following lines—which may be echoing Edgar Poe—evoke this loss of protection.

> La première venue en forme d'oiseau
> Frappe à ma vitre au minuit de ma veille.
> J'ouvre et saisie dans sa neige je tombe
> Et ce logis m'échappe où je menais grand feu.   (P, 68)

The first to arrive in the form of a bird
Taps at my window in the midnight of my vigil.
I open and caught in its snow I fall
And this dwelling where I lit great fires vanishes from me.

Paradoxically, too, although the reality of death provides the dislocations associated with movement, death will be presented in a recurring posture of immobility: *tomber* ("to fall"), *s'interrompre* ("to break off"), *coucher* ("to lay down"). Similarly, the notion of *place*, conceived of as a protecting structure, is undermined by the images of the *site funèbre* ("funereal site"), the *pièce blanche* ("white room"), the deserted *château*, the *logis dévasté* ("ruined dwelling"), even the Brancacci Chapel toward which one directs his steps "in vain." [19] And the poem, of course, on one level, traces the sobering, the *quieting* effect of finitude on the extravagances and delusions of artistic movement and evasion.

The section entitled "L'Orangerie" contains perhaps the strongest suggestion of a narrative line of all the sections of the poem. It evokes the search for protecting structure or habitation and the illusory effort to escape death through erotic fusion with another. (The section draws certain phrases and resonances from the early narrative *L'Ordalie*—that enigmatic and symbolical *récit* of which only the last chapters have survived. Bonnefoy had hoped, in the elaboration of the story, to manifest "our woundedness," to incorporate "bloodshed" as a sudden revelation of authenticity and truthfulness. [20] Paradoxically, however, the story seemed to become a closed form, "luring" its author toward "atemporal worlds," while encouraging him to despise "imperfection and danger" (ibid.). Bonnefoy sees the hero's refuge in the Orangery, where he is neither alive nor dead, as a retreat into the structure of intelligible forms, as the escape from contingency and chance—as the movement toward excarnation.)

There is less explicit violence in the poem than in the narrative (in which Jean Basilide is "covered with blood," and Anne is shot "right in the forehead"—ibid., 14, 38). The poetic text does strive to make manifest our vulnerability in mortality, however, and the sense of futility and loss reverberate strongly in this part of the poem.

Gaëtan Picon, writing of the new poets who had emerged after World War II, said of them that they felt totally disinherited from all poetic tradition. Marked by war, by a history "so monstrous that it denies all poetic possibility," the new generation of poets, in Picon's view, felt itself "separated from the word it might be, from the universe it might name." The new poets were not unaware that it was the very nature of previous poetic enterprises, the uncritical proliferation of imaginary worlds, which had to a degree abandoned the real world of mortal men and women to the onslaughts of violence and war. Appropriately, Picon placed the efforts of the new poets "between the fact of ruin and the desire for reconstruction."[21]

Bonnefoy's section "The Orangery" begins in a crepuscular atmosphere, suggestive of both the transition of twilight and the end of an era:

> *Ainsi marcherons-nous sur les ruines d'un ciel immense,*
> *Le site au loin s'accomplira*
> *Comme un destin dans la vive lumière.*
>
> *Le pays le plus beau longtemps cherché*
> *S'étendra devant nous terre des salamandres.*
>
> *Regarde, diras-tu, cette pierre:*
> *Elle porte la présence de la mort.*
> *Lampe secrète c'est elle qui brûle sous nos gestes,*
> *Ainsi marchons-nous éclairés.*   (P, 71)

> So we will walk among the ruins of a boundless sky,
> The site, from afar, will be made clear
> Like a destiny in the bright light.
>
> The most beautiful country sought for so long
> Will lie before us, land of the salamanders.
>
> Consider, you will say, this stone:
> Death shines from it.
> Secret lamp it is what burns beneath our steps,
> And so we walk in light.

The poem may be read as the modernist response to Baudelaire's "Vie antérieure" and as a continuation of his critique of the imaginary. The past tenses of the earlier, more nostalgic poem yield here to future and present tenses. The first line, on one level at least, seems to speak of a painful period of decline—the end of a certain idealist tradition, the repudiation of the now invalid images of an excarnate reverie which once were rolled toward the languishing poet in "The Previous Life." The heavens which have collapsed with their images represent precisely the infinite imaginary which is the extreme form of alienation. On the other hand, the "ruins" of the first line of the poem already conjure up the image of the guiding stone which will appear at the end of the poem.

The future tense of the verb is suggestive of the search or quest for meaning in an age of spiritual eclipse. The "site" of which the poem speaks indicates the ground upon which the future dwelling will be established. This ground is the land of the salamander, spirit of resurrection, survivor of fire and flood, and symbol for Bonnefoy, through its silent, unpretentious adherence to earth, of "all that is pure" (*P*, 89). This land "so long sought after" by excarnate dreaming, is perhaps nothing so much as the simple evidence before us, the most common features of which—water, stone, tree—are improbable and miraculous presences for the vision purified of an unbounded nostalgia, or, put another way, infused with the energy normally expended on transcendence or dream. "Long is the road," Bonnefoy has said in another place, "that brings us back to the ordinary house—which is our place" (*NR*, 113).

The exhortation of the last stanza is the poet's determination to convert the futurity of the projected quest of the first two parts of the poem into a present apprehension of both limitation and plenitude. This intuition is granted, as it so often is in Bonnefoy's work, by the stone. Bonnefoy's stone is related to those sepulchers in Poussin's *Et in Arcadia Ego* pictures which rise up as a reminder of death's presence even in Arcadia to control an absent-minded absorption in nature's splendors; it has something, too, of those skulls in Georges de la Tour which seem, more than the light from the nearby candle, to be the real source of the illumination on the penitent's face. If Baudelaire's ideal landscape in "La Vie antérieure" is undermined by the remembrance of a "sorrowful secret," which may be understood as the intuition of that finitude which jars complacency in irreality and forbids the desertion of the real world of limitation and tears, Bonnefoy may be said to have made this "secret" the very source of orientation and grounding in his poem. It is what now illuminates the poetic effort, the act of "knowing and naming." The lamp of stone will accompany the poet through much of the rest of the poem and will provide light during the crises recorded by future books. As is the case for other poems in *Douve*, this text may be said, through its "movement" in the first two parts and its return to a kind of timeless present in the last, to reflect many of the major preoccupations of the book as a whole. In this sense, it may be said to trace, through its very organization, that search for "true place"— "where mute or distant reality and my own existence reunite with one another, turn into one another, and rejoice in the sufficiency of being"— which constitutes the deepest aspiration of the struggle recorded by this book.

The section "The Orangery" is, of course, extremely enigmatic. In a general way, the section opposes the daytime of words and distinct realities with the passion of the wind and the indistinctness of night: "C'était jour de parole et ce fut nuit de vent" ("It had been day of words and it was night of wind") (*P*, 72). The Orangery appears as "a bit of stone among the branches" (*P*, 73). It is the place of "necessary repose" (*P*, 73) for one who is "returning" (*P*, 72). It is abandoned. It is here in some ultimate night-experience of being, in "the last room of summer" (*P*, 74) that the narrator identifies the presence of Douve with burning wood and with the salamander he sees frozen on a wall in the light of his lamp and whose closeness is converted into an awareness developed more fully in the poem "Lieu de la salamandre."

The section suggests powerfully but imprecisely some experience of union, "the moment when the closest flesh turns into knowledge" (*P*, 76). This experience is presented in an oblique and ambiguous manner, however, and it is difficult to determine what exactly is being suggested. It is characteristic of Bonnefoy to present erotic experience in the general terms of participation in natural being. Thus the fire, as may be observed in certain poems from the later *Pierre écrite*, as I hope to show, may be said to both reflect presence as such and to suggest what in erotic fusion presents itself as fire. In any case, dawn comes to shatter this experience of union; the sun breaks apart "that last / Attachment which is the heart one touches in the darkness" (*P*, 78). A vision seems to have been developed which comes from "deeper than the lover's gaze" (*P*, 79). Silence is welcomed joyfully (*P*, 80), and the narrator leaves behind in the Orangery the memory of past love to pursue an unsure quest.

Critics have been quick to cite the "classical" elements in *Douve*. I have already spoken of Gordon's comparison of the poem to a classical tragedy; and, in my first chapter, I spoke of the use of a classical versification. In addition, Bonnefoy uses, for his own purposes, the diction of the classical vocabulary: *gloire, victoire, force, foudre*. On the other hand, Bonnefoy seems to be suggesting the vacancy, the insufficiency of classical structures and categories in the face of our finitude, the inability of the forms of classical order to reflect our true condition. He has said of the Orangery that it is the "house of the intelligible"; [22] it represents for him "the emblematic key, the latent consciousness" (*I*, 112) of the classical era. These are the structures, he says, whose large windows open onto the "sun of being," that have no dark parts. They prefigure, for Bonnefoy, "through the exemplary flowers and plants they harbour, the future gardens of Mallarmé" (*I*, 112). But this atmosphere of artificial clarity is invaded by "the night, or the memory of the night," which fills it with the hint of blood, sacrificial blood, "as if some momentous act had once taken place there" (*I*, 112). Bonnefoy, of course, will consciously bring out this hint of blood and have it fill his Orangery.

Similarly, Bonnefoy has spoken of the great works of the classical era as comparable to "a temple . . . the dwelling of a god" (*I*, 110). Through proportion and number, through the essential reduction of form, the temple "seeks to establish the safety of law in the dangerous region."

> Here in the crystal of the atemporal we escape the indefinite and the darkness. But in the secret recesses of the temple, on the altar or in some crypt, the unforeseeable is present. Nothing more than gleaming on a face of stone, but the whole storm is suddenly present again in the midst of the symmetry. (*P*, 110)

In the poem, the approach to the Orangery suggests, in fact, the entrance to a temple: a vase adorns the threshold (*P*, 72). But, as I have said, the "secret recesses" of the classical structures, the intuition of finitude which is repressed but unconsciously experienced there—these "recesses" are brought into sharp focus in the modern poem. The "odor of blood" is the "blessing" sought for, the "frugal blessing shining on an orangery" (*P*, 83). Even the erotic experience, while it destroys our enclosures, the illusory protection of an idealistic structure, brings with it a painful knowledge of limits—an awakening into the inevitably material realities of love and death brought out by the "odor of blood." Similarly, the "burial" of Douve in the Orangery, "on the table set up in another light" (*P*, 82), seems to suggest both the potential lifelessness and vacancy of classical forms in an age of spiritual desolation and the idea that the classical structures, if they are to continue to exist at all, must house our finitude in a central place. If dawn comes to shatter the last possible attachments, poetic consciousness will now strive to reunite the "awkward gestures" of the heart with the "rediscovered" mortal body. Nevertheless, the section ends with a variation on the question asked at the end of the section "Derniers Gestes" ("Last Acts") (i.e. "En quel âtre dresser le feu. . . ?" "In what hearth can the fire be built. . . ?").

> *Tu as pris une lampe et tu ouvres la porte,*
> *Que faire d'une lampe, il pleut, le jour se lève.*   (*P*, 84)

> You took up a lamp, and you open the door,
> What use is a lamp, it is raining, day is coming on.

A solitary consciousness pursues, in the final section, the quest for place, hoping in those indomitable powers of resurrection which insure the continuity of forms and enable a tireless aspiration to spring from the ashes of disillusionment and death. This consciousness will strive to see the presence of Douve in the simple evidence before it, the *being* of which constitutes a true place to the extent that it may be seen to participate in timeless and universal being.

*   *   *

An analysis of what one might call the "movement" of the poem—the sense one has of progression, of quest unfolding—does not exhaust all that one might say about it. There is, as I have said, an equally strong sense of recurrent process. A number of poetic resources contribute to the impression of an endless dialectic of loss and recovery, and I shall focus here on three such resources: on the use of nonverbal utterances (the "cry" and "laughter"), on the use of color, and finally on the elaboration of essential gesture.

To the extent that movement in *Douve* is associated with spiritual searching, the quest invariably encounters the obstacle so overpowering, so impenetrable that the result is the recurrent "cry." The word is of seminal importance in Bonnefoy's work, and it is found again and again in the pages of *Douve*. The word first occurs in connection with Douve's agony.

> *Je t'ai vue ensablée au terme de ta lutte*
> *Hésiter aux confins du silence et de l'eau,*
> *Et la bouche souillée des dernières étoiles*
> *Rompre d'un cri l'horreur de veiller dans ta nuit.* (P, 29)

> I saw you, sunk in sand at your struggle's end,
> Falter at the edges of silence and water,
> And your mouth stained with the last stars,
> Pierce with a cry the horror of waiting in the night.

This passage sets forth a number of recurrent conditions of the cry. The cry is sent out at a moment or a place of threshold or of hesitation. It is a kind of resistance to and protest against the unknown, the unnamed. It is the response to the death of the secure self, to the disappearance of the protecting structure. ("There are things that it is better not to understand, not to explain," Shestov wrote in his *Potestas Clavium*. "Strange as it may be, it is often better to weep, curse, and laugh than to understand. It does no harm not only for poetry but for prose as well to be, at times, not too intelligent and not to know everything.")[23] Dante feels this loss of understanding on the back of the Geryon or just before crossing through the Purgatorial wall of fire. Of his descent into the void of Hell on the back of the monster, Dante says:

> *vidi ch'i'era*
> *ne l'aere d'ogne parte, e vidi spenta*
> *ogne vedute fuor che de la fera.*[24]

> I saw that I was
> in the air on every side, and I saw extinguished
> every sight except that of the beast.

Before the wall of flames in Purgatory, Dante is like "colui che nella fossa e messo"[25] ("one who is put in the pit")—a state reminiscent of the narrator of *Douve* who is "dans un trou de mort" ("in a pit of death") (*P*, 26). Dante summons the Geryon by throwing a rope girdle into the abyss. With this belt, he had at one time hoped to subdue the fearful leopard. The movement foreshadows the confrontation with the wall of flames in Purgatory when Dante must throw his entire body into the pass of fire. In both cases something must be surrendered, and in both cases Dante resists.

In *Douve*, the limitations of language, of representation in the face of what is, explode in a cry which is specifically compared to the void.

> *Et dans le vide où je te hausse j'ouvrirai*
> *La route de la foudre,*
>
> *Ou plus grand cri qu'être ait jamais tenté.* (*P*, 60; emphasis mine)

> And where I lift you in the void I will open up
> The road of lightning,
>
> Or the greatest *cry* a man ever attempted.

The sense of things retreats from them and poetic speech (*la parole*) must resurrect on the "other side" of silence:

> *Que le verbe s'éteigne*
> *Dans cette pièce basse où tu me rejoins,*
> *Que l'âtre du cri se resserre*
> *Sur nos mots rougeoyants.* (*P*, 63; emphasis mine)

> Let the word die out
> In this low room where you return to me,
> Let the hearth of the *cry* close down
> Over our glowing words.

The void of silence is suggestive of the moment when consciousness realizes that it has attached itself to language, to the world image proposed by representation, and that this image is an autonomous construct separated from the awesome realities of finitude. The world image must be shattered, Bonnefoy seems to be saying, language must explode in a cry, and the void of silence must be passed through. These are the first steps to be taken, steps of consciousness among the stones which are both the result of ruin and the material of reconstruction.

"Whatever is in the process of becoming," Kierkegaard once wrote, "is in a state of alternation between being and non-being."[26] The movement toward reconciliation between language and reality in an inspirational perception and their inevitable separation and disjuncture as the language of the initial perception becomes formulistic and autonomous is one of the interpretive levels of the strange verses—

> *. . . à chaque instant*
> *je te vois naître, Douve,*
>
> *A chaque instant mourir.* (*P*, 26)

> . . . every moment
> I see you being born, Douve,
>
> Every moment dying.

I have already spoken at length of the "sin" of language. It is related to the Orphic error of assurance and possession. For Euridyce is lost through the glance of appropriation. But *Douve* will never cease reminding us that the cry, while it is the explosion of habit and form and the movement toward silence and the void, also announces the desire for new relationship and for the new speech which translates it. In short, death can lead to resurrection, as the Phoenix is born from the ashes of defeat, and as the Salamander passes through the trials of fire undaunted. Repeatedly, Bonnefoy will evoke the image of the "hearth" of being and the few words left glowing there. In *Pierre écrite*, for instance, a "voice" will say: ". . . je veille / Sur quelques mots éteints dans l'âtre de nos cœurs" (". . . I keep watch / Over a few words that have died out in the hearth of our hearts") (*P*, 212). *Douve* will insist on the necessity of the extinction of passion and extravagance and on the need for the sort of focusing and restraint—the "immobility"—signaled by the verb *se resserrer* ("to close down," "to tighten or contract"), a verb that will also be applied to the salamander, which emerges as the exemplary or "allegorical" figure of the poem. The witness is led to a kind of absolute limit in the recognition of death. And yet the realization of finitude, while it poses an ultimate threat to the status of representation, is nonetheless seen as a starting point. The "humus," the ashes and decomposition, which indicate the fate not only of the individual human being, but of his dreams and aspirations as well, is the ground for a future and more painfully sober "kingdom." A voice in the section "Douve Parle" will speak of this principle of death and resurrection.

> *Tant de chemins noircis feront bien un royaume*
> *Où rétablir l'orgueil que nous avons été,*
> *Car rien ne peut grandir une éternelle force*
> *Qu'une éternelle flamme et que tout soit défait.*
> *Pour moi je rejoindrai cette terre cendreuse,*
> *Je coucherai mon cœur sur son corps dévasté,*
> *Ne suis-je pas ta vie aux profondes alarmes,*
> *Qui n'a de monument que Phénix au bûcher?* (*P*, 65)

> So many blackened roads will make up a kingdom
> Where we can restore the pride we once knew,
> For nothing can swell an eternal force

But an eternal flame and that all be undone.
For myself I will go back to that earth of ashes,
I will lay down my heart on its ravaged body.
Am I not your life in its deepest alarms,
Whose only monument is the Phoenix on its pyre?

The passage emphasizes the importance of disillusionment and loss in the new vision. Not only does the life of the spirit "maintain" itself in death; it grows stronger, it would seem, in the midst of what menaces it. (In his essay on Morandi of 1968, Bonnefoy makes this extremely interesting observation: "When one speaks of nothingness, especially with insistence . . . does one not already, by that very act, acknowledge meaning? God is not dead as long as a 'bitter knowledge' denounces him" [*NR*, 112].)

The "Chevalier de deuil" (the "Knight of mourning"—perhaps an echo of Kierkegaard, or even of Nerval's "El Desdichado") in the last section, "Vrai Lieu" ("True Place") is also seen in this position of dying in order to resurrect.

> *Il se tait. Que peut dire au terme du combat*
> *Celui qui fut vaincu par probante parole?*
> *Il tourne vers le sol sa face démunie,*
> *Mourir est son seul* cri, *de vrai apaisement.*[27]
>
> (*P*, 87; emphasis mine)

He says nothing. What can he say now that the battle is over,
He who was vanquished by the word of truth?
He turns his helpless face to the ground,
To die is his only *cry*, of true appeasement.

In this vision, death is purgation: on the other side of the void of silence and the flames of death, the poetic word will resurrect and presences seem closer to the regard which has learned that appropriation is impossible ("J'ai apporté de la lumière, j'ai cherché / Partout régnait le sang. / Et je *criais* et je pleurais de tout mon corps." "I brought light, I looked / Blood reigned everywhere. / And I *cried out* and I wept with my whole body" [*P*, 54; italics mine].) Here one is perhaps, as Dante would have it, "presso piu a Dio" ("closer to God").[28] And in this sense, the cry of "death" and the despair of the night and the void are to be desired.

> *Demande pour tes yeux que les rompe la nuit,*
> *Rien ne commencera qu'au delà de ce voile,*
> *Demande ce plaisir que dispense la nuit*
> *De* crier *sous le cercle bas d'aucune lune,*
> *Demande pour ta voix que l'étouffe la nuit,* (*P*, 66; emphasis mine)

Ask for your eyes that night tear through them,
Nothing will begin except beyond this veil,
Ask for this pleasure that night bestows

Of *crying out* beneath the low circle of an absent moon,
Ask for your voice that night smother it.

What Bonnefoy is suggesting is an end to established representations of the world which tend to censor the fact of our finitude. The destruction of this reassuring tyranny is accomplished with a cry of anguish, and it leads, of course, to a night of painful silence. This "passage," on the other hand, opens into the space of a more authentic, if bleaker and more bitterly cold, point of departure.

The "cry" is opposed, as has been suggested, by a certain notion of the "song," for the poet is searching for that "listless shore beyond all song" (*P*, 52). The "mighty singer" is thrown from his peak to illuminate vast, unutterable matter (*P*, 63). Nevertheless, the poem "Justice," from the section "The Orangery," seems to reestablish the song, after the passage through disillusionment and silence.

> *Mais toi, mais le désert! étends plus bas*
> *Tes nappes ténébreuses.*
> *Insinue dans ce cœur pour qu'il ne cesse pas*
> *Ton silence comme une cause fabuleuse.*
>
> *Viens. Ici s'interrompt une pensée,*
> *Ici n'a plus de route un beau pays.*
> *Avance sur le bord de cette aube glacée*
> *Que te donne en partage un soleil ennemi.*
>
> *Et chante. C'est pleurer deux fois ce que tu pleures*
> *Si tu oses chanter par grand refus.*
> *Souris, et chante. Il a besoin que tu demeures,*
> *Sombre lumière, sur les eaux de ce qu'il fut.* (*P*, 80)

But you, but the desert! spread lower
Your gloomy sheets of sand.
Wind through this heart so that it never ceases
Your silence like a legendary cause.

Come. Here a thought breaks off,
Here a beautiful country runs out of roads.
Move out to the edge of that icy dawn
Given you as your due by an enemy sun.

And sing. You mourn twice over what you mourn
If you dare to sing, denying death.
Smile, and sing. He needs you to stay,
Dark light, on the waters of what he was.

It is significant that this poem is called "Justice" as it seems to respond to an earlier poem which begins on a note of questioning and doubt.

Où maintenant est le cerf qui témoigna
Sous ces arbres de justice,
Qu'une route de sang par elle fut ouverte,
Un silence nouveau par elle inventé.   (*P*, 49)

Where now is the stag who testified
Beneath these trees of justice
That a pathway of blood was opened by her,
A new silence invented by her.

The poem "Justice" will make of the desert world of silence and cessation not only the stuff of a new form of song, but its very "cause." The new dawn, if freezing and cold, is nonetheless not without a bitter joy, seen as the "just" return for the suffering and painful lucidity that will not "deny death," that steep the poetic song with death.

If a voice will affirm—

Je ne suis que parole intentée à l'absence,
L'absence détruira tout mon ressassement.
Oui, c'est bientôt périr de n'être que parole,
Et c'est tâche fatale et vain couronnement   (*P*, 67)

I am nothing but words set against absence,
Absence will destroy all my reiteration.
Truly, to be only a word is to die out soon,
The task is doomed and its crowning vain

—the poem, as a whole, will seek to attach poetic speech to something, to unite the consciousness of the narrator first with the anguished cry of disenchantment and then with "des mots qui soient le signe et l'oraison" ("words that are both sign and prayer") and for which his silence will have prepared him, with "des mots de guérison" ("healing words") won through struggle and the fatigue of a painful vigilance (*P*, 85).

The section "Douve Parle" begins with this poem:

Quelle parole a surgi près de moi,
Quel cri *se fait sur une bouche absente?*
A peine si j'entends crier *contre moi,*
A peine si je sens ce souffle qui me nomme.

Pourtant ce cri *sur moi vient de moi,*
Je suis muré dans mon extravagance.
Quelle divine ou quelle étrange voix
Eût consenti d'habiter mon silence?   (*P*, 57; emphasis mine)

What word has surged up next to me,
What *cry* is forming on an absent mouth?
I scarcely hear this *cry* against me,
I scarcely feel this breath that names me.

And yet this *cry* near me comes from me,
I am walled up in my own extravagance.
What divine or what strange voice
Would have agreed to live in my silence?

The identification of the cry with the consciousness of the narrator is accompanied by the notion of imprisonment in "extravagance." The term recalls the state of the narrator in Baudelaire's "A une passante" (one of the poems of Baudelaire Bonnefoy most admires), who is drinking, "crispé comme un extravagant" ("tense" or "on edge, as one a little out of his wits"), when the fugitive beauty passes. It is Baudelaire who, in Bonnefoy's view, gives "the supreme value to what is only mortal," who has understood that death "is not that simple negation of the Idea secretly loved by Racine but, rather, a profound dimension of the presence of beings, in a sense, their only reality" (*I*, 114). And so, too, the "witness" of *Douve* must undergo the process of assimilation of death's realities, must come to see that the truest presence is not in intellectual contrivances but in blood which flows and is shed, that our only true experience of eternity and our only hope of immortality resides in what passes. And if at first the incontrovertible truth that "everything dies . . . everything vanishes" is cause for despair, if awareness of the limitations imposed by finitude reduces the illusions of men to a cry of anguish, soon this painful awakening will appear as the very basis of our authentic encounter with the world of beings as presences.

Bonnefoy's discreet use of color also underlines his principal dynamics. Although there is a reference to *verdure* in "Théâtre V" and to a *statue verte* in "L'Orangerie" (*P*, 75), the use of color is otherwise generally restricted to black and white, with a significant reference to the "cloth of red and grey" of the second room of the Orangery (*P*, 73).

The use of color is related to the convictions which emerge in a number of "choral" poems.

> La lumière profonde a besoin pour paraître
> D'une terre rouée et craquante de nuit.
> C'est d'un bois ténébreux que la flamme s'exalte.   (*P*, 52)

If it is to appear, the deep light needs
An earth broken and cracked with night.
It is a somber wood that gives life to the flame.

The predominant use of the colors black and white highlights the play of being against the backdrop of nothingness. (Much later, Bonnefoy will speak of the tension of these colors as "celle du néant et de l'être" [*NR*, 361].)

The color white is often associated with the *pâleur* (*P*, 28) of death. Douve is seen "white under a ceiling of insects" (*P*, 31), and later she is perceived "in a white room / her eyes circled with plaster" (*P*, 36). Black, too, is an index of death: moribund, Douve proffers gestures "already grown slower, black gestures" (*P*, 27). The "witness" will say of Douve in death:

> *O plus noire et déserte! Enfin je te vis morte,*
> *Inapaisable éclair que le néant supporte,*
> *Vitre sitôt éteinte, et d'obscure maison.* (*P*, 50)

> O blacker and more desolate! At last I saw you dead,
> Unappeasable lightning flashing against the void,
> Window no sooner lighted than gone out, and in a darkened
>   house.

Her lips are black; so, too, is the writing that would speak of her reality (*P*, 58). But the "blackened roads" (*P*, 65) of death's kingdom provide the site for restoring "the pride we once knew" (*P*, 65), for the black and white color pattern is mainly suggestive of *illumination* in death. When Douve speaks, she will tell of ". . . ce vent par quoi mes comédies / Se sont *élucidées* en l'acte de mourir" (". . . that wind which cast light / Upon all my theatrics in the act of dying") (*P*, 61; italics mine). The destiny of death is illuminating; it shines forth painfully now in the poetic act ("ce destin *éclairant* dans la terre du verbe") (*P*, 55; italics mine).

The section "Vrai Lieu" speaks of a "homeless" consciousness, ". . . drawn by the murmur of a lamp / By the lighted doorway of a lonely house" (*P*, 85). Recognition of death provides the stony lamp of illumination which accompanies, in talismanic fashion, the steps of the searcher. And this illumination makes rigorous demands of confrontation, for it inhabits a single "place" of acceptance.

The color red is, of course, associated with blood. Blood is life. As menstrual blood, it contributes to the overthrow of purely aesthetic and "lifeless" constructions of a female Ideal. More generally speaking, spilled blood is the sign of presences declaring themselves in all their precariousness and vulnerability. The red serves, then, to awaken. It is the color with which Delacroix, for instance, "ensanglantait l'Idéal" ("covered the Ideal with blood") (*NR*, 117). A first room of the Orangery cries out "of dead leaves and desertion."

> *Sur la seconde et la plus grande, la lumière*
> *S'étendait, nappe rouge et grise, vrai bonheur.* (*P*, 73)

> Over the second and the largest the light
> Was streaming, cloth of red and grey, true happiness.

If the "red" is the blood of a transient and insecure life, what is the "grey," and how does it contribute to the notion of a true happiness? The grey is the color of the stone, the exemplary concrete reality. For Bonnefoy, the grey is *instaurateur* (i.e. "what founds or establishes") (*I*, 291). Because of its association with the stone, the grey would seem to color the "land of the salamanders." (The salamander, in turn, through its silent constriction and patient waiting, is the allegorical figure for "the first step of consciousness among the stones"; its very "look" has "turned to stone." Holding its breath and clinging to the ground, it is, for the narrator, the "allegory / Of all that is pure" because of its identification with death, with earth, with silence—and finally with victory [*P*, 89].) The colors red and grey—and I am not suggesting that Bonnefoy is using them in a self-conscious or programmatic way—do evoke the dynamic of the movement and elusiveness of reality, on the one hand, and the patience of a vigilant consciousness on the other. The union of the colors is the sign of an approach to a "true happiness," even if the Orangery symbolizes an incomplete and vacant structure for their harmonization.[29]

Most readers of *Douve* notice the emphatic use of the word *gestes* ("gesture" or "act"). The word is used repeatedly, and one section of the poem will be entitled "Derniers Gestes" or "Last Acts." It may be that, on one level, Bonnefoy is attempting to mark the distance between the heroic exploits of the *Chansons de geste* tradition and the austere restrictions of the modern poem. In any case, the elaboration of gesture in the poem serves to "mimic" Bonnefoy's central concerns. What happens is something like what Bonnefoy notices in Degas's work and which he expresses in an essay published two years after *Douve*. The facile ontology of the traditional portrait is replaced in Degas's work, writes Bonnefoy, by "that art of gesture, that art of painting gesture through which the elusive and anonymous being appears only in the slightest brush strokes" (*I*, 169). For Bonnefoy, the gesture is "the more concise, the more allusive evocation" (*I*, 168).

Bonnefoy mentions having taken Marcel Jousse's course on the "anthropology of gesture" in Paris in the forties.[30] An unclassifiable, Jousse combined peasant origins with wide scientific curiosity (in physiology, neurology, linguistics, psychology, ethnology) and a vocation to the priesthood in the Society of Jesus. His mother, who was not literate, taught him the Gospels orally, as she herself had learned them. This early experience was the origin of Jousse's refusal of a *Scientia cum libro* in favor of a *Scientia in vivo*.[31] Jousse's principal intuition was that man is a mimicking animal who acts out—or "re-acts" (*rejouer*)—the world by means of his entire body. The "language" of gesture was for Jousse "at the origin of human expression" (ibid., 10). "It is with these gestures which are like 'actions acting on other actions,' it is with these interactional gestures that man preserves his experiences and even projects them" (ibid., 12). Jousse would maintain, then, that "man thinks with his entire body," that he is "essentially only a complex of gestures." His investigations, as he said, were not "in textual space . . . but in gesticulative duration (*la durée gestuelle*)" (ibid., 29, 33, 36). "The human being must be grasped from the soles of his feet to the top of his head. There is no such thing as a *right-thinking* head, there is a human composite which knows and mimics with its entire body" (ibid., 36).

The human being receives the impression of the world, and this receptivity accumulates in him what Jousse calls "les 'Mimemes' des choses"—that is, "the replay of gesture imposed by the object" (ibid., 15).

Jousse also had a clear notion of the atrophy produced by Greco-Latin civilization. "The original and supreme sin of our civilization of writing is to think of itself as civilization par excellence" (ibid., 33). All the sciences of man have begun "by being static, for it is easier to cut into a dead and unmoving object than into a moving and living being" (ibid., 34). What Jousse calls *le Formulisme*—that is, the tendency to stereotype gestures (man finding mere spontaneity of gesticulative expression impossible)—is a source of life for a people when it lends itself to living formulas which carry realities. *Formulisme* can also, however, be a cause of sterility and atrophy if the stereotype eventually falls into the *algébrose* or *nécrose* of the formulas of society, religion, liturgy, and art.

Jousse was particularly led to find the authenticity of the living word of an Aramaean Jesus under the Greek "envelope" of the written gospels. He conceived of a world of "*in*-formation" received by the human being who is capable of its "*ex*-pression."

> The three-phased gestures (actor-acting-acted) form a succession of gears, and this is what constitutes the justness of gestures. This is what gives us that word which is no longer properly understood: the *Justness* of gestures, which has been reduced to justice. . . . All our gestures must be just in order to be effective. (Ibid., 18)

For Jousse, it is "the play and replay of living gestures which constitute memory" (ibid., 35). And Jousse will maintain that "only the practice of acting out reality in its living complexity convinces us that there is but one reality which is only cut up for the purpose of study because of our limitations" (ibid., 22–23).

Jousse also recognizes that he is proposing an orientation rather than absolute discoveries. He knew the dangers of *l'algébrose* and would insist: "We are only working toward that goal which always eludes us. . . . We will never know the essence of phenomena. We can only propose solutions which strive to bring us closer to this essence. . . . I do not claim to be closing the road, I am simply saying: this is the road that one should follow." (ibid., 26).

Bonnefoy clearly follows this way. All of his poetry is concerned with fundamental gestures. In fact, what he wrote of Mallarmé could easily be applied to himself: "His poetry is built in practice on verbs which refer to

the human gesture, either as what receives the impression, or as what pro-
longs it" (*NR, 194*).

At first, Douve is seen in elevated, protected positions—on that "ter-
race," for instance, which may be meant to suggest the Symbolist poetic
tradition. From the initial "tearing apart," the passing before the flames of
death, the lifting of an arm in which death declares itself and by means of
which the narrator is "enlightened across the ages," from the "noble ges-
ture of coal" the dying Douve casts "into the air suddenly hard as rock" (*P*,
29), the fundamental gestures of the poem depict the movement down-
ward in death and then upward again in resurrection. Thus Douve "slowly
gains access to the lower levels" (*P*, 38); she delivers her head to the "low
flames of the sea" (*P*, 45); fire "washes" her face. And the narrator says,

> *Sur un fangeux hiver, Douve, j'étendais*
> *Ta face lumineuse et basse de forêt.* (*P*, 50)

> Over a muddy winter, Douve, I spread out
> Your face, luminous and rank like a forest.

Essential gestures underline a characteristic posture of horizontality ("I
see Douve stretched out") in death.

> *Pour moi je rejoindrai cette terre cendreuse,*
> *Je coucherai mon cœur sur son corps dévasté.* (*P*, 65)

> For myself I will go back to that earth of ashes,
> I will lay down my heart on its ravaged body.

The narrator busies himself with the futile preparation of the dead body of
Douve.

> *Je prendrai dans mes mains ta face morte. Je la*
> *coucherai dans son froid. Je ferai de mes mains sur ton*
> *corps immobile la toilette inutile des morts.* (*P*, 81)

> I will take your dead face in my hands. I will lay it out
> in its coldness. With my hands I will perform on your
> motionless body the useless preparation of the dead.

The knight of mourning "turns his helpless face to the ground" (*P*, 87).

But if he weeps, he may also "flower"—"on the courtyard of November's
muddy waters" (*P*, 88). Douve, too, will ask that "the cold through [her]
death *rise up* and take on meaning" (*P*, 63; italics mine). If a characteristic
posture for Douve will be *étendue* ("stretched out"), and if a number of
verbs (*coucher, tomber, gésir*) participate in this posture, many poems will
insist upon her *elevation* after death, on her resurrection. She is the "de-
composed being that invincible being recomposes, / Presence recaptured
in the torch of the cold" (*P*, 31). And thus,

> *Au pas noir de la terre, Douve ravagée, exultante,*
> *rejoint la lampe noueuse des plateaux.* (*P*, 34)

76

> With the black tread of earth, Douve, ravaged, exultant,
> rejoins the gnarled lamp of the highlands.

One might imagine, as one way of reading these lines, Douve's reemergence as a presence in the face of the moon on the plateaus. The adjective "exultante" from the verb "exulter" has a primary meaning of "to leap or spring up" (from the Latin verb *exsultare*, from *saltare*, "sauter"—to "jump" or "leap"). The trees assure that "Douve même morte / Sera lumière encore n'étant rien" ("Douve even dead / Will again be light being nothing") (*P*, 43). She flees toward the willows (*P*, 46). *S'élancer, se lever* are the verbs which cooperate in this upward movement in "the vertical net of death." The Phoenix (*"refusing* any death inscribed on the branches" [*P*, 53; italics mine]) dares "to pass beyond the summits of the night" (*P*, 53). The mortal body becomes the tree-top on which he joyfully closes his wings.

> *Il fermera joyeux ses ailes sur le faîte*
> *De cet arbre ton corps que tu lui offriras.* (*P*, 53)

And one of the "Voix basses" ("Low Voices") will articulate this movement downward in death and upward in resurrection.

> *D'un geste il me dressa cathédrale de froid,*
> *O Phénix! Cime affreuse des arbres crevassés*
> *Par le gel! Je roulais comme torche jetée*
> *Dans la nuit même où le Phénix se recompose.* (*P*, 69)

> With a single gesture he raised me a cathedral of cold,
> O Phoenix! Frightful summit of the trees cleft
> by the frost! I fell end over end like a torch thrown
> Into the very night in which the Phoenix is remade.

Bonnefoy's book on Rimbaud will remind us that, among other things, the "body of the Phoenix of freedom . . . is made from hopes burned out" (*R*, 178). And if we see Douve "stretched out" in the horizontal postures of death, she is as often caught up in vertical resurrections. And this "cross," as I hope to show in greater detail in a later place, is the symbol of contradiction taken on and accepted—the essence of Bonnefoy's "faith."

Certain gestures evoke the struggle against death and destruction. Thus, *bâtir le feu* ("to build the fire"); *dresser une maison* ("to put up a house"); *veiller sur l'âtre* ("to watch over the hearth"); *prendre une lampe* ("to take up a lamp"); *garder une source* ("to guard a spring") are all activities which indicate the refusal of human desire "to consider limitation and death as manageable and 'natural'" (*R*, 175). And so, if the dominant season of *Douve* is the "muddy winter" with its "frost," its "cold," its "snow," its "January nights," one is constantly reminded of the feeble fires lit against it and of the spirit "that watches . . . / Over the hearth" (*P*, 69).

The dynamics of the death-and-rebirth cycle are not without involving a characteristic "gay science." *Rire* (laughter) and *sourire* (smile) recur with astonishing frequency, for death infuses itself in Douve's laughter (*P*, 40), and "des liasses de mort pavoisent [s]on sourire" ("bundles of death deck out [her] smile") (*P*, 41). In this sense, Bonnefoy seems to have conceived of his poetic "theater" along the lines developed by Antonin Artaud in his book *Le Théâtre et son double.* The contemporary theater had become decadent, Artaud felt, "because it [had] lost the feeling on the one hand for seriousness and on the other for laughter." [32] The theater had lost touch with both the sense of danger and "laughter's power of physical and anarchic dissociation." [33] In Bonnefoy's poem, the "smile" of the willows envelops the body of the dead Douve—"feigning / The simple joy of some game" (*P*, 46). Douve is seen again "laughing forever" (*P*, 50), just as "she who still watches / Over the hearth," without face or body, "is always laughing, with the laughter that once was dead" (*P*, 69).

*   *   *

The poem "Lieu de la Salamandre" ("Place of the Salamander"), which I have already mentioned a number of times, embodies some of the complexities of organization I have been discussing with respect to the book as a whole. It exemplifies the coexistence of a kind of "story" with a network of associations and thus brings into play both narrative and allegory, metonymy and metaphor. The poem establishes more precisely the nature of the moment of illumination presented briefly and obliquely in "The Orangery" and constitutes an example of the "true place" as a place in meaning.

In the third poem of the series "La Salamandre," the narrator says:

> *Je suis près de toi, Douve, je t'éclaire. Il n'y a plus*
> *entre nous que cette lampe rocailleuse, ce peu d'ombre*
> *apaisé, nos mains que l'ombre attend. Salamandre*
> *surprise, tu demeures immobile.*
>
> *Ayant vécu l'instant où la chair la plus proche se mue*
> *en connaissance.*   (*P*, 76)

> I am close to you, Douve, with the light. There is nothing between us but this stony lamp, this bit of quiet shadow, our hands that the shadow awaits. Startled salamander, you remain motionless.
>
> Having lived the moment when the closest flesh turns into knowledge.

The transformation of "flesh" into "knowledge" is the poetic way of evoking the allegorical implications inherent in an experience that might other-

wise seem perfectly banal. The narrator says that there is "nothing be-
tween" him and the salamander with which the presence of Douve seems
to have become identified. This is a way of suggesting the "true place," and
the poem "Place of the Salamander" will explore more fully the implica-
tions of this moment of epiphany and oneness—the "moat" of separation
crossed over for an instant—during which consciousness has an intuition
of the eternal in the here-and-now and in the midst of "temporal finitude,"
and of the universal in spite of "spatial frailty" (*I*, 123).

> La salamandre surprise s'immobilise   1
> Et feint la mort.
> Tel est le premier pas de la conscience dans les pierres,
> Le mythe le plus pur,
> Un grand feu traversé, qui est esprit.
>
> La salamandre était à mi-hauteur   6
> Du mur, dans la clarté de nos fenêtres.
> Son regard n'était qu'une pierre,
> Mais je voyais son cœur battre éternel.
>
> O ma complice et ma pensée, allégorie   10
> De tout ce qui est pur,
> Que j'aime qui resserre ainsi dans son silence
> La seule force de joie.
>
> Que j'aime qui s'accorde aux astres par l'inerte   14
> Masse de tout son corps,
> Que j'aime qui attend l'heure de sa victoire,
> Et qui retient son souffle et tient au sol.   (*P*, 89)

The startled salamander freezes   1
And feigns death.
This is the first step of consciousness among the stones,
The purest myth,
A great fire passed through, which is spirit.

The salamander was halfway up   6
The wall, in the light from our windows.
Its look had turned to stone,
But I saw its heart beating eternal.

O my accomplice and my thought, allegory   10
Of all that is pure,
How I love what draws up thus in silence
The only force of joy.

How I love what is in harmony with the stars through   14
    the inert
Mass of its whole body,
How I love what awaits the hour of its victory,
And holds its breath and clings to the ground.

The story or principal subject is contained in lines 1 and 2, and 6 through 9, while the references to "myth" (line 4), "thought" or "idea" (line 10), and "allegory" (line 10) point to the associations developed from the principal subject. That the salamander is conceived of as an "accomplice" is perhaps a way of suggesting poetically the "crime" of the purely excarnate Idea. Located in common experience, the salamander is what gives authenticity to the Idea. It is the "substance" poetic speech needs.

The salamander frozen on the wall may be said to mimic the death which approaches all beings. Its "immobility" is suggestive of that sobering enlightenment in death which curtails the aimless "running" that characterized the earlier theater of Douve. In this sense, it may be said to "accept" what is its destiny. It may perhaps be thought to represent Heidegger's notion of an anticipating Dasein that gains "an impassioned freedom towards death"[34] ("What saves from death," Bonnefoy would write much later, "is the acceptance of death" [*NR*, 179]).

The pivotal, central line of the poem—"But I saw its heart beating eternal" (line 9)—indicates that the poet has perceived in the posture and being of the salamander something eternal, that it has become, as Bonnefoy would say in a later essay to which I will return in some detail, "the gently beating heart of the earth . . . the origin of all that is" (*I*, 248). The word "eternal" (which is itself placed about exactly in the middle, or at the heart, of the words of the text) points to the more general and metaphysical implications of the salamander's presence which are developed in lines 12 through 17. The repetition of the wide-ranging and impersonal *Que j'aime qui* ("How I love what") extends the simple evidence of the salamander to the proportions of an existential stance. The salamander has passed through the fires of disillusionment unvanquished; its adherence to the stony real is marked by the signs of a voluntary attachment (*resserrer*, "to draw up or contract"; *tenir*, "to hold"); in motionless silence, it awaits rebirth in meaning, the emergence of those few saving words which will establish its "victory."

*   *   *

I have called this chapter "The Baptism in Death." In fact, the sacramental events most often referred to are the last rites and marriage. This is only an apparent misnomer, however, for "the humblest marriage" is, on one level, the union of the decomposing body with earth, and on another, the espousal of the principle of death by the poetic vision. The last rites are repeatedly seen as futile for the body. These awarenesses, evoked by sacramental institutions, have as consequence the kind of elucidation or illumination one might justifiably call initiatory or baptismal.

Douve works out a shattering death rite. The poem delivers the shocks to complacency and the dislocations to "everyday" thinking Artaud had demanded in his polemical texts. But if the poem deals in destruction, if it strives to reestablish a primitive sense of mystery and awe, it does so largely in a mythic, atemporal setting. While the poem sets out to record the devastations of being and the travail of becoming, it does so without exactly incorporating what Bonnefoy calls existential time, or *le temps vécu*. The next book of poems, *Hier Régnant Désert*, will mark this crisis of consciousness.

Nevertheless, it is the recognition of the reality of death, the "fall" into matter, the outrage to the idealizing mind, which constitutes a first threshold to be crossed—a pass of fire to be braved by the consciousness unafraid of somber truths. In the situation of "alarm," of sorrow and eclipse, a desperate alternative presents itself: if specific lives perish, general life persists in the continuity of being. The faces and the voices of the dead may be sought in nature, in the trees, for instance—those "impassibles garants que Douve même morte / Sera lumière encore n'étant rien" ("impassive guarantors that Douve even dead / Shall still be light being nothing") (*P*, 43). The intuition of this book, the challenge that it develops for the poet, is that one can use a present apprehension of mortality and finitude as the foundation of a *vita nuova* by consenting to that larger unity of being whose greater existence seems to require our disappearance in order to translate indifference or evasion into not only painful awareness of limitation but also celebration of being and presence. This is the intuition that gives direction to the poet's quest.

The questions with which three of the sections of *Douve* end are calls for proper poetic orientation. "En quel âtre dresser le feu?" ("In what hearth can the fire be built?") "Que faire d'une lampe?" ("What use is a lamp?") To what ends, in other words, should one consecrate the poetic fire? The future tense of the verb of the last verse of the book—"O notre force et notre gloire, pourrez-vous / Trouer la muraille des morts?" ("O our strength and our glory, will you be able / To pierce through the walls of the dead?")—points to the challenges and the tests to come. It announces the search for the "éternité praticable" (*R*, 175) which can be won by our obstination and our freedom—by that capacity for resurrection and new dawning which constitutes for Yves Bonnefoy "our strength and our glory."

4   Trial by Ordeal

Make light, make dawn, have us invoked,
have us adored, have us remembered by
Created man, by made man, by mortal man.
Thus be it done.

Popol Vuh

"Day and Night are One"

Heraclitus

Hier régnant désert (*Yesterday's Desert Dominion*), published in 1958, was
originally to have been called *L'Ordalie* (*Trial by Ordeal*), emphasizing the
suffering of a rite of passage.[1] That Bonnefoy changed the title to *Hier ré-
gnant désert* is an indication of the extent to which the book's force is in the
process of exorcism. The title comes from one of the last poems of the last
section "A une terre d'aube" ("To an Earth of Dawn") and insists through
the use of the word *hier* ("yesterday") on a torment surmounted and sus-
pended, on a dominion reversed. The emphasis on past crisis resolved
points to a characteristic effort at self-mastery, to that equilibrium of an-
tagonistic tensions which is a hallmark of Bonnefoy's poetic and moral
determination.

The collection reflects the greatest suffering of the major works. It is also
the most painfully self-conscious. Interrogation of methods, the effort to
constitute a "self," the struggle with the question of time, the search for
artistic values, for new departure—the problems which pervade *Hier rég-
nant désert* constitute the painful coming of age of the poet and reflect his
struggle to establish both a poetical and an ethical identity.

Had Bonnefoy discovered after the profoundly searching recognition of
death in *Douve* that outside of its articulation in a formal system, mortality,
our passage through duration to inevitable extinction, has a more paralyz-
ing and less easily mastered dimension than he might have hoped when he
was in his twenties? If *Douve* was struggling to find the "inerte rivage au-
delà de tout chant" ("the listless shore beyond all song") (*P*, 52), *Hier* will
be laboring for that song trembling "au-delà de toute forme pure" ("be-
yond all pure form") (*P*, 137), for the song which rises from the "fond
morne du chant de l'oiseau qui s'est tu" ("mournful depths of the hushed
bird's song") (*P*, 130). But this search is full of dangers, since the poet
must wander in a night of silence in which he risks losing himself com-
pletely. The bird now leads "toutes voix dans la nuit où les voix se perdent"

82

("every voice into the night where voices are lost") (*P*, 131), and the poet "qui a tant détruit" ("who destroyed so much") (*P*, 107) will admit: "J'ai fait naître un silence où je me suis perdu" ("I brought to birth a silence in which I lost myself") (*P*, 130).[2] *Douve* and *Hier* tell of destructions, of their necessity. But one can lose oneself in destruction, and *Hier* records this crisis. For here is the poet *nel mezzo del cammin*, in a state of apathy and inertia, perhaps calling his very sincerity into question, separated from his deepest self, in the grip of what the medieval world knew as *acedia*, recoiling from spiritual imperatives.

The poem from which the title of the book is taken reads as follows:

UNE VOIX
Écoute-moi revivre dans ces forêts
Sous les frondaisons de mémoire
Où je passe verte,
Sourire calciné d'anciennes plantes sur la terre,
Race charbonneuse du jour.

Écoute-moi revivre, je te conduis
Au jardin de présence,
L'abandonné au soir et que des ombres couvrent,
L'habitable pour toi dans le nouvel amour.

Hier régnant désert, j'étais feuille sauvage
Et libre de mourir,
Mais le temps mûrissait, plainte noire des combes,
La blessure de l'eau dans les pierres du jour.   (*P*, 144)

A VOICE
Hear me come to life again in these forests
Beneath the foliage of memory
Where green I pass,
Charred smile of plants that once were on the earth,
Carbonaceous descendant of day.

Hear me come to life again, I lead you
Into the garden of presence,
What was abandoned at evening and covered by shadow,
The place where you can live now in newfound love.

In yesterday's desert dominion, I was the wild leaf
That might have died,
But time deepened, dark plaint of the valleys,
The wound of water in the stones of day.

The lines include a number of the principal preoccupations of the book: the notion of rebirth, of course, of a "wounded" self seeking healing through maturity; the journey through the night of loss into the daytime of rediscovered presence; the temptation of death and freedom from becoming; the problem of time; the relation of the "dream" of an ideal world to the realities of limitation and opacity. The "voice" which springs up again here is the feminine voice ("vert*e*") associated with Douve and the emergence of epiphany and presence. The green of revitalization is related to the love the poet must reestablish with the real, with the world of those stones which were the talisman of *Douve*. For the major questions of the earlier work had already pointed to that loss of orientation *Hier* will trace. As if sensing the trials to come, the absence of direction, the movement toward spiritual chaos, the fears, the apathy and self-hatred, the poet had provided himself in *Douve* with a talisman, a special light:

> Regarde, diras-tu, cette pierre:
> Elle porte la présence de la mort.
> Lampe secrète c'est elle qui brûle sous nos gestes,
> Ainsi marchons-nous éclairés. (*P*, 71)

> Consider, you will say, this stone:
> Death shines from it.
> Secret lamp it is what burns beneath our steps.
> And so we walk in light.

The poet carries this lamp, as it were, into the experiences to come. At once a reminder of death and an appeal from the real, the lamp of stone will provide direction at the moment when "tous chemins que tu suivais se ferment" ("all roads you followed are closed now") (*P*, 96). *Hier régnant désert* will be the theater of an immense struggle (as Rimbaud had warned that "spiritual battles are as brutal as the wars of men").[3] And the outcome of this struggle will be to restore "le pas dans son vrai lieu" ("the step in its true place") (*P*, 149) where "l'inquiète voix consent d'aimer / La pierre simple" ("the troubled voice agrees to love / The simple stone") (*P*, 149).

* * *

Many of the conventions used in *Douve* are employed again here, but with notable variations. The *you* of the first poems of the section "Menaces du témoin" ("Threats of the Witness") is a masculine *you* who is lost and indifferent. This indifference is thought of as the most dangerous indication of spiritual apathy and the *tu* is urged to struggle against it by voices Bonnefoy has said come from *la conscience morale* (*AP*, 120).

The images and symbols used in *Douve* to insist on the principle of resurrection are here called into question. "L'Oiseau . . . s'est dépris d'être Phénix" ("The bird . . . has grown weary of being the Phoenix") (*P*, 101). And,

> Déjà le feu n'est plus que mémoire et que cendre
> Et bruit d'aile fermée, bruit de visage mort. (*P*, 99)

Already the fire is nothing more than memory and ashes
And the sound of closed wings, the sound of dead faces.

The poet's ship no longer moves: "Ainsi noircit au vent des sables de l'usure / La barque retirée où le flot ne va pas" ("Thus blackens in the windy sands of erosion / The bark brought up to the shore the waves never touch") (*P*, 102). The new dawn, recompense for the nights of suffering and despair, is no longer espoused: "Tu n'aimes que la nuit en tant que nuit, qui porte / La torche, ton destin, de tout renoncement" ("You only love the night as night, which carries / The torch, your destiny, of every renunciation") (*P*, 100).

In his essay on Balthus, published in 1957 (that is, during the same period as the composition of *Hier régnant désert*), Bonnefoy had said that at certain moments of an artist's life it is perhaps necessary that "this place of the loss and the reaffirmation of the real be itself lost in order to be better recovered" (*I*, 41). The basic structure of the poem *Hier régnant désert* is from loss to recovery, from night into day, from "the steps which no longer go anywhere" to "the step in its true place." The book marks a kind of turning point for the poet: an experience of disorientation and disintegration and subsequent recovery, of a fall into a "sin" which will become a *felix culpa*—for Bonnefoy will discover that for him, too, "it is in the very place where there is sin that grace superabounds" (*I*, 41).

What is the nature of this "sin"? How has the sacred fire died out? The *tu* is accused of a kind of spiritual inertia, of dying "longuement comme en sommeil" ("slowly as if in sleep") (*P*, 97).

> *Et vois, tu es déjà séparé de toi-même,*
> *Toujours ce même cri, mais tu ne l'entends pas,*
> *Es-tu celui qui meurt, toi qui n'as plus d'angoisse,*
> *Es-tu même perdu, toi qui ne cherches pas?*　　　　　(*P*, 98)

> And look, you are already far away from yourself,
> Always this same cry, but you do not hear it,
> Are you the one who is dying, you who no longer feel anguish,
> Are you even lost, you who are not searching?

The Middle Ages knew of this kind of dreadful unconcern, as I have said, under the name of *acedia*. Aquinas referred to it as a "weariness of doing."[4] The term was applied, specifically, to the spiritual *ennui* which was known to plague monastic life. (The first poem of *Hier* will complain that "le feu s'est retiré qui était mon église"—"the fire which was my church has withdrawn" [*P*, 95].) Dante reserves a circle of Purgatory for those exorcising its power.[5] Significantly, Dante saw the sluggishness of *acedia* as the result of an insufficiency of love. In her commentary on the *Commedia*, Dorothy Sayers writes of *acedia* that "it is that whole poisoning of the will which beginning with indifference . . . extends to the deliberate refusal of joy and culminates in morbid introspection and despair."[6] One form of it, she continues, is "that withdrawal into an 'ivory tower' of Isolation which is the peculiar temptation of the artist and the contemplative" (ibid.). *Acedia* is associated with the demon of psalm 91 who devastates at noontime, and the cruelly ironic poem "Le Bel Été" ("The Beautiful Summer") evokes the suffocating atmosphere of a fire-haunted summer, "fade, brisant et sombre" ("stale, exhausting and somber") (*P*, 105). Not yet the season of plenitude and fruitfulness celebrated in *Pierre écrite*, the summer of *Hier régnant désert* is one of horror and sterility.

In his *Arrière-pays*, Bonnefoy provides an analysis of his state of mind at the time of *Hier régnant désert*. He had fallen, he says, "into the unremitting sorrow of dream and inhibition toward it" (*AP*, 120).

> In fact what I accused in myself, what I thought I could recognize and judge, was the pleasure of creating artistically, the preference given to created beauty over lived experience. I saw correctly that such a choice, in devoting words to themselves, in making of them a private language, created a universe which guaranteed the poet *everything*; except that by withdrawing from the openness of days, by disregarding time and other people, he was in fact headed toward nothing except solitude. (*AP*, 120–21)

Bonnefoy has often said that the "stuff" of excarnation, of dream, should be recognized and confronted and then diffused through the real, mingled with lived experience: one cannot "blot out like a bad dream the thousand excarnations one has been; they must be converted; they must, in a way, be preserved."[7] The problem for Bonnefoy at the time of *Hier régnant désert* is that he has not as yet taken the dream seriously: it must be acknowledged, lived, and hence, simplified; and Bonnefoy speaks specifically of a kind of acquiescence to, and yet inhibition about, the dream.

It is clear that impatience and pride are the causes of the stagnation described in *Hier*. The menacing voices will accuse the *tu* of evasion:

> *Tu n'aimes pas le fleuve aux simples eaux terrestres*
> *Et son chemin de lune où se calme le vent.* (*P*, 100)

> You do not love the river with its simple earthly waters
> And its moon path where the winds grow calm.

The *tu* is lured by the vague idea of "une lumière / Plus heureuse, établie dans l'autre monde obscur" ("a happier light / Set up in the dark other world") (*P*, 102). The movement of excarnation is underscored by a characteristic use of such words as *plutôt* ("rather"), *mieux vaut* ("it is better"), and *autre* ("other").

> *Plutôt, dis-tu, plutôt sur de plus mortes rives* (*P*, 100)

> Rather, you say, rather on more lifeless shores

Mieux vaut marcher plus près de la ligne d'écume
Et nous aventurer au seuil d'un autre froid.　　　　　　(*P*, 103)

It is better to go out closer to the line of sea foam
And venture to the threshold of another coldness.

What one hears in these passages is the longing for death, the ultimate extension of excarnation.[8] This movement will confirm the separation of the *tu* from himself. And this separation is especially disastrous in that it constitutes estrangement from the suffering and alarms which were the proof, the test, of spiritual vocation. Writing itself, for Bonnefoy, must be "not the unfolding of dream, with its infinite ambiguities, on the fringes of real time, but the test by which one proves oneself, and to oneself first of all, worthy of living where life makes its place, that is, 'here,' 'now,' in the presence of other beings."[9] The witness will exclaim,

Oh, souffre seulement de ma dure parole
Et pour toi je vaincrai le sommeil et la mort.　　　　　　(*P*, 99)

Oh, only suffer from my harsh words,
And for you I will vanquish both sleep and death.

Now this lethargy and indifference, contested by the accusations of the witness, are not easily vanquished. They are supported both by pride and by probity—for the bird is this voice "qui ne veut pas mentir" ("that will not lie") (*P*, 102). Are not death and night our inescapable lot, impenetrable matter the stuff of these dark realities? Hasn't one the obligation in spite of "incurable hope" (*P*, 104) to recognize our aspirations as mirages and forms of art as inadmissible escapes into the atemporal? Furthermore, to progress truly, one must leave the shores of what one knows, of what one has said, and search for "la côte longtemps vue / Et dite par des mots que nous ne savions pas" ("the coast seen for a long time / And told of by words we did not know") (*P*, 103). The dislocations and destructions recorded in *Douve* must themselves be risked if the poet is to avoid the fall into convention and the establishment of some "fine art" of desolation. "There is no writing which can be lastingly revolutionary," Barthes wrote in 1953, "and . . . any silence of form can escape imposture only by complete abandonment of communication."[10] And so the poet will say, "J'ai risqué / Le sens et au-delà du sens le monde froid" ("I risked / Meaning and beyond meaning the cold world")(*P*, 116).

This sincerity (or the poet's doubts about his sincerity which push him toward apathy and self-laceration) has as its end point the temptation Hamlet also knew to venture toward absolute stillness "in the land that knows neither birth nor death," where one is free from time and becoming.

Souvent dans le silence d'un ravin
J'entends (ou je désire entendre, je ne sais)
Un corps tomber parmi des branches. Longue et lente
Est cette chute aveugle; que nul cri
Ne vient jamais interrompre ou finir.

Je pense alors aux processions de la lumière
Dans le pays sans naître ni mourir.　　　　　　　　　　　(*P*, 106)

Often in the silence of a ravine
I hear (or want to hear, I cannot tell)
A body falling among the branches. Long and unhurried
Is this blind cascading; which no cry
Ever comes to interrupt or finish.

Then I think of the processions of light
In the land that knows neither birth nor death.

The abyss evoked here is the inevitable void of becoming: the state of alternation between being and nonbeing that Kierkegaard speaks of. Normally, as I tried to show in my discussion of *Douve* (chapter 3), the passage across this void is accompanied by a *cry*. In this poem, a falling is imagined which meets no resistance of any kind; at this point, even the hope in poetry, that "pont de fer / Jeté vers l'autre rive encore plus nocturne" ("iron bridge / Thrown out toward the other still more nocturnal shore") (*P*, 111), is abandoned. This is Hamlet's desire "to die; to sleep; no more"— the temptation to escape from "the whips and scorns of time." Here, the lure of an unopposed fall is accompanied by the vision of a world all of light and free from time. Bonnefoy will come to the awareness—and *Hier régnant désert* will trace the emergence of this conviction—that our being exists neither in light nor in darkness alone, but in light and darkness together. A sign of his maturity will be the acceptance of "the ceaseless resurgence of hope based on nothing" (*R*, 128). If the last poem of "Menaces du témoin" already sees that *aube dure, en ténèbre venir* ("harsh dawn, in shadow come forth"), it is because the collection as a whole is the struggle to recognize and consent to Heraclitus' profound intuition that "Day and Night are One." [11]

*　　　*　　　*

Many of the poems of the section "Le Visage mortel" ("The Mortal Face") seek to elaborate a poetics. If the passage of time, if mortality and limitation are man's fate, then the atemporality and formal perfection of works of art must be contested, and the emergence of beauty willfully and self-consciously undermined. In this poetics, "imperfection is the summit."

Il y avait qu'il fallait détruire et détruire et détruire,
Il y avait que le salut n'est qu'à ce prix.

Ruiner la face nue qui monte dans le marbre,
Marteler toute forme toute beauté.

Aimer la perfection parce qu'elle est le seuil,
Mais la nier sitôt connue, l'oublier morte,

L'imperfection est la cime. (P, 117)

And so it was that you had to destroy and destroy and destroy,
And so it was that salvation is only at this price.

Ruin the naked face rising out of the marble
Batter all form all beauty.

Love perfection because it is the threshold,
But once known disown it, once dead forget it,

Imperfection is the summit.

Perfect forms are traps; they falsify our situation in time; they must be de-
stroyed. Salvation is achieved through a process of continual destruction of
form, by passing beyond the lure of perfection and static beauty. It is sig-
nificant, it seems to me, that Bonnefoy will never seek to deny or exclude
the reality of the lure of beauty. The desire for beauty ("Notre désir pour-
tant étant ton corps infirme"—"And yet our desire being your frail body"
[P, 114]) is the threshold of the creative act; its destruction is the measure
of our self-awareness. For beauty "ruins being": it is *la menteuse, la pur-
voyeuse du ciel noir* ("the liar, the purveyor of black sky") (P, 114). Beauty
must be dishonored, humiliated, turned into that cry in the night, into
those signs of blood which are the indication of mortality and presence.

The poem "L'Ordalie II" uses the Arthurian image of a sword lodged in
stone to render the same conviction. The poem compares the sword to
"being" and the stone to "the greyness of the word" (P, 116). Releasing
the sword from the stone is suggestive of the process by means of which
being is freed from the bondage of representation and form. This effort is
placed in the context of a modest heroism: "Je ne sais pas si je suis vain-
queur" ("I do not know if I have conquered") (P, 116). For this disloca-
tion can be accompanied by the sense of vertigo and loss.

Un instant tout manqua,
Le fer rouge de l'être ne troua plus
La grisaille du verbe (P, 116)

For a moment everything failed
The red blade of being no longer pierced
The greyness of the word

The poem ends with the evocation of victory, however.

Mais enfin le feu se leva,
Le plus violent navire
Entra au port.

Aube d'un second jour,
Je suis enfin venu dans ta maison brûlante
Et j'ai rompu ce pain où l'eau lointaine coule.   (*P*, 116)

But at last the fire rose up,
The most violent ship
Entered port.

Dawn of a second day,
I have at last come into your blazing house
And I have broken this bread in which the distant water flows.

   This insistence upon destruction of formal beauty, upon the necessity to free being from the autonomy of art, is related to Bonnefoy's belief that the work of art must acknowledge lived experience and the passage of time, or, as he said in his essay on the Italian Quattrocento, "the reaffirmation of the atemporal must first of all have confronted the resistance of time" (*I*, 78). Thus, a number of poems of the section "Le Visage mortel" will evoke, like a torch carried into daylight, memories from the past, from childhood in particular. The remembrance of things past is a kind of first dawning, although the poet who abolishes the present to reconstruct a past is not sure "s'il a droit d'aimer cette parole d'aube" ("if he has the right to love this word of dawn") (*P*, 109). The poems of this section do, of course, trace a specific human face, give us a clear impression of a lonely and vulnerable childhood; and in this sense, *Hier régnant désert* is the most overtly and self-consciously "autobiographical" of the major works, as though, by invoking the notion of *le fleuve du passé* ("the river of the past") (*P*, 109), Bonnefoy were insisting on the movement of time, were seeking to make concrete those words which are so often repeated in *Hier: j'ai vieilli* ("I have grown older"). And if the remembrance of childhood nightmares ("Les Guetteurs"—"The Watchers"), the obsession with darkness and death in these poems seem to underline the strong current of submission and passivity in *Hier régnant désert*, it is nonetheless true that recognition of the wounded past is a way of eventually assuming and delivering it.

LES GUETTEURS I

Il y avait un couloir au fond du jardin,
Je rêvais que j'allais dans ce couloir,
La mort venait avec ses fleurs hautes flétries,
Je rêvais que je lui prenais ce bouquet noir.

Il y avait une étagère dans ma chambre,
J'entrais au soir,

Et je voyais deux femmes racornies
Crier debout sur le bois peint de noir.

Il y avait un escalier, et je rêvais
Qu'au milieu de la nuit un chien hurlait
Dans cet espace de nul chien, et je voyais
Un horrible chien blanc sortir de l'ombre.   (*P*, 112)

THE WATCHERS I

There was a passage at the end of the garden,
I dreamt that I was walking in this passage,
Death came forward with his tall withered flowers,
I dreamt that I took from him this black bouquet.

There was a shelf in my bedroom,
I would go in in the evening,
And I would see two shriveled women
Standing up shrieking on the black painted wood.

There was a staircase, and I dreamt
That in the middle of the night a dog was howling
In that space of no dog, and I saw
A horrible white dog come forth from the shadows.

The recurrence of the phrase *il y avait* is used to designate a particularly dark "season" of the poet's past. There was, Bonnefoy has written, "a season which marked the end of childhood," during which he was regularly seized by the specter of a *guetteur*—that terrifying force that seemed to lie in wait for him to menace him with the sense of the brutal futility of the world. This was the season of the Stranger.

> It always happened in the same way: voices falling silent in the substance of the world, things losing their flavor, how can I put it? the world turning black and white where once everything was full of color. . . .
>   . . . when the Stranger has appeared, what is left to us but the object, opaque and frigid, impenetrable, *unfamiliar*. This feeling of the unfamiliar is the question "Why?" associated with each thing. And this question without an answer. And the invasion by chance—that further enigma—of this confusion we call the world. The object, in the modern sense of the word, has just come into being from the ashes of the symbol. What once was is no more. (*I*, 318–20)

Thus, in "Le Visage mortel," Bonnefoy will remember "au bout d'une longue rue / Où je marchais enfant une mare d'huile, / Un rectangle de lourde mort sous le ciel noir" ("at the end of a long street / Where I would walk as a child a pool of oil, / A rectangle of heavy death beneath the blackened sky") (*P*, 111). The self he tries to constitute in time is the child haunted, and even perhaps fascinated (see "Guetteurs II"), by the Stranger whose presence does at least provide for a kind of terrible metaphysical distancing or awakening. In any case, the evocation of morbid obsession, of *hantise*, is the particular perspective chosen for the elaboration of an historical or psychological self. These recollections enforce the impression of trials undergone and even, perhaps, suggest a kind of complacency in suffering, a disquieting submission. They will yield, however, to the poet's conviction that memory is structured on a deeper level by more fundamental and universal experience: "Pierres sur pierres / Ont bâti le pays dit par le souvenir" ("Stones upon stones / Have built the land told of by memory") (*P*, 150).[12]

Hier seems to come to terms with the impossibility of constituting the historical self, to acknowledge what a line in the later *Dans le leurre du seuil* will call "l'inutilité de se souvenir" ("the uselessness of remembering") (*P*, 238). For the imagination has supplied a *representation* for an original intuition or experience which is absent or dead in the sepulcher of the image. The present is thus inhabited by fragments of representations from memory. In one of his "Spleen" poems, for instance, Baudelaire wrote,

> *J'ai plus de souvenirs que si j'avais mille ans.*
>
> *Un gros meuble à tiroirs encombré de bilans,*
> *etc.*
> *Cache moins de secrets que mon triste cerveau.*
> *C'est une pyramide, un immense caveau*
> *Qui contient plus de morts que la fosse commune.*

> I have more memories than if I had lived a thousand years.
>
> A huge chest of drawers stuffed with accounts,
> etc.
> Hides fewer secrets than my unhappy brain.
> It is a pyramid, an enormous burial vault
> That holds more dead than a potter's field.

Eugenio Donato calls the pyramid "a symbol of the death of 'Natural Object' in the sign."[13] Secondary memory created by language is nothing but an archaeological cemetery populated by funerary monuments. And Bonnefoy, by the end of *Hier régnant désert*, will be looking for a new origin based on active forgetfulness, an apprehension of the eternal which has confronted the reality of time:

> *L'oiseau des ruines se dégage de la mort,*
> *Il nidifie dans la pierre grise au soleil,*
> *Il a franchi toute douleur, toute mémoire,*
> *Il ne sait plus ce qu'est demain dans l'éternel.* (*P*, 153)

The bird of the ruins frees itself from death,
It builds its nest in the grey stone out in the sun,
It has passed beyond all sorrow, all memory,
It no longer knows what tomorrow is in the eternal.

Furthermore, the problematics of the historical self, of the self reconstructed by the images of memory is related to the general question of *perspective*. History, as Bonnefoy knows, is *la fatalité de la perspective* (*I*, 73). In painting, around the year 1400, the problematics of time and perspective becomes crucial. Perspectivists, while unsettling established symbolisms and traditional representations of mythic order and unity, nevertheless, because of their attention to specific sensorial qualities, create an image which is closely related to the concept: "the image is no longer to the model it sets for itself but what is to a thing its definition, its concept" (*I*, 72). And this conceptualization is based on the fact that perspective "makes a cut in the visible, at some very precise moment" and therefore "will only be able to retain a *trace* of the moment, a petrifaction of the human gesture which will be to the moment really lived what the concept is to being" (*I*, 73). The true sense of gestures and events escapes us "because we are missing their past and also their future, I mean the energy which flows from the one to the other in the continuity of all true duration" (*I*, 73). One senses in the struggle of *Hier régnant désert* that Yves Bonnefoy is seeking to confront the realities of time and mortality, to embody them in the poems themselves, while at the same time searching for the universal and ahistorical context in which to place them. Poetry, the bridge between worlds, is his hope: "to *see* death . . . or dissipate it in the universal . . . is perhaps a same effort, at least for a project in us . . . which we can call poetry" (*I*, 84).

*   *   *

It is the section "A une terre d'aube" ("To an Earth of Dawn") which records the return to a *terre seconde*. One of the poems of the section reflects Bonnefoy's determination to "convert" the past, to transcend the Oedipal "fatalities" by responding to them. What is needed for this transformation is that *ardente patience* of which Rimbaud speaks and which, as Bonnefoy says, "will change what one endures into what one takes on, suffering into being, those 'dead bodies which will be judged' into that vigilance of which we have always been capable and whose truth dawn will see firmly established in an existence which begins anew" (*R*, 132).

La voix de ce qui détruit
Sonne encor dans l'arbre de pierre,

Le pas risqué sur la porte
Peut encore vaincre la nuit.

D'où vient l'Oedipe qui passe?
Vois, pourtant, il a gagné.
Une sagesse immobile
Dès qu'il répond se dissipe.

Le Sphinx qui se tait demeure
Dans le sable de l'Idée.
Mais le Sphinx parle, et succombe.

Pourquoi des mots? Par confiance,
Et pour qu'un feu retraverse
La voix d'Oedipe sauvé.   (*P*, 151) [14]

The voice of destruction
Still resounds within the stony tree,
The step risked at the door
Can still vanquish the night.

Whence comes the Oedipus who passes?
Look, though, he has prevailed.
A motionless wisdom
Once he responds is dispelled.

The Sphinx that says nothing remains
In the sands of the Idea.
But the Sphinx speaks, and succumbs.

Why words? Because we trust,
And so that a fire pass again through
The voice of Oedipus delivered.

Already in his early essay "Les Tombeaux de Ravenne," Bonnefoy had written: "Conceptual thought makes it a point of honor to question rather than to answer. It is a point of honor with all thought. The Western world began badly with Oedipus" (*I*, 121). The "motionless wisdom" of which the poem speaks is a concept, an "image" of (or perspective on) man, which can imprison him; it is dissipated by the response to what Bonnefoy calls the "misunderstood . . . or to put it better . . . the *unloved* (*NR*, 242). In his book on Rimbaud of 1961—that work which sheds so much light not on Rimbaud alone but also on Bonnefoy himself—Bonnefoy wrote: "To be for oneself this Son of man who delivered man from sin by giving him his love, to accept oneself such as one is, imperfect and incomplete, and thus to break down pride, the possessive instinct, and the impatience which can so profoundly separate us from the real, this is what . . . deepens the willingness to hope . . . and contributes to its future" (*R*, 132). Response, acceptance, love, *parole*—these are the arms to be seized to save

Oedipus, or which enable him to save himself: "Vois, pourtant, il a gagné" ("Look, though, he has prevailed"). There is a certain childhood, Bonnefoy has said in another place, which "one must abandon if one wants to drive out the Stranger" (*I*, 326).

Bonnefoy has held that "human freedom—*la parole*—has something miraculous about it" (*NR*, 242). "Like Shestov, I believe that it has chains to break in a certain silence of the world. And therefore it is a question of being in this world, even if it seems silent, since a patient utterance can replace the initial vacancy with meaning" (*NR*, 242). It is important, however, as Bonnefoy remarks in his essay on Ubac entitled "Des fruits montant de l'abîme" ("Fruits Rising from the Abyss"), to distinguish *absence* from *nothingness*.

> There is *nothingness* when some order is perpetuated, with everything in place—except devoid of all real content, so that our experience of things through it is no longer anything but one long dreary concept, through which the feeling of absurdity will triumph over all our hopes. The devil is the master of appearances, as is well known; the dead letter is his weapon, reason closed up on the abstraction of principles, the means cut off from the ends: but it is certainly never the stone, even the most naked and sterile one—and *absence* is of another spirit. One experiences it—one is sometimes intoxicated by it—when the collapse of mediations, often endured as a result of history, throws us brutally, suddenly, outside every human order, and into the great silence of the world in all its frightful evidence. And as no myth has survived to refract or to filter its violence, we are blinded by this day which so many mystics have therefore called dark night. (*I*, 299)

Hier will sometimes use these terms with the distinctions developed above. Thus, in the early accusatory poems, one reads, for instance:

> Lui qui a tant détruit; qui ne sait plus
> Distinguer son néant de son silence. (*P*, 107)

He who destroyed so much; who no longer knows how
To distinguish his nothingness from his silence.

These lines seem to suggest the very danger I mentioned earlier, namely, the capacity for any project to become a convention; or, put another way, the lines seem to evoke the impasse which may always arise when a project becomes a program, when the systematic striving for innocence through the disintegration of habits of language becomes silence. They also speak, of course, to the greater danger of preferring the elaboration of the work of art to lived experience—"in devoting words to themselves" (*AP*, 120).

A later poem, from the section "Le Chant de Sauvegarde" ("The Song of Safekeeping" or "The Safeguard Song"), on the other hand, will speak of absence as the road to salvation.

> *Entre dans le ravin d'absence, éloigne-toi,*
> *C'est ici en pierrailles qu'est le port.* (*P*, 139)

> Go into the ravine of absence, go in deeply,
> The homecoming is here in the bits of stone.

Absence has two faces: on the one side, the direct and unmediated experience of the real in the *hic-et-nunc* is our chance of encountering the world of presences; on the other side, this experience can have the overwhelming or sinister dimension associated with the Stranger or the Dark Night. How does one master the more terrifying side of absence? How does one banish the *guetteurs*, the terrors that lie in wait for us? The Stranger is irrefutable, Bonnefoy has said,

> There is no *reason* not to see through its eyes that the world is empty, unintelligible even though it can be formulated, with neither horizon nor center in spite of the futile procession of the gods. But at the same time, the Stranger is nothing; it is enough to hold onto anything—to "no matter what," be it only a stone—for that specter over there who was lying in wait for us to vanish. And thus, it is enough simply to love; but however important this may be, one knows as well that it cannot be forced. There is no power for making sure of this power. (*I*, 324)

As I said earlier, many poems of *Hier* will emphasize the adherence to the simple and the concrete as a means of salvation: "C'est ici en pierrailles qu'est le port" ("The homecoming is here in the bits of stone"); "Ici l'inquiète voix consent d'aimer / La pierre simple" ("Here the troubled voice agrees to love / The simple stone"); "Ici dans l'herbe ancienne tu verras / Briller le glaive nu qu'il te faut saisir" ("Here in the ancient grass you will see / Gleaming the naked sword you must take up"). Each line contains the word *ici* ("here"), emphasizing the importance of the *hic-et-nunc*; "simple" and "ancient" suggest the quality at once evident and perennial of the real, while the word "port" insists that we must journey and struggle toward this real, that we return to it, after losing it, and "know the place for the first time." And if this recovered love for simple earth is a grace, it is nonetheless one which is sought by that *forme orante* ("praying form") of which Bonnefoy speaks in his essay on Valéry: "the new praying figure whose face this time is free, which, beyond theology and science, man owes it to himself to invent" (*I*, 103).

The fourth poem in the series "Le Feuillage éclairé" ("The Foliage Lit up") from the section "Le Chant de Sauvegarde" speaks of a kind of angel of grace—"l'ange de vivre ici, le tard venu" ("the angel for living here, the one who comes late") (*P*, 133).

> *Il est la terre, elle l'obscure, où tu dois vivre,*
> *Tu ne dénieras pas les pierres du séjour,*
> *Ton ombre doit s'étendre auprès d'ombres mortelles*
> *Sur les dalles où vient et ne vient pas le jour.*
>
> *Il est la terre d'aube. Où une ombre essentielle*
> *Voile toute lumière et toute vérité.*
> *Mais même en lieu d'exil on a aimé la terre,*
> *Tant il est vrai que rien ne peut vaincre l'amour.* (*P*, 134)

He is the earth, the dark earth, where you must live,
You will not deny the stones of your stay here,
Your shadow must be cast beside other mortal shadows
On the flagstones where the day comes and does not come.

He is the earth of dawn. Where an absolute shadow
Veils every light and every truth.
But even in the place of exile the earth has been loved,
So much is it true that nothing can vanquish love.

The poem is the affirmation of the earthly situation; the poet consents both to mortality and to uncertainty, for earth is the place of obscurity and ambiguity. The angel is associated with that dawn invoked throughout the entire poem. The new beginning, the new day begins with acceptance and love. This love, if a gift of grace, is nevertheless seen as invincible.

This poem announces the title of the last section with the words *la terre d'aube* ("the earth of dawn"). Dawn is addressed in the first poem of this section in the imperatives—at once supplications and exhortations—normally associated with prayer.

> *Aube, fille des larmes, rétablis*
> *La chambre dans sa paix de chose grise*
> *Et le cœur dans son ordre. Tant de nuit*
> *Demandait à ce feu qu'il décline et s'achève,*
> *Il nous faut bien veiller près du visage mort.*
> *A peine a-t-il changé. . . . Le navire des lampes*
> *Entrera-t-il au port qu'il avait demandé,*
> *Sur les tables d'ici la flamme faite cendre*
> *Grandira-t-elle ailleurs dans une autre clarté?*
> *Aube, soulève, prends le visage sans ombre,*
> *Colore peu à peu le temps recommencé.* (*P*, 143)

Dawn, daughter of tears, restore
The room to the peacefulness of what is grey
And the heart to its order. So much night

97

Asked of this fire that it grow still and die out,
We must keep watch over the dead face.
Scarcely has it changed. . . . Will the ship of the lamps
Enter the harbor it had asked for,
Will the flame turned to ashes on the tables here
Rise up again elsewhere with a new and stronger brilliance?
Dawn, come forth, take on the shadowless face,
Give color, little by little, to time begun anew.

Dawn is the recompense for suffering; it is related to what another poem calls "l'inlassable patience / Qui fait aube pour nous de tout branchage mort" ("the tireless patience / Which makes a dawning for us out of every dead branch") (*P*, 147). Lines 6 through 9 seem to constitute a tentative restatement of faith in the principle of resurrection from impasse and defeat. The time which begins again for the poet is that time associated with the simple, falling fruits of the poem "Ici, toujours ici" ("Here, Forever Here") (*P*, 150), with those quiet hours in *le lieu clair* ("the bright place") which will pass like a rose "soundlessly shedding its pedals" (*P*, 150). This is the time "which will heal" (*P*, 150). The entreaty that dawn should "color" the time which begins the new day is a prayer to exorcise the Stranger who robs life of its bright hues and its savor.

*   *   *

The entire movement toward the dawn of a new day described here is contained in a recurrent "scene" of the poem. As was the case in *Douve*, the mythic or metaphoric development of *Hier* will occasionally yield to the metonymic. The book begins with the image of sacred fire which has become extinguished. The altar celebrates only death and disillusionment. The accusatory poems situated in a symbolic interior cease abruptly with the finely specific lyric "A San Francesco, le Soir," suggesting that the inner searching of the poetic consciousness is structured by lived experiences in real time and space. This notion is further supported by the elaboration of a night scene in the Roman catacombs. There, the "Veneranda" fresco depicts a woman in vigil, praying over the remains of a dead loved one. The first of the "Veneranda" poems is especially rich.

L'orante est seule dans la salle basse très peu claire,
Sa robe a la couleur de l'attente des morts,
Et c'est le bleu le plus éteint qui soit au monde,
Écaillé, découvrant l'ocre des pierres nues.
L'enfance est seule, et ceux qui viennent sont obscurs,
Ils se penchent avec des lampes sur son corps.

Oh, dors-tu? Ta présence inapaisable brûle
Comme une âme, en ces mots que je t'apporte encor.

Tu es seule, tu as vieilli dans cette chambre,
Tu vaques aux travaux du temps et de la mort.
Vois pourtant, il suffit qu'une voix basse tremble
Pour que l'aube ruisselle aux vitres reparues.   (*P*, 118)

She prays alone in the lowly, darkened room,
Her dress has the color of the waiting for the dead,
The most faded blue the world could know,
Peeling away to show the ocre of the naked stones.
Childhood is lonely, and those who come forward are dark,
They bend over her body with their lamps.
Oh, are you sleeping? Your undying presence burns
Like a soul, in these words I bring to you once more.

You are alone, you have grown old in this room,
You tend to the work of time and of death.
Look, though, the trembling of a single low voice
Is enough for dawn to stream forth from the windows,
      reappearing.

The poem is one among many examples in Bonnefoy's work of the capacity of art to instruct perception and encourage wisdom and acceptance. Alone in the somber rocky chamber, the praying woman, in her situation of vigil, provides a variation on the interior—there of despair and impatience—evoked at the beginning of the book. Here, the posture of the *orante* teaches acceptance of limitations: her dress has the character or color of a deathwatch, and this notion is reinforced by the fact that even her image is invaded by the ocre of the underlying stone. A first example among many to follow of one "world" or dimension of reality mingling with another, the intrusion of stony material here into the contrivance of art underscores Bonnefoy's notion of an awakened and deliberately imperfect beauty which refuses that notion of the beautiful Baudelaire also seems to suspect with its *grandes attitudes*[15] and hatred of *le mouvement qui déplace les lignes*. Mortality is not only the subject of the fresco, the representation itself is menaced. Art and its theme are here consubstantial. The *orante* is a presence to the extent that she is herself torn and faded. In this sense, she may be said to oppose the petrified mask of the "aesthetic self," the frozen statue of the image, construed by arrogance or blind dreaming. The *orante* seems to have grown old in patient acceptance of time and death. And yet her presence is "unappeasable" and burns like a soul. She is one in a series of images developed by Bonnefoy to suggest the quality at once resigned and indefatigable of spiritual vigilance. In this, as well as in her close association with the stones, she reminds us of that other exemplary figure, the salamander of *Douve*. The strange lines 5–8 seem to suggest that the figure or archetype exists at a deeper and more absolute level than the visitors who are perhaps suggestive of the poet's temptation to evoke a specific past or an overly determined psychological perspective. They seem to yield to the discovery of a more profoundly universal presence. The words of the poet collaborate here to make of the figure not only a symbol of spiritual wakefulness and patience but also a harbinger of dawn. Her influence burns in his words; his quiet reverence is a dawning. The *vois pourtant* ("look, though,") of line 11 echoes the *vois, pourtant, il a gagné* ("look, though, he has prevailed") of the Oedipus poem cited earlier, just as the *il suffit* pattern of the same line echoes the remedy proposed for the sense of despair wrought by the Stranger, also already cited: *il suffit d'aimer* ("it is enough to love").

The praying figure—and she is the most immediate and personal form of the feminine in this book of crisis and isolation—is the image of the soul's labor. Does she also represent what has been stifled and buried by a proud but sterile and lifeless masculine spirit?

A series of evocations of this figure provides a kind of correlative for the more general, symbolical movement through night to dawn. The *orante* keeps up a dying fire she knows does not burn in vain. And the poet will discover his own death in the figure and will sleep in confidence. Nevertheless, he seems to waken in despair—

> *Rien ne réunira ces globes étrangers*   (P, 124)

Nothing can bring together these foreign worlds—

to pass a night of horrible anxiety, trapped in a duration which brings only unexplained suffering.

> *Toute la nuit la bête a bougé dans la salle,*
> *Qu'est-ce que ce chemin qui ne veut pas finir,*
> *Toute la nuit la barque a cherché le rivage,*
> *Qu'est-ce que ces absents qui veulent revenir,*
> *Toute la nuit l'épée a connu la blessure,*
> *Qu'est-ce que ce tourment qui ne sait rien saisir,*
> *Toute la nuit la bête a gémi dans la salle,*
> *Ensanglanté, nié la lumière des salles,*
> *Qu'est-ce que cette mort qui ne va rien guérir?*   (P, 125)

All night the beast has prowled about the room,
What is this road that does not want to end,
All night the bark has sought the missing shore,
What are these absent wishing to return,
All night the sword has coupled with the wound,
What is this torture that seizes on nothing,
All night the beast has groaned within the room,

Covered with blood, denied the light of the rooms,
What is this death that does not cure a thing?

The sense of an unending crisis is underscored by the absence of line stops.
The poem is a somewhat more specific and personal evocation of night
placed in the heart of the more symbolic, spiritual night journey which
culminates in dawn—the dawn which will discover the face of the praying
woman on the stones which had been lost in the darkness.

Je regarde le jour venir parmi les pierres,
Tu es seule dans sa blancheur vêtue de noir.   (P, 145)

I watch the day rising among the stones,
You are alone in its pale beauty clothed in black.

Again, the emphasis is on a dawn based on the acceptance of real limita-
tion: the whiteness of dawn serves to set off the mourning clothes of the
orante and places its appearance in the context of death confronted and
acknowledged. The dawn, constantly invoked in this book, is ultimately
seen, therefore, as inseparable from the "night" which calls it forth, from
the darkness which entreats it into being.

*   *   *

What Bonnefoy was coming to see clearly now—and if *Hier régnant dé-*
sert records the crisis of this faith, one can only say that this crisis passed
through has served to strengthen the conviction—is that one must consent
to contradiction as an inevitable dimension of our being-in-the-world: "we
must no longer seek," he would write in his book on Rimbaud, "to deny
the spiritual fatalities that are ours" (R, 130). His *Rimbaud*, published just
three years after *Hier*, discusses the spiritual contradictions of Western
man "at the end of his history" (R, 130). Bonnefoy's analysis of *Une Saison*
en Enfer contains passages of great penetration and sympathy, for Bon-
nefoy comes to meet the earlier poet's anguish and suffering with the expe-
rience of his own. I would like to cite a rather substantial portion of this
analysis.

> I really believe that Rimbaud, at that hour before dawn, was con-
> verted to hope. And by this I mean that that fluctuation he would
> call his "hell"—impatience, impulse, disillusionment, bitterness—
> he came now to understand that, unending and anguished, it is
> the same as life itself, and as far from the credulity he once knew as
> from the detachment he strove for in vain, he could see it as the
> only true being that exists in this universe of absence, and that one
> should therefore accept its "lies" and its devastations, confide

one's bark to it as to the waves of an ocean, show it respect and love. An affirmation of endless contradiction. . . . The absence of an "eternal sun," the seasons of death during which all the limitations of man are revealed in the context of temporal restriction, the "port of misery," the human condition so irrevocably material, even if a glowing does appear in its sky. And, on the other hand, the unappeasable desire for the absolute in those who remain committed to the "discovery of the divine splendor," and soon that illusion, as tenacious as it is futile, which allows Rimbaud, in spite of disappointment and "despair," to write in the present: "Sometimes I see endless beaches in the sky covered with white nations full of joy"—the mirage, forever illusory, of the "true life." . . .

And thus, at the end of *A Season in Hell*, Rimbaud comes to recognize Western man at the end of his history, denouncing in the ambitions and dreams, in the myths and the "ravings" which had been too easily accepted from the centuries of Christianity a credulity which is the most serious form of alienation, but refusing as well that our consciousness resign itself, and proposing a realism to it beyond religious phantasmagoria, a realism in the existential sense of the term. "One must be absolutely modern," writes Rimbaud. For him, it would seem, the fact of alienation is not, in the last analysis, either political or economic, but moral, man becoming alienated when he grows impatient and gives in to his dream, since he thereby loses the sense of his limits which is the foundation of and approach to his deepest reality. Modernity is the *peasant*'s knowledge of a reality surrounded by nothing miraculous, of a difficult but healthy duality in man's condition, at once misery and hope—and the future will be neither in possession nor in glory, but in truth, the obsession with salvation or its useless repudiation having made place for that creative recognition that we only have being because of that desire in us which never obtains and which never gives up—our endless confrontation with finitude, far from both the resigned and the credulous, "far from the people who die according to the seasons." (*R*, 129–30)

What Bonnefoy sees as the basis for new hope for Rimbaud, and what by extension may be seen as his own most fundamental conviction, is a certain notion of truthfulness: our authentic situation resides in oppositions, and integrity consists in denying neither our aspiration for absolutes, nor our state of limitation and defeat. One cannot abandon oneself to either side of this tension without suffering the alienation of credulity and evasion, on the one hand, or of cynicism and despair on the other. This *réalité rugueuse*, to use Rimbaud's own phrase, if difficult and painful, is nevertheless our chance for wholeness and appreciation. An ardent patience will help us to see that it is the very contradictoriness of our condition which is the source of our creativity and strength. (Thus the poem "A la Voix de Kathleen Ferrier" affirms the spirit which knows the two shores—"extreme joy and extreme sorrow"—and evokes those tears smiling "higher than anguish or hope" [*P*, 137].)

A number of poems in *Hier* speak of the contradictions which are man's fate. This one is from "Le Visage Mortel":

> *Tu te coucheras sur la terre simple,*
> *De qui tenais-tu qu'elle t'appartînt?*
>
> *Du ciel inchangé l'errante lumière*
> *Recommencera l'éternel matin.*
>
> *Tu croiras renaître aux heures profondes*
> *Du feu renoncé, du feu mal éteint.*
>
> *Mais l'ange viendra de ses mains de cendre*
> *Étouffer l'ardeur qui n'a pas de fin.* (*P*, 126)

You will lie down upon the simple earth,
From whom did you come to think it was yours?

From out of the unchanging sky, the wandering light
Will begin eternal morning once more.

At the deepest hours you will feel yourself springing to life again
From the fire you gave up but could not extinguish.

But the angel will come with his ashy hands
To put out the ardor that cannot end.

The poem is made up of paradox and contradiction. In the first place, the two realities of man: on the one hand, his destiny in the "horizontality" associated with finitude ("You will *lie down* upon the simple earth"; italics mine); on the other hand, his "vertical" reality, his desire for the ideal, for perfection, the "incurable" (*P*, 104) movement of aspiration ("At the deepest hours you will feel yourself springing to life again"). Dawn is a fatality; man's spiritual energy is never quite extinguished. And if the angel comes to defeat an aspiration which could estrange us from the real, from our sense of limitation, that aspiration remains, nonetheless, limitless and indomitable.

To live out our wounded condition, to assume totally the cross of our contradictions—this is the resolution of the crisis of *Hier régnant désert* and the essence of Bonnefoy's poetical approach in general. One of the last poems of the collection makes clear this effort to maintain oneself in the tension of contradiction.

> *Combien d'astres auront franchi*
> *La terre toujours niable,*

Mais toi tu as gardé claire
Une antique liberté.

Es-tu végétale, tu
As de grands arbres la force
D'être ici astreinte, mais libre
Parmi les vents les plus hauts.

Et comme naître impatient
Fissure la terre sèche,
De ton regard tu dénies
Le poids des glaises d'étoiles.   (*P*, 146)

How many stars will have passed beyond
The earth which can always be denied,
But you, you have kept clear
An ancient freedom.

Are you plantlike, you
Have the power the great trees have
Of being tied down here, but free
Among the highest winds.

And as to be born impatient
Cracks the arid earth,
You with your gaze you refuse
The pull of starry clay.

The simple evidence of earth can always be scorned or forgotten. The poem sets in opposition the liberty of the transcendent stars and the freedom in rigorous adhesion of the earthbound tree. The lofty condition of the star is not for man. Like certain forms of credulity or dream, it represents alienation. Man cannot deny the reality of his limits. ("Il tombera dans l'herbe," another poem will say, "ayant trouvé / Dans l'herbe le profond de toute vérité"—"He will fall down in the grass, having discovered / In the grass the depths of all truth" [*P*, 101].) To confront the absence of freedom in limitations is to enter into relation with that other freedom, no longer illusory, but real, which man has always possessed ("une *antique* liberté"), but rarely accepted. For it must be kept *claire* (another version of the poem will say *pure*);[16] it demands patience, although its force is in this patience; and the subjection to a difficult situation, which is suggested by the verb *astreindre*, is the foundation of this freedom. The earth is "arid" for an untempered and impatient thirst, but the "anxious" or "troubled" voice of the early poems will come to love that olive tree which has learned to flourish amidst the dry stones (*P*, 149). The denial of earth of the first lines is countered by the refusal of the lure of the stars in the last. The "clay" of these stars may indicate that in Bonnefoy's view the place "over there" is not apt to be substantially different from the place we know right here. On the other hand, the "clay" of the ideal stars may be suggestive of the artist's materials and world. The poet finds in the image of the tree a symbol for his own condition: rooted in earth, yet reaching upwards,[17] the tree, with its vertical and horizontal tendencies, is the *locus* of contradiction assumed and made fruitful—at once the tree of knowledge and an eternal cross.[18]

*   *   *

The epigraph for this collection—"'You want a world,' said Diotima. 'This is why you have everything, and you have nothing'"—is in part related to the problem of impatience and the power of the artist. Bonnefoy was specific about the paradoxical condition of the artist whose relation to words seems to assure him everything, but whose very power, in abolishing the real world and the true being of others, can place him in a situation of extreme solitude. The temptation of the artist is the lure of possession—the hope of Mallarmé, for instance, who, according to Bonnefoy, "must have turned with real interest toward the words thanks to which what one conceives of but fails to find here may take shape again, having found in words, or so one might think, the undiscoverable 'place to live'" (*NR*, 185). If the poem cited above insists "You will lie down upon the simple earth," this insistence on mortality and limitation is connected to a realization of the emptiness of the claim of appropriation and artistic autonomy: "From whom," the poem will ask, "did you come to think that [the earth] was yours?"

To want a world: this desire for possession leads, in fact, to dispossession and estrangement.

> Tu es seul maintenant malgré ces étoiles,
> Le centre est près de toi et loin de toi,
> Tu as marché, tu peux marcher, plus rien ne change,
> Toujours la même nuit qui ne s'achève pas.   (*P*, 98)

You are alone now in spite of all these stars,
The center is close to you and far from you,
You have walked, you can keep walking, nothing changes
     anymore,
Always the same night that refuses to end.

The fall into dream, the retreat into nostalgia for some ideal world destroys the world at hand and robs the poet of his capacity for appreciation. He is plunged into darkness and confusion. The oil in the lamp of vigilance has blackened and grown old and useless (*P*, 101). The dark night of the soul, as conceived of by a mystic such as St. John of the Cross,[19] is the proper preparation for clarification and spiritual progress: "God places . . . souls in the dark night," he writes, "so as to purify them . . . and make them advance."[20] Bonnefoy seems to have some experience of the mystical literature, but he appears to have found the mystical orientation "too abyssal." The study of this literature seems only to have contributed to his morbidity and loneliness, to his "fever not to live" (*P*, 176). (For more on Bonnefoy's reservations about the mystical tradition, see my note 19.) Nevertheless, the "everything and nothing" of the spirit of appropriation and pride which results in the disorientation recorded in *Hier* becomes, for the mystic, more properly a "nothing and then everything," since, as St. John of the Cross says, "the spirit purged and annihilated of all particular knowledge and affection, not finding satisfaction in anything, nor understanding anything in particular, and remaining in . . . emptiness and darkness, embraces all things with great preparedness. And St. Paul's words are verified: *Nihil habentes, et omnia possidentes.*"[21] The "bird of the ruins," evoked in the last poem of *Hier*, seems to suggest this preparedness through self-abnegation and the trials of darkness.

> *Il a franchi toute douleur, toute mémoire,*
> *Il ne sait plus ce qu'est demain dans l'éternel.* (*P*, 153)

It has passed beyond all sorrow, all memory,
It no longer knows what tomorrow is in the eternal.

There is considerable irony in the epigraph, of course, and a number of poems will be marked by a voice *d'ironie pure* (*P*, 132). Irony is the register of a certain detachment and distance—of self-judgment. For Kierkegaard, irony is the boundary zone in the passage from the *aesthetic* to the *ethical* stage (just as humor often marks the passage from the ethical to the religious stage). Bonnefoy seems clearly to have measured a certain distance between his writing and his life. *Hier régnant désert* traces the development of a more passionate and decisive commitment.

I spoke earlier of an act of forgetfulness, of a certain break with the past which *Hier régnant désert* seeks to mark. The poem "La Mémoire" suggests that a process of overcoming *les tristes forces gardiennes* ("the sorrowful protective forces") (*P*, 127) of early wounds must be accomplished in order to recognize and deliver the past. Claudel, in his rather muscular way, speaks of a moment in his life when he broke with "the last traces of [his] attachment to the past."[22]

> In a railway car there is the seat facing forward and the seat facing backward; there are people who watch the past fading away, and others who watch the future arriving; well, that dramatic moment in my life marks the turning point. It was at that moment that I changed seats, if you will; from the seat facing backward, I went to the seat facing forward. (Ibid.)

Something of the same sort seems to have happened for Bonnefoy. *Hier régnant désert* unquestionably reflects a period of crisis and a turning point. Later, he would say of Valéry, for instance, "we have to forget Valéry" (*I*, 103), for Valéry was doubtless a *possibility* which existed in Bonnefoy. Certain writers, he said, "exist *in us*" (*I*, 103). "We have to struggle against them, just as we have to choose, and with being in mind. It is a private battle. It is perhaps a wager, in the rather serious sense that has been given to this word" (*I*, 103). Valéry, for Bonnefoy, was a "poet who was cursed—doubtless sheltered from misfortune and from the ability to imagine misfortune, but condemned to ideas, to words (to the intelligible part of the word) because he never learned how to love things, and deprived of that essential joy mingled with tears which all at once rescues the work of poetry from its night" (*I*, 102).

Jean Grosjean had complained that *Douve* was bookish and contrived. Its heroine, he felt, had passed through too many universities. "If the best poetry," he wrote testily, "were the poetry which solves literary problems, we would be in the presence of a major work. I have no doubt that the alexandrine spirit everywhere today will hail the advent of *Douve*, and that the literary manuals in their literary manual hearts will be delighted with such an event."[23] It is undeniable that *Hier régnant désert* is a starker book than *Douve*, even though the latter is supposed to be focusing on our desolation. If *Douve* proposes to deal with spiritual deprivation and bleakness, it does so by means of an unusually rich poetic tapestry and through an indisputable technical brilliance and rhetorical diversity. Grosjean's criticisms of the book were aimed, as he said, at making Bonnefoy's voice "more itself." But if these doubts about the sincerity of a young poet's first major work are understandable—and they do seem extraordinarily hostile and mean—the suffering of *Hier régnant désert*, its deliberate celebration of "the voice mingled with the color grey / That wavers in the distances of the song that died out / As if beyond all pure form / There trembled another song and the only absolute" (*P*, 137), must have put them to rest. By the end of the fifties, Bonnefoy will have definitively taken his stand against a purely aesthetic poetry: "The real curse in this world," he would say, "is to be reduced to playing games" (*I*, 102).

*   *   *

Bonnefoy will begin his work on Shakespeare during the period of *Hier régnant désert*. Ironically, his *Hamlet* appeared the same year the book of poems was published. Bonnefoy has said of Hamlet that he confronts "a world without structure, truths which henceforth are only partial, contradictory, in competition with one another—as many signs as one could wish and quickly far too many, but nothing which will resemble a sacred order, or meaning."[24] In a world without sense, in a world of absence and nothingness, Hamlet feels that "a single act still has some logic and is worthy of being carried out: and that is to take great pains to detach oneself from every illusion and to be ready to accept everything—everything, but first of all and especially, death, essence of all life—with irony and indifference" (ibid., 14). Bonnefoy will characterize the "ripeness" of Lear as "the quintessence of the world's order, whose unity one seems to breathe," whereas the "readiness" of Hamlet is "the reverse side of that order, when one no longer sees anything in the greyness of the passing days but the incomprehensible weave" (ibid., 22).

Did Bonnefoy also know a "sharpening of the unvanquished suffering, its reduction to a single shrill note"—that suffering which is the fate of "a being who believed himself to be the depositary of the absolute, and who has not yet resigned himself to the breakup of that heritage which remains centered on the self"? (ibid., 15). One might, in any case, characterize *Hier régnant désert*—Bonnefoy's greyest book[25]—as a kind of "Hamlet phase" or "Hamlet crisis."[26]

The next collection of poems—*Pierre écrite*—which appeared seven years later, would have as epigraph a quotation from *The Winter's Tale*—that play which Bonnefoy sees as "in fact solar" and which "may be superimposed on *Hamlet* point for point":[27] "Thou mettest with things dying; I with things newborn." Something of the same sort of distinction might be established, with reservations, between *Hier régnant désert* and *Pierre écrite*, since the four-part structures of each work allow for some interesting comparisons and contrasts, as I hope to show in the next chapter. The experience recorded in *Hier régnant désert* clearly involved purgation and trial, but in the dissolution of credulities and dream, of an illusory self, a world of plenitude and daily fruitfulness appears, like boats arriving in music.

5 Marriage

In our contact with being, we cannot do without the mediation of specific beings.

When the poet, at the end of *Hier régnant désert*, sends out his prayer to Dawn that she "color" time on the mend, the reader cannot but join in the supplication. The unrelenting greyness of *Hier* creates a rather uncomfortable impression of stagnation and sterility. The rains which fall on "la terre surprise," promising new ardor, new beginnings in time, presage the flowering and fruitfulness in the garden scenes, so full of new colors, with which *Pierre écrite* (*Words in Stone*) (1965) begins. If grey is, as Bonnefoy has maintained, the color "that founds" (*I*, 291), the native hue of the real, it is nonetheless true that "we are not cured of the garden," that we long for "le jardin dont l'ange / A refermé les portes sans retour" ("the garden whose gates / The angel has closed forever") (*P*, 163). And it is this garden with its foliage and rich fruitfulness which is evoked in the opening pages of *Pierre écrite* where "le vert, et l'orangé des fruits mûrs, s'est accru" ("the green, and the orange of the ripened fruit has deepened").[1] For, as a later poem of the collection maintains, "la grisaille se perd dans le fruit mûr" ("the greyness vanishes in the ripened fruit") (*P*, 220). The earlier struggling gives way to a peaceful acceptance of the rich substantiality of earth.

> *Le fer des mots de guerre se dissipe*
> *Dans l'heureuse matière sans retour.* (*P*, 220)

> The iron of the words of war dissolves
> Into joyful matter without end.

Where has this garden, which may be seen as replacing the "lost" garden of the poet's youth in Toirac, come from? How do we explain the new sense of peacefulness and reconciliation? The emphasis in the book on maturation is a key. The last poem of the book—on "The Art of Poetry"—insists that transformation has come, in part, because "on a dit au cœur / D'être le cœur ("the heart was told / To be the heart") (*P*, 227). *Pierre écrite* celebrates new feelings and honors an eroticism whose languorous peacefulness may be contrasted to the violent ruptures and despairing dislocations recorded in *Douve*. Night, here, is no longer the obscurity of aimless suffering: it is the *Nacht der Liebe* lovers know—in which, as Tristan says, "there is no more name, only oneness"; it is the world Juliette dreads to see shattered by dawn. This "Summer of Night" is the lovers' context.

> *Tout ce qui est bougeait comme un vaisseau qui tourne*
> *Et glisse, et ne sait plus son âme dans la nuit.* (P, 168)

> The whole world swayed like a ship that veers
> And glides, and loses itself in the night.

These years will have marked a decided change in Bonnefoy, in part reflected by the important insight that "in our contact with being, we cannot do without the mediation of specific beings."[2] In his own life, this conviction will be supported by a new marriage and by the discovery in the region of "les Basses-Alps" of a specific place to which "he became attached at once" and "where he lived for long moments."[3] The notion of a "shared soul" ("L'Ame partagée") pervades the book. The collection, which distinguishes itself sharply in this respect from the sense of solitude and despair of the preceding volume, incorporates and makes manifest (as perhaps only *Dans le leurre du seuil* will as powerfully) the reconciliation, the alliance, of the nostalgia for transcendence and the capacity for the transfiguration of the here and now. And the dissolution of dream, of the longing for another, more perfect place is accomplished, in great measure, by the earthly presence of the other:

> *Ces frêles mains terrestres dénoueront*
> *Le nœud triste des rêves.* (P, 167)

> These frail earthly hands will untangle
> The sorrowful knot of dreams.

The feminine *tu* who emerges in the pages of *Pierre écrite* has all the resonances of a specific other and no longer the merely emblematic character of the "Veneranda" figure of *Hier régnant désert* or the richly polysignifying associations of Douve with the metamorphoses of representation and the transmutations of poetic inspiration in a dark age. It is true, of course, that for all her specificity, the feminine *tu* is also part of a larger complex of relationships and that the intimacy of the couple in *Pierre écrite* is the foundation for a closer association with both nature and the dead. She too will have her impact on the poet's relation with his own inner "voices," for the experience of the other person in this collection is never entirely dissociated from the experience of language and the poetic act. In this sense, the *tu* so often addressed in these poems seems to represent the poet's emerging confidence in life, a new and more trustingly affirmative relationship with his muse.

And it is with the reverberations of the specifically "other" that this feminine presence arrests the attention. She emerges like a "Venus," or like Nerval's April Nymph "fraîche éclose, / Qui, souriante, sort de l'eau" ("fresh blooming, / Who, smiling, comes forth from the water"). She is "happy" and "uncaring."

> *Souriante, première, délavée,*
> *A jamais le reflet d'une étoile immobile*
> *Dans le geste mortel.*   (*P*, 165)

> Smiling, pristine, sea-washed,
> Forever the reflection of an unmoving star
> In the mortal gesture.

She seems to exercise a calming effect on those "cries of alarm" which characterized some of the poetic voices of an earlier time. A "pure hand" now sleeps next to the "careworn hand."[4] And one of the last poems of the collection will exclaim,

> *Nous n'avons plus besoin*
> *D'images déchirantes pour aimer.*
> *Cet arbre nous suffit, là-bas . . .*   (*P*, 221)

> We no longer need
> Rending images to love.
> That tree over there is enough . . .

Douve had already suggested the breakdown of intellectual and conceptual mediations provided by the erotic experience:

> *C'était jour de tes seins*
> *Et tu régnais enfin absente de ma tête.*   (*P*, 25)

> It was day of your breasts
> And you reigned at last far from my head.

Pierre écrite continues and develops this experience, but the violent eroticism of *Douve*, whose heroine is presented "all bent on death on the exulting drums of [her] gestures," yields here to a languid and dreamy communion between lovers—a drowsy, gentle sensuality evoked in the context of a setting which also communicates a sense of concrete specificity. The material of the poetic texture—simple, daily realities such as the bedroom and mirror, a red dress, myrtle branches, the sound of bees—distinguishes *Pierre écrite* from the more symbolic and hieratic volumes which precede it. The poet's attention goes to the real birds of his experience; the emblematic "bird" of the earlier work is replaced by "ces oiseaux qui se parlent, indéfinis, / Qui se mordent, lumière" ("these birds that speak to one another, indefinite / That bite one another, light") (*P*, 207). Even the phoenix only appears once (*P*, 183). And one could say, I think (to take up Bonnefoy's own terms once again), that the excarnate, purely formal dimensions of the earlier works have been transformed and made incarnate in a fresh experience of the world—at once simpler and more accepting—

and that *Pierre écrite* represents a new level of immediacy and concreteness. This is not, of course, a repudiation of the earlier works. One is tempted, in fact, to think of the earlier work as preparation, as having, as it were, "called" the present experience into existence.

The book strives to make manifest Plotinus's notion that "there is nothing yonder which is not also here," and to convert the poet's nostalgia into a new vision and acceptance of what is. Many poems of the collection are supplications or prayers for this kind of conversion:

> *O de ton aile de terre et d'ombre éveille-nous,*
> *Ange vaste comme la terre, et porte-nous*
> *Ici, au même endroit de la terre mortelle,*
> *Pour un commencement. Les fruits anciens*
> *Soient notre faim et notre soif enfin calmées.*
> *Le feu soit notre feu. Et l'attente se change*
> *En ce proche destin, cette heure, ce séjour.* (P, 224)

> O wake us with your wing of earth and shadow,
> Angel vast as earth, and carry us
> Here, to the same place on the mortal earth,
> For a beginning. May the fruits that always were here
> Calm our hunger and our thirst at last.
> May the fire be our fire. And may our waiting be changed
> Into this destiny close by, this hour, this place.

And the poet finds a number of striking natural images to suggest the blending of dream and evidence, the merging of that fatal desire for transcendence with the realities of mortality:

> *Toi aussi tu aimes l'instant où la lumière des lampes*
> *Se décolore et rêve dans le jour.*
> *Tu sais que c'est l'obscur de ton cœur qui guérit,*
> *La barque qui rejoint le rivage et tombe.* (P, 201)

> You too, you love the moment when the light of the lamps
> Grows pale and dreams in the daylight.
> You know that it is the darkness in your heart that is healing,
> The bark that meets the shore and falls.

The severe "black and white" color patterns of *Douve*—the violent flashings of being against the black backdrop of nothingness—will yield here to a gentler mingling of light and darkness, as *Pierre écrite* focuses particularly on the merging lights of evening.

Two incomplete images of man had been confronted and rejected by Bonnefoy—Oedipus and Hamlet. Here, in an Arcadian setting which, for all its color and beauty, will never exclude the greyness of the stone, the poet seems to have achieved a new degree of maturity and affirmation, to have found the means of reconciling and allying what otherwise might have

112

remained in dangerous opposition. In this garden, "simple . . . are the fruits that have ripened" (*P*, 217).

*   *   *

The collection begins with a series of nine love poems entitled "Été de nuit" or "Summer of Night." The title suggests an inversion of Shakespeare's "Midsummer Night's Dream" ("Songe d'une nuit d'été"), and Bonnefoy is conceivably underlining the possibility of a dominance by Night-Oneness, by the *Liebesnacht*. And in fact, this languorous night of love is controlled poetically in much the same way as is the "dark night" of *Hier régnant désert*—that night from which the poetic voice ("bloody and mournful") has been "dredged" and "cleansed" (*P*, 227). Starlit heavens make this night "less dark" (*P*, 163). No longer the fearful dark night "that does not want to end" and in which the beast prowls (*P*, 125), this night is the context in which "l'éternité montait parmi les fruits de l'arbre" ("eternity rose among the fruit of the tree") (*P*, 164).

The poem begins "dans [un] rêve de mai" ("in a May-dream") (*P*, 164). The suspension points which precede the indication for the sixth poem of the series (i.e., ". . . VI") are doubtless used to reinforce the feeling that "for a long time it was summer" (*P*, 168).[5] Time ceases to be: "voici presque l'instant / Où il n'est plus de jour, plus de nuit . . ." ("here is almost the moment / When there is no more day, no more night . . .") (*P*, 167). Summer is to be crossed "comme un large / Océan immobile" ("like a huge / Unmoving ocean") (*P*, 169). The beloved is the figurehead at the prow of the "navire de vivre" ("the ship of living")—"happy, uncaring . . . smiling, pristine, sea-washed" (*P*, 165). At first, this peaceful immobility seems like an eternity far from death.

> *Vaguent au loin les morts au désert de l'écume,*
> *Il n'est plus de désert puisque tout est en nous*
> *Et il n'est plus de mort puisque mes lèvres touchent*
> *L'eau d'une ressemblance éparse sur la mer.*   (*P*, 164)

Far off the dead are wandering in the deserts of surf,
There is no desert anymore since everything is in us
And there is no death anymore since my lips touch
The water of resemblance scattered on the sea

The poet longs for "a greater summer where nothing can end" (*P*, 169). The fourth poem of the series, however, already seems to shatter the illusion of timelessness and unity; the figurehead is "spotted with red" ("tachée de rouge") (*P*, 166), either because of the appearance of that dawn which ushers in day distinctions or because poetic consciousness has suddenly apprehended her in the essential vulnerability of her mortality.[6] She bends her neck "comme on pèse l'âme des morts" ("as one weighs the soul of the dead") (P, 166).

The eighth poem, beginning with the qualifying "mais" very certainly substantiates this impression of rupture and awakening.

> Mais ton épaule se déchire dans les arbres,[7]
> Ciel étoilé,[8] et ta bouche recherche
> Les fleuves respirants de la terre pour vivre
> Parmi nous ta soucieuse et désirante nuit.
>
> O notre image encor,
> Tu portes près du cœur une même blessure,
> Une même lumière où bouge un même fer.
>
> Divise-toi, qui es l'absence et ses marées.
> Accueille-nous, qui avons goût de fruits qui tombent,
> Mêle-nous sur tes plages vides dans l'écume
> Avec les bois d'épave de la mort,
>
> Arbre aux rameaux de nuit doubles, doubles toujours.   (P, 170)

But your shoulder is torn apart in the trees,
Heavens bright with stars, and your mouth searches for
The breathing rivers of earth to live out
With us your night full of anguish and desire.

O once more like us,
You carry near your heart the same wound,
The same light in which the same sword is stirring.

Break yourself apart, you who are absence and its tides.
Gather us to you, we who have the taste of fruit that falls,
Mingle us in the surf of your empty beaches
With the wreckage left by death,

Tree with twofold branches of night, always twofold.

The disintegration of Night-Oneness is placed specifically in the context of the movement of love and desire. Somehow, Bonnefoy seems to be saying, unity and eternity are fractured through love to allow for multiplicity, division, mortality.[9] We, "who have the taste of fruit that falls," are nonetheless invited, through our adherence to specific forms of a common finitude, to participate in those momentary intuitions of the essential unity of being which often remain just beyond the reach of language, which ordinarily separates in order to name. And so one poem will speak, for instance, of "le nom presque dit d'un dieu presque incarné" ("the name almost uttered of a god almost incarnate") (P, 221). The night which ends in an "awakening" is the night of wordless oneness; the ninth and concluding poem of

the series evokes "cet autre jour . . . / Ce plus bas rougeoiement mêlé de
sable noir" ("that other day . . . / That deeper glowing mingled with black
sand") where "un langage se fait, qui *partage* le clair / Buissonnement
d'étoiles dans l'écume" ("a language is formed which *splits up* the bright
clustering of stars in the surf") (*P*, 171; italics mine). In the period of *éveil*
or "awakening," dream folds up her painted cloths and the poet returns to
his familiar "darkened road," to "the stones / Of mortal earth" (*P*, 173)—
but with the moral exhortation that

> *L'Ame se fait d'aimer*
> *L'écume sans réponse.*
> *La joie sauve la joie,*
> *L'amour le non-amour.* (*P*, 178)

The soul is formed through loving
The surf that does not answer.
Joy saves joy,
Love what is not love.

*   *   *

The structure of *Pierre écrite* will remind some readers (John E. Jack-
son mentions it, for instance, in passing)[10] of Poussin's *Et in Arcadia Ego*
paintings, which represent shepherds in an Arcadian setting examining a
tomb they have discovered and on which they make out the words "I, too,
in Arcadia." Whether the words are to be interpreted as if coming from the
dead person in the tomb (i.e., "I, too, once lived in Arcadia") or from
Death itself (i.e., "I, Death, exist even in this Arcadia") is a matter of some
dispute.[11] Bellori, a contemporary of Poussin, wrote of the second of these
paintings (the one in which a priestess-like figure[12] has replaced the earlier
shepherdess) that it exemplifies a philosophy of life he calls "'la felicità sog-
getta alla morte.'"[13] In just such a way the idyllic timelessness of the love
described in the first poems is tempered and controlled, in the arrange-
ment of the texts Bonnefoy chooses to give, by a remembrance of death
commemorated by the "inscriptions" of the poems in the section "Pierre
écrite."[14] These poems, many of them of great power and simplicity, cen-
tered on their pages, suggest the epitaphs written on tombstones. Many
tell the story of a particular existence stopped by death. Even something of
the ambiguity in the *Et in Arcadia Ego* expression is preserved, since the
inscription may be interpreted variously as either the voice of the dead per-
son or as the voice of Death itself as it evokes some futile existence. And so,
one "tombstone" will read,

Nicolas Poussin, *Et in Arcadia Ego.* Courtesy of the Musée du Louvre, Paris.

Je fus assez belle.
Il se peut qu'un jour comme celui-ci me ressemble.
Mais la ronce l'emporte sur mon visage,
La pierre accable mon corps.   (*P*, 184)

I was rather beautiful.
Perhaps as beautiful as a day like today.
But the brambles have more power than my face,
And stone crushes my body.

But another will say,

Il désirait, sans connaître,
Il a péri, sans avoir.
Arbres, fumées,
Toutes lignes de vent et de déception
Furent son gîte.
Infiniment
Il n'a étreint que sa mort.   (*P*, 182)

He desired, without knowing,
He perished, without having.
Trees, smoke,
Rows and rows of wind and disappointment
Were his home.
Endlessly
He embraced only his own death.

In order to enter into the strange mixture of love and death, of participation in plenitude and the inescapable sense of personal limitation which characterizes *Pierre écrite*, it would be well to recall Bonnefoy's own assessment of Poussin as it appears in his study of the early Baroque period entitled *Rome, 1630*. The poet recognizes in the sensibility of the painter two fundamental aspects:

> The first, and of course the more readily apparent, is a sensuality which can extend to the point of violence and which is always fundamentally erotic; while the other, more secret, elusive like anguish, is an obsessive feeling of personal limitation. By this, I mean that, too conscious of itself, too attached to its own particular form, the *ego* cannot commit itself to being absorbed into the heart of the real (as in a way sensation asks it to). In short, it knows itself as a kind of object, the aspects and ways of which are perfectly defined—and because of this, the real appears infinite to it, and it therefore will always remain regretful (given the sensuality I mentioned a moment ago) of the riches it has been unable to capture. A constant conflict ensues, a state of anguish, and a dream as well, which seeks the solution. In how many of his pictures has Poussin, encouraged in this by the example of the *Bacchanales* of Titian, by Venetian "color," abandoned himself to the

dream of an infinite participation in the riches of the senses, a plentiful golden age for a human being without limits! It is in this that he is sometimes so close to Cortona. But soon the wound reopens: and then there are those inscriptions on tombs, those inaccessible cities on the hills that remind us that the glimpse of plenitude is but forever an illusion. Poussin will always be torn by these two opposing intuitions of a profusion of the real and the limits of the individual.[15]

Something of the same sort of opposition is seeking resolution in *Pierre écrite*.

Now Bonnefoy has repeatedly insisted that "we *exist* only by elaborating our difference" (*I*, 310). The Arcadian dream, "the hunger for immediacy" (*I*, 39) is a reality, and so too is our estrangement. And if Bonnefoy has seemed to some a "philosophical" poet, if his analyses of works of literature and art tend to place them into general or abstract categories, to read them as allegories of being, if he is inclined to celebrate the real in the most "essential" and intellectual of discourses, it is because there is a contradiction at the heart of his project which he has affirmed in a particularly eloquent and moving way.

> But so that this movement of return be more than mere simulation, it is essential that the two terms of the contradiction be kept face to face, and that this separated and unhappy life of the mind, which would like to return to the substantiality that was lost, be itself affirmed to the very end in its profound difference. We are from the Western world, and this cannot be denied. We have eaten of the tree of knowledge, and this cannot be denied. And far from dreaming of a cure for what we are, it is through our irrevocable intellectuality that we must try to reinvent presence, which is salvation. (*I*, 40)

For Bonnefoy, it is a special kind of highly concentrated love which, while seizing the particular in its difference, yet dissolves that distinctiveness in a vision of the participation of the separate in the universal. If we exist only through the elaboration of our difference, "we *are* only by knowing how to give [this difference] back to the earth."

> And between the art which develops the ideal figure, made entirely of dream, and that which, elemental like the plowshare, is inscribed on the shadow cast by the body of being, we need poetry which longs for their union and helps us to establish it in us, that patient work of the spirit on a specific being—on a face first grasped, then dissolved, but recreated as well and transfigured by the profoundest of our possibilities. (*I*, 310)

The section "Un feu va devant nous" ("A Fire Goes Before Us") is the poetical manifestation of this "transformation"; the poems of the section

118

"Pierre écrite" constitute the grey passage through opacity and disintegration where, as one "stone" will say, "Mourir a fait le lit de la nuit dans mon cœur" ("Dying has made the bed of the night in my heart") (*P*, 192).

It is this passage through the underworld, however, this remembrance of those "ancient dead who are the rust of being" (*I*, 311), which allows for the return to "the menaced earth" (*P*, 217), to "the simple hour" (*P*, 214), to "the ripened fruit" (*P*, 217). And the dead are incorporated into the transformed vision of "Un feu va devant nous." In the lovely lyric "Andiam, compagne belle. . . ," the poet says of the river, "more radiant with evening,"

> J'entends tomber sur vous, qu'une musique emporte,
> L'écume où bat le cœur introuvable des morts.   (*P*, 216)

> I hear falling on you, who are carried along by music,
> The spray in which the undiscoverable heart of the dead is
>   beating.

The reference to Don Ottavio's line in the third scene of the first act of Mozart's *Don Giovanni* ("Let us go, my dear friends") would seem to represent, in this context, a kind of mastery over an earlier moment of discouragement recorded in the poem "L'Écume, le récif" ("The Surf, the Reef"):

> Il ne faut plus tenter d'unir voix et prière,
> Espoir et nuit, désirs de l'abîme et du port.
> Vois, ce n'est pas Mozart qui lutte dans ton âme,
> Mais le gong, contre l'arme informe de la mort.   (*P*, 175)

> We must no longer strive to bring together voice and prayer,
> Hope and night, longings for shipwreck and for shore.
> Look, it is not Mozart who struggles in your soul,
> But the gong, raised against the shapeless arms of death.

In his *Rimbaud*, Bonnefoy had referred to man as "une musique latente" (*R*, 152). And the effort to harmonize the reality and presence of death with an accepting and loving vision of life would seem to constitute a desire to transform and enrich "the frightful music" of the earlier *Douve* (*P*, 34).[16]

*   *   *

The collection establishes a discrete chronological line, beginning, as I said, "in a May-dream," and ending in that "pays du début d'octobre" ("land of early October") which

> *n'avait fruit*
> *Qui ne se déchirât dans l'herbe* . . .   (P, 215)

> had no fruit
> That was not rotting in the grass . . .

The passage from plenitude to fall reinforces the notion of the presence of death, even in Arcadia. The memory of death permeates the poetic consciousness, and a number of allusions contribute to this pervasive feeling, in particular the allusion to the myth of Kore in the last section of the book, "Le Dialogue d'angoisse et de désir." I said earlier that *Pierre écrite* distinguishes itself from the previous collections by a greater concrete specificity, that it strikes us as less "symbolic" and allusive than the other books. This not to say that Bonnefoy now refuses allusions, that he is entirely in a world of unmediated immanence. Aglauros, Kore, Porphyry, Tintoretto, Mozart, for instance, are evoked for special meditations, sometimes to suggest the insufficiency of artistic or intellectual representation in the face of death,

> *Le livre de Porphyre sur le soleil,*
> *Regarde-le tel qu'un amas de pierres noires.*
> *J'ai lu longtemps le livre de Porphyre,*
> *Je suis venu au lieu de nul soleil.*   (P, 193)

> Porphyry's book on the sun,
> See it as a heap of black stones.
> I read Porphyry's book for a long time,
> I have come to the place where there is no sun,

sometimes to contemplate the need of our emotional life for images and forms—

> *Oh, qui est plus réel*
> *Du chagrin désirant ou de l'image peinte?*
> *Le désir déchira le voile de l'image,*
> *L'image donna vie à l'exsangue désir.*   (P, 225)

> Oh, which is the more real
> Longing sorrow or painted image?
> Longing tore the veil of the image,
> The image gave life to bloodless desire.

The story of Kore recapitulates, in mythic form, the movement the poem itself will trace.

One of the "tombstone" voices of the section "Pierre écrite" will say,

> *En tête du cortège je suis tombé*
> *Sans dieu, sans voix audible, sans péché,*
> *Bête trinitaire criante.*   (P, 187)

> At the head of the procession I fell
> Godless, voiceless, sinless,
>   A howling three-personed beast.

The cruel substitution of a "three-personed beast" for the traditional notion of a divine trinity suggests the three-headed monster Cerberus, guardian of the underworld, and thus anticipates the poem on the myth of Kore in the last section of the.book.

> *Et je pense à Coré l'absente; qui a pris*
> *Dans ses mains le cœur noir étincelant des fleurs*
> *Et qui tomba, buvant le noir, l'irrévélée,*
> *Sur le pré de lumière—et d'ombre. Je comprends*
> *Cette faute, la mort. Asphodèles, jasmins*
> *Sont de notre pays. Des rives d'eau*
> *Peu profonde et limpide et verte y font frémir*
> *L'ombre du cœur du monde. . . . Mais oui, prends.*
> *La faute de la fleur coupée nous est remise,*
> *Toute l'âme se voûte autour d'un dire simple,*
> *La grisaille se perd dans le fruit mûr.*
>
> *Le fer des mots de guerre se dissipe*
> *Dans l'heureuse matière sans retour.*   (*P*, 220)

> And I think of the absent Kore; who took up
> In her hands the glittering black heart of the flowers
> And who fell, unrevealed, drinking the darkness,
> On the meadow filled with light—and with shadow. I
>   understand
> What is missing because of death. Asphodels, jasmine,
> These are from our land. Banks of water,
> Shallow and limpid and green, cause
> The shadow of the heart of the world to stir. . . . Yes, do take.
> The sin of the cut flower is forgiven us,
> The whole soul is arched over a few simple words,
> The greyness vanishes in the ripened fruit.

> The iron of the words of war dissolves
> Into joyful matter without end.

The myth is familiar to most, especially to readers of Ovid, who deals with it in the fifth book of his *Metamorphoses*. Kore (i.e., "the maiden" or "daughter") is another name for Persephone, the wife of Hades and daughter of Zeus and Demeter. As she was picking flowers in the meadows of Enna in Sicily, she was, as Ovid puts it, "in one moment, / Or almost one, . . . seen and loved, and taken / In Pluto's rush of love."[17] Ovid notes that, before her capture, Persephone lived in unending springtime (*Metamorphoses* 5.389). Her mother, Demeter, searched for her all over the world, and, on the strength of her lamentations, an agreement was reached according to which Persephone would spend part of the year in Hades, during the barren months of earth, and part of the year with her mother, during the period of fruitfulness and growing. The periods are said to represent the burying of corn seeds in the ground and the eventual fruition of the corn. Kore or Persephone is sometimes depicted with Hades, the three-headed Cerberus at their feet. Kore often carries a scepter or torches. The righteous in Hades were thought to dwell amid the sweet blooms of asphodel in the Elysian fields.[18]

The German painter Adam Elsheimer treats the myth in his painting of the early seventeenth century called *The Mocking of Ceres*—a work for which Bonnefoy feels a particular affection.[19] It is, he has said, one of a small number of works which touch him particularly because of the effort it makes to render explicit an intuition as yet uncertain and laboring (*NR*, 97). In his essay on Elsheimer, first published in *L'Éphémère* in 1968, just three years after *Pierre écrite*, Bonnefoy devotes to the work one of his most sustained analyses. The essay, which introduces many of the ideas to be developed more fully in the book *Rome 1630*, published in 1970, provides an excellent example of Bonnefoy's manner of approaching the visual arts and gives some insights into the poetic texts, particularly into texts from *Pierre écrite*.

Elsheimer focuses on the moment of the myth when Demeter (or Ceres), weary from roaming the world in search of the absent daughter, stops at a cottage and knocks on the door. An old woman offers her "a drink sweetened with barley kernels." As she drinks, she is mocked by "a hard-faced youngster, / A loutish country boy." In anger, Ceres throws the drink at him, and immediately he is spotted, his arms become legs, he grows a tail, and he shrinks into a lizard, disappearing through a chink in the rocks. His name, Ovid says, suits his performance—for it is Stellio, that is, the spot-marked. The subject seems to have fascinated Elsheimer since he made a number of drawings and etchings on the theme. Although the myth of the daughter lost to Hades to be returned to earth after months of dormancy may be seen to translate the agricultural cycles, Bonnefoy prefers to see in it "the realization of the precariousness of the sacred" (*NR*, 98)—the god of the Dead being both rich and avaricious, symbol of the spirit "under whose influence all presence is degraded into a richness one hoards, and every symbol as a consequence dies out, every approach to the One vanishes" (*NR*, 99). Thus, Ceres represents, for Bonnefoy, being stifled by the spirit of possession and conceptual order; Persephone symbolizes what could be presence, participation in meaning, but has become estranged from itself and lost.

Ceres therefore must arm herself with torches: she is in a foreign land. It is at this moment of deprivation and wandering that she will knock at a

Adam Elsheimer, *The Mocking of Ceres*. Courtesy of the Museo del Prado, Madrid. Reprinted, with permission, from Keith Andrews, *Adam Elsheimer: Paintings, Drawings* (Oxford, Phaidon Press; New York: Rizzoli International Publications; 1977).

threshold and ask for help. And as the door opens and refreshment is passed, the sacramental life of sacred order which might reintegrate the divided world and restore Persephone seems suddenly possible; and thus Ceres drinks, as Ovid says, with "avidity." And as for the boy who mocks the goddess at this critical moment, he may be thought, in Bonnefoy's view, to mock that desire which is always susceptible to possessiveness, to the influence of the god of the Dead. As such, he represents the earth itself in a reaction of self-defense against the potentially threatening and destructive intrusion of unbounded longing. Yet the mocking of this natural desire is an indifference, and thus the transformation of the boy into lizard (or into the salamander Bonnefoy prefers to see), and which the poet imagines already in progress in the figure, especially about the head—this transformation signifies, in the context of an endangered sacred order, the emergence of the cold opacity of the object, multiplicity abandoned by the One—"the icy gleaming of the surface of being, of meaning" (*NR*, 101). In Bonnefoy's view, Elsheimer seems, therefore, to be saying, "'This is where we are. This exteriority could become our destiny'" (*NR*, 101). But Elsheimer will not resign himself to this *surface déserte* (*NR*, 101), and if he refuses the Renaissance art of numbers and Ideas, so closely related to the protection of conceptual orders, he also refuses the notion of a *fantastique tragique* (*NR*, 101)—the "surreal" obsession with groundless and absurd phenomena—and, as sign of these refusals, Bonnefoy will focus on the foliage lit up in the lefthand part of the picture in which, in Bonnefoy's analysis, the absent Persephone reasserts herself as presence and meaning: "When the mind is in confusion, the earth can reemerge" (*NR*, 101). And this earth of simple realities becomes both an absolute and an infinite; in this sense, the foliage may be seen as the persistence of being in spite of the precariousness of that vision which gives it meaning and coherence. And absence—the painfulness of disappearance—may thus be affirmed, since it calls forth desire which finds satisfaction in the simple evidence of earth.

For Bonnefoy, Elsheimer is at the beginning of a movement which will extend to Poussin and Rembrandt, namely the refusal of "a complacent system of signs" (*NR*, 96)—those *belles images* in which "being withdraws from the figures proposed for it" (*NR*, 96), the music of appearances which denies the contradictions of being. Bonnefoy senses at work in Elsheimer the "obscure, but tenacious premonition of what could be an earth" (*NR*, 97), an interest, unfounded by God and haunted by vertigo, for *le silence du simple* (*NR*, 103), for that bit of foliage lit up against the gathering night. In a word, the poet senses something like his own feeling of estrangement and searching reflected in the painter's work—the quest for "an earth . . . that teaches finitude, but while keeping it substantial and not tragic" (*NR*, 101).

Already in *Douve*, the image of the wandering and searching goddess is present. How can one not think of the Ceres figure while reading the first poem of the concluding section of the book "Vrai Lieu" ("True Place")?

> *Qu'une place soit faite à celui qui approche,*
> *Personnage ayant froid et privé de maison.*
>
> *Personnage tenté par le bruit d'une lampe,*
> *Par le seuil éclairé d'une seule maison.*
>
> *Et s'il reste recru d'angoisse et de fatigue,*
> *Qu'on redise pour lui les mots de guérison.*
>
> *Que faut-il à ce cœur qui n'était que silence,*
> *Sinon des mots qui soient le signe et l'oraison,*
>
> *Et comme un peu de feu soudain la nuit,*
> *Et la table entrevue d'une pauvre maison?*   (*P*, 85)

Let a place be made for the one who is approaching,
The one who is cold and homeless.

The one who is lured by the sound of a lamp,
By the bright doorway of a lonely house.

And if he remains worn out by anguish and toil,
Let the healing words be said to him once more.

What could it need, this heart lost in silence,
If not the words that are both sign and prayer,

And like a bit of fire suddenly at night,
And the glimpse of a table in a poor man's house?

Douve insists in a number of places on the importance of death and dormancy, absence and silence, in the process of new birth, in the emergence of authentic poetic speech.

> *La lumière profonde a besoin pour paraître*
> *D'une terre rouée et craquante de nuit.*
> *C'est d'un bois ténébreux que la flamme s'exalte.*
> . . . .
> *Il te faudra franchir la mort pour que tu vives.*   (*P*, 52)

If it is to appear, the deep light needs
An earth broken and cracked with night.
It is a somber wood that gives life to the flame.
. . . .
You will have to pass through death in order to live.

The horrible night of *Hier régnant désert* ("Always the same night that refuses to end" [*P*, 98]) calls the new dawn into being. Death to *la langue* leads to resurrection in *la parole*. Even the "sin" of excarnation, the lure of preferring words and forms to real experience can become the *felix culpa* of a vision cleansed and defined, of resolution strengthened through trial.

Bonnefoy places his poem on the myth of Kore in the last section of the book, "Le Dialogue d'angoisse et de désir" ("The Dialogue between Anguish and Desire"). The very title of the section is another indication of that effort to reconcile opposing forces which, as I have said, is a distinguishing feature of Bonnefoy's poetic determination and places his work in the same context as that of those Baroque artists who labor, in Bonnefoy's view, for "the synthesis between nostalgia and hope, between what is senseless and what is capable of founding" (*NR*, 105). This "ambiguity between grace and suffering" (*NR*, 95) is precisely what Bonnefoy celebrates in Elsheimer. Bonnefoy's reading of the myth of Kore is related to the epigraph from Shakespeare's *The Winter's Tale* chosen for the book: "Thou mettest with things dying; I with things new born." The sense of the myth informs the entire structure of *Pierre écrite*. The book is a more luminous and smilingly affirmative acceptance of the essential contradictions of our mortal state than was the case in the more tormented and anguished earlier volumes. The poem on the myth of Kore is a recognition of the ephemeral and the unrevealed. To participate in passing beauty, to cut the flower, is to accept mortality, and with it, opacity. The field on which Kore falls is filled with both light and shadow. Acceptance of this condition dispels what it might otherwise allow for of "sinfulness" and sorrow, possessiveness and flight. Former struggling yields here to a mature consent, confirmed by a later poem of the same section.

> —*Je ne sais pas, je ne suis plus, le temps s'achève*
> *Comme la crue d'un rêve aux dieux irrévélés.* (*P*, 226)

> —I know not, I am no longer, time comes to an end
> Like the rising of a dream whose gods are unrevealed.

The imagination and the mechanisms of self-reflexiveness are subsumed in this powerful affirmation, as the sun on the river fills the mirror of another poem with smiling, silver light:

> . . . . *Imaginer*
> *S'est déchiré dans le miroir, tournant vers nous*
> *Sa face souriante d'argent clair.* (*P*, 223)

> . . . . Imagining
> Has burst apart in the mirror, turning toward us
> A smiling face of bright silver.

An unmoving star comes to drink at great closed roads; it brings its message—*d'aimer, de prendre et de mourir* ("to love, to take, and to die") (*P*, 209). In this atmosphere of reconciliation, "la mort / Encercle le bonheur de la flame qui bouge" ("death / Encircles the happiness of the moving flame") (*P*, 204).

To say, therefore, that *Hier régnant désert* is Bonnefoy's "darkest" book and that *Pierre écrite* is a work full of color and light is misleading: the former struggles for its clear places and the latter does not forget the darkness or the swarming dead. Each work struggles for a kind of equilibrium, and the sustained use of such categories as "night" and "dawn," for instance, never settles into system. Bonnefoy does not evoke these realities in any single way: the horror of dawn for the beleaguered lovers in *Douve* is converted to the hope of new beginnings in *Hier*; the dark night of *Hier*, as I have said, becomes in *Pierre écrite* a *Liebesnacht*.[20] This preoccupation with polarities is everywhere accompanied by the desire for reconciliation, by the affirmation of contradiction. "I recognize and celebrate," Bonnefoy would write in an essay published in 1961,[21] "that unswerving attention to the contradictions of what is—whether life or the order of numbers, accident or law, shadows or reassuring light in the distance—which is the vocation of the highest consciousness and the principle of the greatest art."

*   *   *

If *Hier régnant désert* focused particularly on the emergence of dawn, *Pierre écrite* finds a characteristic setting for the marriage of opposites in the crepuscular atmosphere of evening: the great sun—of the intelligible, of Western man's need for logical structure, permanence, order—in decline to offer, martyrlike, its last light to the simple earth, to the "mortal ground." Closer, as if merging with it, the light gives itself to earth, as earth is lit up by gentle fire.

> *Imagine qu'un soir*
> *La lumière s'attarde sur la terre,*
> *Ouvrant ses mains d'orage et donatrices, dont*
> *La paume est notre lieu et d'angoisse et d'espoir.*
> *Imagine que la lumière soit victime*
> *Pour le salut d'un lieu mortel et sous un dieu*
> *Certes distant et noir. . . .*   (*P*, 223)

Imagine that some evening
The light lingered on the earth,
Opening its stormy and giving hands, whose
Palm is our ground both for anguish and for hope.
Imagine that the light gave itself up
For the salvation of a mortal place and under a god
Certainly distant and dark. . . .

The play of light on the finite beings of earth creates the conspicuous "shadows" of *Pierre écrite*. These are those "cast shadows" which, "in the law of geometry and the unity it assures, bear witness to a resistant opacity" (*I*, 194). They invade the garden of the opening poems with a reminder of mortality.

> Les étoiles voûtaient les murs du haut jardin
> Comme les fruits de l'arbre au-delà, mais les pierres
> Du lieu mortel portaient dans l'écume de l'arbre
> Comme une ombre d'étrave et comme un souvenir.
>
> Étoiles et vous, craies d'un pur chemin,
> Vous pâlissiez, vous nous preniez le vrai jardin,
> Tous les chemins du ciel étoilé faisant ombre
> Sur ce chant naufragé; sur notre route obscure. (*P*, 173)

The stars arched over the walls of the lofty garden
Like the fruit in the tree beyond, but the stones
Of the mortal ground carried into the surf of the tree
Something like a bowsprit shadow, and a memory.

Stars and you, chalky stones on a pure path,
You grew pale, you took from us the true garden,
All the paths in the star bright heavens casting shadow
On this shipwrecked song; on our darkened way.

Born from the chance meeting of light and volume, the shadow "maintains the sense of irreducible chance in the structures built by number."

> And one sees that the shadow brings to life there, along with chance, the sense of time, the being of this furtive moment. . . . What the cast shadow designates, profoundly, like the hands of a clock, is *such and such a place at such and such a moment* . . . the reality of encounter, which has no name in the world of the Idea. In a word, finitude. The mystery of the presence of a being and our melancholy at seeing it excluded from the coherence of numbers. (*I*, 194–95)

It is for this reason that a "voice" will speak of "une ombre aimant une ombre" ("a shadow loving a shadow") (*P*, 209), and that another poem will evoke the mystery of presence in the following terms:

> Cendre qui te détaches de la flamme
> Dans la lumière du soir,
> O présence,
> Sous ta voûte furtive accueille-nous
> Pour une fête obscure. (*P*, 210)

Ember, you who fall from the flame
In the light of evening,
O presence,

Under your furtive arches welcome us
For a dark celebration.

As I have already indicated, "presence" for Bonnefoy is inseparable from
the backdrop of absence, and the moment of epiphany in his work is often
recognition of imperiled being, an encounter with the reality of finitude
which exceeds intellection and conceptual category. The momentary and
serene participation in unity can be shattered by an awakening into this
awareness of mortality: "Mais l'Un se déchirant contre la jambe obscure, /
Tu te perds, où la bouche a bu à l'âcre mort" ("But the One tearing apart
against the dark leg, / You are lost, there where the mouth has drunk
of bitter death") (*P*, 205). This obscurity is "l'obscurité propre de /
l'homme" ("the darkness fitting to / Man") (*P*, 181). Nevertheless, Bon-
nefoy is striving in *Pierre écrite*, through love of mortal and shadowy pres-
ences, for an intuition of invisible and luminous unity.

The last poem of the section "Pierre écrite" in a way prepares us for the
serene beauties of "Un Feu va devant nous." Already "Sur un Eros de
bronze" had spoken of new coloring in the horizon and of the passage of
the heart toward unknown foliage (*P*, 196). In the last poem of the sec-
tion, a voice rises to say:

> *Nous vieillissions, lui le feuillage et moi la source,*
> *Lui le peu de soleil et moi la profondeur,*
> *Et lui la mort et moi la sagesse de vivre.*
>
> *J'acceptais que le temps nous présentât dans l'ombre*
> *Son visage de faune au rire non moqueur,*
> *J'aimais que se lêvat le vent qui porte l'ombre*
>
> *Et que mourir ne fût en obscure fontaine*
> *Que troubler l'eau sans fond que le lierre buvait.*
> *J'aimais, j'étais debout dans le songe éternel.*   (*P*, 197)

> We were growing old together, he the foliage and I the hidden
>   water,
> He the bit of sun and I the depths below,
> And he a part of death and I the wisdom for living.
>
> I was glad that time would show us in the shadows
> Its faunlike face and that we would hear its gentle laughter,
> I loved to feel the wind rise up and carry off the shadow
>
> And that dying be no more than the stirring
> Of bottomless water in a dark fountain at which the ivy drank.
> I was in love, I was standing upright in the endless dreaming.

The opening emphasis on aging contributes to the sense of an ongoing
and maturing relationship in which recognition of death and limitation is
diffused through a tempered acceptance of life, as the wind gently stirs the

dark water of a fountain. Time here has the face of a laughing faun, and laughter and humor may be taken in Kierkegaard's sense as marking the passage from the ethical to the religious stage.[22] The recurrent *J'acceptais*, *J'aimais* place the poem in the context of an affirmation coming from the deep sources of life. The precarity of particular lives is not forgotten: the voice describes a relationship, speaks of a *nous*. The key to the profound sense of contentment and serenity in this piece is doubtless the stress on love: "J'aimais, j'étais debout dans le songe éternel" ("I was in love, I was standing upright in the endless dreaming"). This upright position, fortified by love and adherence, is in sharp contrast to the typical posture of the earlier Douve, *jetée la tête en bas* ("thrown head downward"), and recalls the pilgrim Dante who emerges, *dritto*, from his passage through the underworld. The "endless dreaming" seems to align itself with other verses in the collection which speak of *l'être sans retour* ("endless being") (*P*, 178), or evoke "l'effraie . . . / Tournant vers nous ses yeux de terre sans retour" ("the owl . . . / Turning toward us its eyes filled with endless earth") (*P*, 209). The *immense matière indicible* ("vast unutterable matter") of *Douve* has become *l'heureuse matière sans retour* ("joyful matter without end") (*P*, 220).

*   *   *

It is in part because of that passage through opacity, darkness, and death which is the section "Pierre écrite" that the section immediately following it, "Un Feu va devant nous," strikes us as so extraordinarily luminous and beautiful. It appears, in some ways, as the succession of moments or poems for which Bonnefoy's life and art have been struggling: a series of intense, deeply felt experiences, evoked in specific time and place, but seen in the context of eternity and the universality of being—the "fragments of duration consumed by the eternal" of which he had written earlier. (The poet was doubtless trying to suggest the presence of the eternal and the universal burning at the heart of this deeply lived experience of oneness and simplicity in earlier lines from the book—lines in which he speaks, for instance, of "the foliage burning *beneath* the foliage" (*P*, 163; italics mine) or of "the beating of hidden light" (*P*, 163) or of "the day lower than day" (*P*, 179).) And although these moments cannot be "possessed," the poet seems to have developed an increasing confidence that they will be recovered after (and perhaps because of) loss. The thirst for the "true place" is calmed by these scenes of daily familiarity: the cries of birds, the presence of trees, the color of a dress, the sound of bees.

The section begins with an evocation of the marriage place in the poem entitled "La Chambre." "Un Feu va devant nous" will proliferate images of merging and marrying to suggest the dissolution of barriers in the apprehension of oneness. The first lines of "La Chambre," for instance, speak of the relation between the light from a stream and the reflected light of a mirror:

> Le miroir et le fleuve en crue, ce matin,
> S'appelaient à travers la chambre, deux lumières
> Se trouvent et s'unissent dans l'obscur
> Des meubles de la chambre descellée. (P, 199)

> The mirror and the surging river, this morning,
> Called to one another across the room, two lights
> Meeting and marrying amid the dark
> Furnishings of the unsealed room.

The lines are suggestive of the interconnection between being and individual consciousness, between the "source" and its reflection.[23] Repeatedly, Bonnefoy sees this movement as inspired by Eros. Here, the two lights "call" to one another. They meet in a context of "obscurity," it is true, but the adjective "descellée" ("unsealed") implies that the vision of the room has been freed from the cover of assumption, that the seal of that "everyday thinking" of which Heidegger speaks has been broken, and that the room is making its appeal to consciousness as a presence. The poem continues in this way:

> Et nous étions deux pays de sommeil
> Communiquant par leurs marches de pierre
> Où se perdait l'eau non trouble d'un rêve
> Toujours se reformant, toujours brisé.

> La main pure dormait près de la main soucieuse.
> Un corps un peu parfois dans son rêve bougeait.
> Et loin, sur l'eau plus noire d'une table,
> La robe rouge éclairante dormait.

> And we were two lands of sleep
> Meeting along their steps of stone
> Where the untroubled water would vanish, a dream
> Always forming again, always broken.

> The pure hand slept next to the careworn hand.
> Sometimes a body would stir slightly in its dreaming.
> And far off, on the blacker water of a table,
> The gleaming red dress was sleeping.

The lovers' communion in a drowsy atmosphere of half-sleep points to a more general blending of dream and wakefulness. Often the focus in the previous books was on a painful vigilance, the extreme limit of which is the poet's assertion in the first poem of *Hier régnant désert*: "je ne dors pas" ("I

131

do not sleep"). *Pierre écrite* allows for sleep, for peace, even for sur-render—and for dream simplified and accepted. The proximity of a pure and of a careworn hand is suggestive, as I have said, of that reconciliation between "anguish and desire" which is a principal concern of the book as a whole. The red dress, associated with the feminine other of his book—that red dress which, as another poem says, "brightens and scatters / Far off, in the sky, ancient sorrow's train" (*P*, 201)—is evoked beautifully as a pres-ence as well, the word *éclairante* ("gleaming" or "full of light") serving to mark, as the stone of *Douve* had done before, the call to consciousness from mortal presence—an appeal which awakens and instructs awareness. Alone on the darkness of the table, the dress is one of many examples of what is isolated by consciousness for the special blend of concentration and care signaled by the recurrent use of the verb *voûter* ("to arch or bend over").[24]

The verb designates a characteristic posture in *Pierre écrite* with its em-phasis on bending, protectingly, over what is one's to care for, like the shepherd in "Le livre, pour vieillir" ("The Book for Growing Old")—

> *Voûté sur le bonheur terrestre.* (*P*, 217)

Bent over the happiness of earth.

The verb sometimes serves to focus an erotic moment,

> *Ton corps voûte pour nous son heure respirante* (*P*, 200)

May your body arch for us its breathing hour

or to evoke the body's response to a loving caress,

> *Et tout ton sang voûté sous une main rêveuse.* (*P*, 202)

And all your blood arched under a dreaming hand.

But it also is used to signify the way in which, suddenly, "an entire god" (*P*, 213) can emerge from a tree, for instance. That is, the verb may desig-nate the manner in which consciousness envelops or is enveloped by presence:

> *O présence,*
> *Sous ta voûte furtive accueille-nous*
> *Pour une fête obscure.* (*P*, 210)

O presence,
Beneath your furtive arches welcome us
For a dark celebration.

The verb also is used to signify the elaboration of a poetic vocabulary: "Toute l'âme se voûte autour d'un dire simple" ("the entire soul arches over a few simple words") (*P*, 220). I shall return to this last consideration in greater detail in a moment.

The book develops two interrelated notions concerning love: one is the idea of *l'impartageable amour* ("the love that cannot be divided"), the other of an *âme partagée* ("shared soul"). The first involves the refusal of dispersion and the *concentration* on both specific, chosen components of the real and the language which places them in a sacred context. The second implies the *opening*, through love shared, to the greater continuity of being, to the "soul" which all being shares.[25]

In one of the last poems of *Pierre écrite*, a voice will address the feminine presence as

> *O moins à contre-jour, ô mieux aimée,*
> *Qui ne m'es plus etrangère.*   (*P*, 222)

> O better seen now, better loved,
> No longer stranger to me.

L'Âme partagée as union with another person who has lost the dark side of otherness seems to facilitate access to the unity of a vast network of being. This experience, which doubtless is lived before it is described, has been expressed very powerfully and movingly by Marcel Raymond in the tribute he wrote to his wife called *Mémorial*:

> There is a very lofty form of simplicity, at once the beginning and end of things. This simplicity has another name, it is unity. What is unalloyed, what is pure or whole, the *alpha* before the fall into diversity, and the *omega* which is the fruit of re-creation in identity. And it is when he strives to rejoin unity that man escapes for a moment from his ceaseless drifting and rediscovers his reason for being. And he rediscovers it nowhere better than in love.[26]

Thus in the beautiful celebration of Eros which is the poem "Le Myrte," the beloved is compared both to earth and to burning myrtle.

> *Parfois je te savais la terre, je buvais*
> *Sur tes lèvres l'angoisse des fontaines*
> *Quand elle sourd des pierres chaudes, et l'été*
> *Dominait haut la pierre heureuse et le buveur.*

> *Parfois je te disais de myrte et nous brûlions*
> *L'arbre de tous tes gestes tout un jour.*
> *C'étaient de grands feux brefs de lumière vestale,*
> *Ainsi je t'inventais parmi tes cheveux clairs.*

> *Tout un grand été nul avait séché nos rêves,*
> *Rouillé nos voix, accru nos corps, défait nos fers.*

Parfois le lit tournait comme une barque libre
Qui gagne lentement le plus haut de la mer.   (*P*, 203)

Sometimes I knew you as earth, and I would drink
From your lips the anguish of the fountains
When it wells up from the warm stones, and summer
Would loom high above the happy stone and the drinker.

Sometimes I would say you were myrtle and we would spend
A whole day burning the tree of all your gestures.
These were great brief fires of vestal light,
Thus I would invent you amid your bright hair.

A whole vast empty summer had dried out our dreams,
Rusted our voices, strengthened our bodies, loosened our
    chains.
Sometimes the bed would shift like a ship set free
And which slowly moves out to high sea.

The poem is organized around the notion of an intermittent experience of presence, signaled by the repetition of the word *parfois* ("sometimes"). The "you" doubtless designates the presence of a coherence or innocence in the simple realities of daily existence which the poet encounters as a "beloved" unity experienced on different levels, this difference in part suggested by the elemental realities of earth, water, and fire which are evoked in succession. The last stanza ("sometimes the bed would shift like a ship set free") establishes the erotic foundation for the other, but similar, experiences of drinking at a fountain or building and watching a fire. On the other hand, the drinking and the fire building remain nicely ambiguous and could as clearly suggest the sexual experience itself. This ambiguity, this richness of presence is part of the poet's capacity for "invention" and discovery—the ability to see hair in fire or fire in hair, for instance, or to feel lips in the earth's water or water in lips. (The connection between the sexual act and the drinking of water is pursued in *Dans le leurre du seuil*, as I hope to show in the next chapter, especially in the section "Deux Couleurs" and "Deux Barques." See, for instances, *Poèmes*, pp. 257 and 262.)

In the same way, the caress of a hand is associated with other daily mysteries in the piece called "Les Chemins" ("Pathways"):

Chemins, parmi
La matière des arbres. Dieux, parmi
Les touffes de ce chant inlassable d'oiseaux.
Et tout ton sang voûté sous une main rêveuse,
O proche, ô tout mon jour.   (*P*, 202)

Pathways, amid
The substance of the trees. Gods, amid
The clusters of this tireless singing of birds.

And all your blood arched under a dreaming hand,
O near, O all my day.

Here the beloved, who has come closer, is the pathway to the beauties of the day. And it is love which seems to have helped the poet to experience the full richness of his days, which gives these days the "wholeness" suggested by *tout mon jour*.[27]

The oneness of being is suggested poetically in the section "Un Feu va devant nous" in part through the elaboration of concomitant sensations, or by what one might justifiably call "synaesthetic" perception.

> *Le jour puise là-bas dans la couleur l'eau fraîche,*
> *Ruisselante, du soir.* (P, 205)

Day draws up from color the fresh,
Streaming water of evening.

Or,

> *Et le feu parle auprès de nous dans l'éternité de la sauge.* (P, 206)

And the fire speaks near us in the eternity of the sage.

The dreamy sensuality described in "Le Sang, la note Si" takes on the specific resonance of the musical note B.

> *Le nageur est aveugle.*
> *Il descend par étages pourpres dans le battement de ton*
> *cœur.* (P, 204)

The swimmer is blind.
He sinks through purple levels in the beating of your
heart.

A line from "L'Abeille, la couleur" ("The Bee, the Color") will put sleep on the window panes ("Le sommeil est léger, en taches sur les vitres"— "sleep is light, dappled on the window panes" [P, 205]), evoking both the experience of a broken sleep on the "window" of consciousness and also perhaps the motley colors of evening. (The hour is precisely indicated: "five o'clock.") In the twilight atmosphere of evening, the birds speak indefinitely to one another, and "bite one another, light" (P, 207). The unmoving star of evening comes to "drink" at great, closed roads (P, 209). The poet locates gods in the clusters or clumps of the bird songs.

For the lovers, sleep is near "in the world's sap" ("dans la sève du monde") (P, 201). Magic moments are in the twilight, in that *lumière du soir* which is the proper ambiance for mature recognitions and peaceful blending—the moments when "time lies around us like pools of color" (P, 207). In this atmosphere, the poet tries to merge "clarté de proche nuit et clarté de parole" ("the light of coming night and the light of words")

(*P*, 215), and for Bonnefoy, the light of evening, "in its sudden depth, but hindered future" (*I*, 268), defines, in its way, the particular richness and limitation of French poetry itself—and, by extension, the gentle radiance of *Pierre écrite*.

*   *   *

Most readers will notice the predominant use of the definite article in "Un Feu va devant nous": "*L'*Arbre," "*La* Chambre," "*Le* Myrte," "*L'*Abeille," "*La* Note Si," "*L'*Épaule," and so on. Now Bonnefoy has developed in his essay "La Poésie française et le principe d'identité" a notion of perception which involves a distinction between the definite and the indefinite article. He considers a salamander[28] he has seen on the wall.

> I can analyze what my perception brings me, and thus, benefiting from the experience of others, mentally separate this tiny life from the other data of the world and classify it, as the language of prose would, telling myself: "*A* salamander," then continue my walk, absent-minded as ever, remaining as if on the surface of the encounter. (*I*, 246–47)

Salamander as "a" salamander—that is, as an object structured by reason—can take on the sinister allure of a *mauvaise présence*, but may be saved by another approach to perception.

> By an act which is always sudden and unexpected, this reality that was falling into separate, external parts, *comes together again*, and this time in a superabundance in which I am taken up and saved. It is as if I had accepted, *lived*, that salamander, and henceforth, far from having to be explained by other aspects of reality, it is the salamander, present now as the gently beating heart of the earth, which becomes the origin of all that is. Let us say—although this experience can barely be put into words—that the salamander has revealed itself, becoming or rebecoming *the* salamander—just as one says *the* fairy—in a pure act of existing in which its "essence" is seized and understood. (*I*, 247–48)

But this "essence" of the salamander is the essence of all that is.

> Let us say—for the word too must be saved, and from the fatal urge to define everything—that its essence has spread into the essence of other beings, like the flow of an analogy by which I perceive everything in the continuity and sufficiency of a *place*, and in the transparency of *unity*. The wall is justified, and the hearth, and the olive tree outside and the earth. And I, having become all this once again, conscious all at once of my deep savor—for this space

arches in me as the interior of my own existence—I have passed from a wretched perception to love, which is foreknowledge of the invisible. (*I*, 248)

Thus apprehension of distinct realities yields to an intuition of the invisible continuity and oneness of being. And so, too, the realities of "Un Feu va devant nous"—tree, shoulder, bee, myrtle, bedroom—become, through love, approaches to this unity. It is important to stress, in this connection, Bonnefoy's insistence on the *heart*. ("What I have tried to show, in short, is that in unity, or in any case under its sign, there is no longer *a* salamander in contrast to this hearth or to one or a hundred swallows, but *the* salamander, present at the heart of other presences" [*I*, 249].) The salamander which might have become separated from other realities by a prosaic perception is present "as the gently beating *heart* of the earth" (italics mine). And the experience of "the deep savor" of being presents itself to the perceiving agent as a characteristic "vaulted or arched space." In fact, as I hope to show in a moment, the heart is isolated for special concentration throughout *Pierre écrite*.

A deep experience of particular realities becomes the groundwork, then, for participation in unity, for each particular carries a kind of divine power, is the "angel" of which Bonnefoy speaks in his essay "La Poésie française et le principe d'identité." "The angel that chased out the demons, the one and only angel, for the One is the great revelation of this limitless moment during which everything is given to me so that I might understand and bring together" (*I*, 248).

This apprehension or intuition of essential unity, however, is never the permanent possession of man. Many of the poems of *Pierre écrite* remind us of the obscurity and limitation which are man's fate. Oneness "tears itself apart"; vision loses itself, "where the mouth has drunk of bitter death" (*P*, 205). Words, too, are "barriers across the evening roads" (*P*, 213). In Plotinus's thought, the One "can be neither said nor written." It is the "indefinable," the "untellable."

> And this name, The One, contains really no more than the negation of plurality. . . . If we are led to think positively of The One, name and thing, there would be more truth in silence: the designation, a mere aid to inquiry, was never intended for more than a preliminary affirmation of absolute simplicity to be followed by the rejection of even that statement: it was the best that offered, but remains inadequate to express the nature indicated. For this is a principle not to be conveyed by any sound; it cannot be known on any hearing but, if at all, by vision.[29]

Nevertheless, "the Soul sees and in its emotion tries to represent what it sees and breaks into speech 'Existent; Existence; Essence; Hestia or

Hearth,' sounds which labour to express the essential nature of the universe produced by the travail of the utterer and so to represent, as far as sounds may, the origin of reality" (ibid., 407–8).

For Bonnefoy, too, language divides in order to signify, and even "the most serious speech, being at every moment engaged in what analyzes and dissociates, can only share in this alienation, and thus must burden itself, indefinitely perhaps, with preliminary tasks in order to avoid drying up" (*I*, 251). But there is radical dissociation when words become concepts or categories or when the poet allows himself to be lured by the merely exterior vision, by "artistic" forms. Desire, feeling, even humor struggle against conceptualization. "Le Verbe" strives for the unity which being possesses in spite of diversification. The *logos* tries to bring "into being" what it names. And poetic language thus creates or re-creates a sacred order in the destiny of the poet speaking; it proposes "no longer to reabsorb what is in a formula, but, on the contrary, to reabsorb the formula in my participation in the real" (*I*, 250). And therefore, in *Pierre écrite*, Bonnefoy will write of [*l*]*es mots fondateurs* ("the founding words") in which the poet finds his "only true warmth" (*P*, 215). These are those "loving" words which save the sense of mystery in "what is only simple" (*P*, 211). They are not new; they are elementary words, invested with vision:

> *Un éblouissement dans les mots anciens.*
> *L'étagement*
> *De toute notre vie au loin comme une mer*
> *Heureuse, élucidée par une arme d'eau vive.*   (*P*, 221)

A resplendence in the ancient words.
Our entire life
Laid far out like a joyful sea
Lit up by a band of moving water.

Being and *logos* are thus intimately interconnected. One poem will ask,

> *Le jour au fond du jour sauvera-t-il*
> *Le peu de mots que nous fûmes ensemble?*
> *Pour moi, j'ai tant aimé ces jours confiants, je veille*
> *Sur quelques mots éteints dans l'âtre de nos cœurs.*   (*P*, 212)

Will the day at the depths of the day save
The small number of words we were together?
As for me, I loved these trusting days so much, I keep watch
Over a few words gone out in the hearth of our hearts.

Poetry is thus the effort to "interiorize the real"; the poem "seeks the ties that unite things *in me*" (*I*, 250). "In the form of poetry which I hold to be the only true one, the words with depth—and they vary of course with each of us—carry the promise of being; they preserve the idea of a *logos* through which an order will be made clear which will "authenticate"—as Mallarmé would say—our life" (*I*, 252). The most intense language will evoke this order without reaching it in itself, "and this because true experience, only seeking the absolute by the threshold of finitude, is, in any case, only our necessarily relative consciousness lived to the depths as such" (*I*, 252). It is only "here where we live" that the poet will speak of having "learned the universal language" (*P*, 224). And "what poetic consciousness has hoped for in words—at least in some words—is that unity, that the divine shine in them" (*I*, 253). Thus, "the true subject of the poem is an existence that takes on new form—a finitude that grows limitless" (*I*, 266).

Many poems of *Pierre écrite* deal poetically with the problematics I have been discussing. "Le Livre, pour vieillir" ("The Book, for Growing Old") is a case in point.

> *Étoiles transhumantes; et le berger*
> *Voûté sur le bonheur terrestre; et tant de paix*
> *Comme ce cri d'insecte, irrégulier,*
> *Qu'un dieu pauvre façonne. Le silence*
> *Est monté de ton livre vers ton cœur.*
> *Un vent bouge sans bruit dans les bruits du monde.*
> *Le temps sourit au loin de cesser d'être.*
> *Simples dans le verger sont les fruits mûrs.*
>
> *Tu vieilliras*
> *Et, te décolorant dans la couleur des arbres,*
> *Faisant ombre plus lente sur le mur,*
> *Étant, et d'âme enfin, la terre menacée,*
> *Tu reprendras le livre à la page laissée,*
> *Tu diras, C'étaient donc les derniers mots obscurs.*　　　　(*P*, 217)

> Stars moving from pasture to pasture; and the shepherd
> Bent over the happiness of earth; and so much peace
> Like this uneven insect cry,
> Fashioned by an impoverished god. The silence
> Has risen from your book toward your heart.
> A wind stirs soundlessly amid the sounds of the world.
> Time smiles from afar at ceasing to be.
> Simple in the orchard are the fruits that have ripened.
>
> You will grow old
> And, losing your color in the color of the trees,
> Casting a slower shadow on the wall,
> Being, and with soul at last, the menaced earth,
> You will take up your book at the place you left it,
> And you will say, So these were the last unclear words.

The poem sets in opposition the peaceful silence of evening and the language of men, symbolized by the book. The uneven cry of an insect seems to give more apt expression to the sense of tranquil unity than any intellectual fabrication would be able to achieve. The silence rises in the midst of peaceful noises and makes its appeal not to the intellect, but to the *heart*. Time has ceased: the poet experiences that *saveur d'éternel* he felt represented by the breaks in the walls at the fortress at Amber. The emphasis on simplicity and silence are reminiscent of Plotinus's discussion of the relation between human thought and speech and the nature of the One. The simple fruits of the orchard are those that have matured like the poetic vision which has learned to accept and love "the mysterious meaning in what is only simple." Growing older, the poet imagines merging with earth— that earth which is "menaced" by the desertion of excarnations, but which may be infused with the consciousness that adheres to it and saved by the soul which binds its destiny to that of evidence. And this "alliance" or "marriage" of poetic vision and the silent simplicity of earth is what allows the poet to return to his book understanding better "its last unclear words." There are at least two ways to regard the last two lines. On the one hand, the lines seem to suggest that it is the language of man which is obscure by comparison to the ineffable simplicity of nature. One may also see in them, however, the suggestion that it is the passage from a wordless experience of unity to the book which struggles to give utterance to vision which allows the words of the book to become less obscure, that it is in this constant *va-et-vient* that the poet develops his perception and discovers "the few words"—"the deep words."[30]

In somewhat the same vein, the piece entitled "On a Pietà of Tintoretto" seems to argue that the intuitions and sufferings of the *heart* call out for and require the shaping of the *hands*.

> *Jamais douleur*
> *Ne fut plus élégante dans ces grilles*
> *Noires, que dévora le soleil. Et jamais*
> *Élégance ne fut cause plus spirituelle,*
> *Un feu double, debout sur les grilles du soir.*
>
> *Ici,*
> *Un grand espoir fut peintre. Oh, qui est plus réel*
> *Du chagrin désirant ou de l'image peinte?*
> *Le désir déchira le voile de l'image,*
> *L'image donna vie à l'exsangue désir.* (P, 225)

Never was sorrow
More elegant behind this black
Grating, consumed by the sun. And never
Did elegance have more spiritual grounds,
A double fire, upright on the gates of evening.

Here,
A great hope was painter. Oh, which is the more real
Longing sorrow or painted image?
Longing tore the veil of the image,
The image gave life to bloodless desire.

The first lines speak of the transformation of suffering into elegance through art. Tintoretto has placed metal grillwork around his subject, which grillwork the poet sees as ravaged by the sun. Perhaps Bonnefoy sees a reminder here of the implacable effacing and reducing of representation through the power of those same natural forces that had diminished the "Veneranda" fresco of *Hier*. He makes the abstract and anonymous quality "hope" the painter. But emotions such as sorrow are seen to "desire" expression in the shaping form of the image through the "veil" of which they nonetheless pierce.

It is perhaps not surprising, then, that *Pierre écrite* should reserve special attention, in its concern with the body, for the heart and the hands. As in *Douve*, there is reference here to a great diversity of bodily members—*flanc, jambe, sein, bouche, lèvres, taille, yeux, bras, cheveux, sang, veines, nerfs, visage, face, cœur, épaule, nuque. Douve*, however, concentrated with great power on that "humbling of the head," noticed by Alex E. Gordon. If few poems have evoked physical dissolution and disintegration with greater frankness than *Douve*, few have captured with equal precision and justice the atmosphere of peaceful reconciliation and gentle, erotic binding which exists in many parts of *Pierre écrite*. It is not as though the recognition of horror has disappeared entirely in this collection. (Or, as one poem says it, "It is not that the old night / Is no longer writhing in you" [*P*, 196].) Many poems, particularly from the "Pierre écrite" section of the book, insist on our rent condition, on our insufficiency and futility. Nevertheless, there is a new emphasis here on feeling and construction, and this emphasis is reflected in the attention given to the heart and the hands.

The heart is the seat of feeling. Even the earlier indictment of beauty in *Hier régnant désert* had said of it: "Notre haut désespoir sera que tu vives, / Notre *cœur* que tu souffres" ("our high despair shall be that you live, / Our *heart* that you suffer") (*P*, 114; italics mine). And if the heart is the place of the wound (*P*, 170), it is also the scene of healing. "Tu sais que c'est l'obscur de ton cœur qui guérit" ("You know that it is the darkness in your heart that is healing) (*P*, 201). In moments of erotic communion, the lover descends through purple worlds into the beating of the beloved's heart (*P*, 204). (And this intense purple or crimson—*pourpre*—is a recurrent color in the book:[31] it is the color the naked horizon turns in the pivotal poem "Sur un Éros de bronze," just as it is the hue of the afternoon "of simple features" in which "happiness / Ripened its bright fruit on absent branches" of another poem [*P*, 223].) The poet watches over the few words which die out in the hearth of the heart. In the lovely song "Le Cœur, l'eau non troublée" ("The Heart, the Untroubled Water"), it is the heart which is shot through with gardens and shadows—principal polarities in the book—and the heart, too, is characterized, along with earth, being, and matter, as *sans retour* or "endless." The silence in "Le Livre, pour vieillir," as I have said, makes its appeal to the heart. The poet imagines Kore seizing "the dark heart" of the flowers to suggest, perhaps, what is imponderable in the ephemeral. And he hears falling on the river of evening, swept along by music, "the spray in which the undiscoverable *heart* of the dead is beating" (*P*, 216; italics mine).

The hands, too, are isolated for special concentration, and, like the heart, recur with a great diversity of resonance. It is the frail earthly hand which disentangles the knot of dreams; the lovers seek each other's hand, "comme éternellement l'écume et le rocher" ("as do eternally the surf and rocks") (*P*, 175). The summer of night carries the summer of day in hands of light (*P*, 168). On the high plateaus, the poet sees one "stony" hand holding another. (*P*, 219)

The hands are associated not only with awakening through physical love, but also with the act of contemplation: they are sometimes "pensive hands" (*P*, 208). The hands of the quiet or simple time know measure and are not sad (*P*, 221). The hands stand out in a number of contexts. They are "alone in light" ("seules éclairées") (*P*, 177). In death, "the hands alone persist upright" ("[l]es mains seules droites persistent") (*P*, 187). These images recall vaguely the depictions of Kore and Ceres with torches in their hands. Here, the waist of Aglauros is reshaped by "diligent hands" (*P*, 190). And the palm of the hand of light is our earth—"our ground both for anguish and for hope" (*P*, 223).

The last poem of the collection, in affirming that vision has been dredged from night, that fever has been calmed and demons banished, a voice cleansed and recalled to order and purity, mentions both the heart and the hands.

> *Dragué fut le regard hors de cette nuit.*
> *Immobilisées et séchées les mains.*
> *On a réconcilié la fièvre. On a dit au cœur*
> *D'être le cœur. Il y avait un démon dans ces veines*
> *Qui s'est enfui en criant.*
> *Il y avait dans la bouche une voix morne sanglante*
> *Qui a été lavée et rappelée.* (*P*, 227)

Vision was dredged from night.
The hands were settled and dried.
The fever was calmed. The heart was told
To be the heart. There was a demon in these veins

Who rushed out screaming.
In the mouth there was a mournful, bloody voice
Which has been cleansed and steadied.

The simple directness of "The heart was told / To be the heart" seems to suggest that the process of exorcism has depended in great measure on the plain affirmation of feeling, that salvation for the poet has resided above all in acknowledging the heart's desires. By the same token, the lines which speak of the hands, "Immobilisées et séchées les mains" ("The hands were settled and dried"), suggest a process of steadiness and calming, a drying out of idle, disorienting longing and dreaming. This is the process of summer's magic: "Tout un grand été nul avait *séché* nos rêves" ("A whole vast empty summer had *dried out* our dreams") (P, 203; italics mine). And if the state of the hands anticipates their posture in death, the course of quieting will have for end result a kind of liberation, for the summer has also "loosened chains," set free the poet's bark (P, 203), and this opening and expansion may be set in contrast to the contraction and enclosure marked in the earlier *Douve* by the verbs "resserrer" (P, 89) and "refermer" (P, 55). Thus the hands, the shaping forces of the body, serve a number of functions here, from the calming caress of erotic caring and communion to the fashioning of art and the movements of resurrection, and in this, they may be thought of as the heart's ministers.

*   *   *

It might be well to return, by way of conclusion, to that poem cited in the first pages of the first chapter of this study: "La Lumière, changée" ("The Light, Changed").

Nous ne nous voyons plus dans la même lumière,
Nous n'avons plus les mêmes yeux, les mêmes mains.
L'arbre est plus proche et la voix des sources plus vive,
Nos pas sont plus profonds, parmi les morts.

Dieu qui n'es pas, pose ta main sur notre épaule,
Ébauche notre corps du poids de ton retour,
Achève de mêler à nos âmes ces astres,
Ces bois, ces cris d'oiseaux, ces ombres et ces jours.[32]

Renonce-toi en nous comme un fruit se déchire,
Efface-nous en toi. Découvre-nous
Le sens mystérieux de ce qui n'est que simple
Et fût tombé sans feu dans des mots sans amour.   (P, 211)

We no longer see each other in the same light,
We no longer have the same eyes or the same hands.

The tree is closer and the water's voice more lively,
Our steps go deeper now, among the dead.

God who are not, put your hand on our shoulder,
Rough-cast our body with the weight of your return,
Finish blending our souls with these stars,
These woods, these bird cries, these shadows and these days.

Give yourself up in us the way fruit falls apart,
Have us disappear in you. Reveal to us
The mysterious meaning in what is only simple
And would have fallen without fire in words without love.

Bonnefoy had noted in Elsheimer's "The Mocking of Ceres" a development from spiritual wandering and the temptation to fixate on a meaningless exteriority, an unfounded multiplicity, to the acceptance of a simple substantiality. And the notion of an absent Persephone sought by the anguished Demeter who will rediscover her presence in the silent simplicity of earth is surely conveyed as well in the poem "La Lumière, changée." The poem is an affirmation of a change in vision. As it often is in Bonnefoy's work, the *nous* is a complex of relationships involving, doubtless, the poet's experience not only of the specific other, but of life itself, his bond with the sources of his own inspiration—those obscure words whose weight is felt against the pensive hands of lovers crossing fields (*P*, 213)—as well as his connection to the dead and the absent. The change in vision is based on a deepening and a maturing of these relationships which guarantees a closer approach to the contradictions of being, here represented by the tree to which the poet has now come so close that it is no longer a merely exterior presence, distinguishable from others, but an approach to the unity of being. The mark of greater maturity is the convinced acceptance of the "mortal place"—its affirmation.

The last two stanzas of the poem are like a kind of prayer to the god of absence. In fact, these two stanzas develop the notion of an incarnate divinity and an excarnate transcendence. The transcendent deity no longer exists for us, is absent, Bonnefoy seems to be saying; this is the fatality of our modernity. But the force of its appeal has not been forsaken. That power has rather been blended with the concrete reality of the stars and woods, has come to light up the real world of shadows and days. Renunciation, yes, for ours is the place of finitude. But the disappearance of hope in transcendence, of nostalgia for an ideal or timeless world beyond our own, is the very foundation for the return of the gods. If the dream of what is now absent is married to the real, the divine will speak to reveal the mysteries of evidence, and simple things will find expression in the few words won through love and adherence.

6 New Life

Further than the star
The child who carries the world
Is bathing, simple,
In what is.

Pierre écrite ends on a note of provisional triumph: vision has been purified, changed. We might expect, therefore, that the next poem, *Dans le leurre du seuil* (*In the Lure of the Threshold*), would reflect this change. And, in fact, the book is very different from the preceding collections. The longest, densest, most complex of Bonnefoy's poetical works, *Dans le leurre du seuil* nevertheless represents a recapitulation of a number of recurrent and major poetic preoccupations. The book reenacts the perennial drama of excarnate yearning and acceptance of limit, and many familiar themes—the search for place, the desire for transcendence, the meditation on death and the act of writing, on the role and status of the image—are treated again in this work. One might say that *Dans le leurre du seuil* gives new expression to lifelong concerns. In this sense, it represents both a "summing-up" and a new departure.

Let us begin with what constitutes the newness and the difference.[1] In the first place, the work is considerably longer than the preceding books—so long, in fact, that some readers, experiencing the text for the first time, might argue, with Poe, that the "'long poem' is . . . a flat contradiction in terms," and that trying to read such a poem at a single sitting is to know "a constant alternation of excitement and depression."[2] Divided into seven sections of varying lengths, *Dans le leurre du seuil* has a continuous narrative flow which distinguishes it from the previous collections, although, as I have attempted to show, there is an element of effaced, barely perceptible narrative line even in these "collections." The narrative aspect of *Leurre* is extremely difficult to follow, as it is interspersed with commentary on our possibilities for knowing and with reflections on the means by which knowing is constituted—that is, the narrative is constantly interrupted by self-reflexivity, by commentary on itself. Nevertheless, the continuity of the book is a distinguishing feature, and once the structural organization of the poem becomes more familiar, its breadth and density seem less overpowering. I shall return to the question of the book as "story" in a moment.

The sense of place is rendered more specific than in any of the other poetical works. The setting for the poem is a former monastery, now in disrepair, located in Provence, near the mountain of Vachères. A number of details about this place substantiate impressions given to us in *Pierre écrite*. Thus, the *chambre* of the previous book and the images of the "ship of a summer" (*P*, 164) are recalled in flaming illumination:

> *Flamme*
> *Notre chambre de l'autre année, mystérieuse*
> *Comme la proue d'une barque qui passe.* (*P*, 274)

> Flame
> Our bedroom of the other year, mysterious
> Like the prow of a passing ship.

Here, however, place is filled out and rendered more complete: a kitchen with its table glistening from the sponge which has cleared "the remains of the bread and wine" (*P*, 315), with its box of salt, an archway, a fireplace, the vineyards outside, the well. The monastery in ruin becomes the symbol for a menaced but persistent sacred order, as well as for a poetry which can no longer "finish or organize" (*P*, 276). The notion of a crumbling habitation is reinforced by such homely details as the "sack of plaster," the mason who has been called for work, the hole by the chimney, and the shattered arch of the threshold, just as the sense of a sacred order is recalled by the remains of bread and wine on the kitchen table, by the names in the attic of those who, at a time not recorded, built a communion rail, by the presence of a light bulb burning above the stable door in a spot once reserved for the presence of God (*P*, 274). Part of the experience recounted by *Dans le leurre du seuil* is the recognition of impermanence as the basis, as the foundation, of vision and becoming.

The metonymic detail is a conspicuous aspect of *Leurre*, not only in the designation of simple household realities, but also in the use of proper names. Place (Vachères) is made specific; the poet's friend, the musicologist Boris de Schloezer, is mentioned by name, as are those who built the communion rail at some time in the dateless past, "Jean Aubry, of Orgon, / And his sons Claude and Jean" (*P*, 320).

Dans le leurre du seuil was begun in the late sixties, and the years of its composition were, of course, years of great cultural and intellectual upheaval for Western society. Bonnefoy's book in many ways reflects change. References to elements of contemporary culture—to vans and television sets, for instance—which would have seemed impossible in the earlier work are made here with decisiveness. By the same token, Bonnefoy seems to evoke the pastoral and romantic aspirations of the generation of "flower children" in a striking passage from the section of the poem entitled "Les Nuées" ("The Clouds"):

O rêves, beaux enfants
Dans la lumière
Des robes déchirées,
Des épaules peintes.

"Puisque rien n'a de sens,
Souffle la voix,
Autant peindre nos corps
De nuées rouges.

Vois, j'éclaire ce sein
D'un peu d'argile
Et délivre la joie, qui est le rien,
D'être la faute."

. . . .

Ils marchent, les pieds nus
Dans leur absence
Et atteignent les rives
Du fleuve terre.

Ils demandent, ils donnent,
Les yeux fermés,
Les chevilles rougies
Par la boue d'images.

Rien n'aura précédé, rien ne finit,
Ils partagent, une eau,
S'étendent, le flanc nu
Reflète l'étoile.

Ils passent, prenant part
A l'eau étincelante,
A toi, pierre jetée,
A des mondes là-bas, qui s'élargissent.

. . . .

Et à leurs pas se joint
Flore la pure
Qui jette ses pavots,
A qui demande.

Et beauté pastorale
Nue, pour ouvrir
A des bêtes mouillées, au froid du jour,
L'enclos du simple

—Mais aussi beauté grise
Des fumées
Qui se tord et défait
Au moindre souffle.

(*P*, 299–301)

O dreams, beautiful children
In the light
Their clothing torn,
Their shoulders painted.

"Since nothing has meaning,"
Breathes the voice,
"Why not paint our bodies
With red clouds?

Look, I brighten this breast
With a bit of clay
And deliver joy, which is nothing,
From being sin."

. . . .

They walk, barefooted
In their absence
And reach the shores
Of the river earth.

They ask, they give,
Their eyes closed,
Their ankles red
From the mud of images.

Nothing will have preceded, nothing ends,
They share, some water,
And when they stretch out, their naked flanks
Reflect the star.

They pass by, taking part
In the shimmering water,
In you, stone flung out,
In worlds over there, growing larger.

. . . .

And their steps are joined
By Flora, the pure
Who throws her poppies
To all who ask.

And naked, pastoral beauty,
To open
For wet animals, at the cold of day,
The shelter of the simple

—But also grey beauty
Of the smoke
That rises, twisting, and comes apart
At the slightest breath.

If the "Flora" of these lines—an allusion to the ancient Roman goddess of fertility and flowers—puts one in mind of a famous painting by Poussin of 1631 and seems therefore to obscure the sense of the modern, the "grey beauty / Of the smoke" seems clearly to suggest those drugs which became so visible in the late sixties and whose practice formed part of the tapestry of change—just as the "shared water" may "reflect" the sexual act a new generation sought to liberate and "deliver." If Bonnefoy knows, as his analysis of Rimbaud's use of them demonstrates, that drugs can "contribute to the overthrow of the power of appearances" (*R*, 158), his devotion to meaning, even knowing *la tache noire dans l'image* ("the black smudge in the image") and "the misery of sense" (*P*, 295), prohibits complete identification with the romantic movement of the sixties. Nevertheless, *Dans le leurre du seuil* works toward its own revolution, and the poetic consciousness will depend upon the arcadian interlude and upon the lost child to reanimate meaning in much the way that these are essential components in Shakespeare's *The Winter's Tale*.

Concern with change is also reflected by a new preoccupation which dominates this work: the question of generation, of paternity. For the poetic work is now conceived of in its futurity, and the few poetic words are seen as "saved for a child's mouth" (*P*, 323). A new and distinctive element in the book is the emergence of a child figure who unites the opposing faces of angel and serpent, a child "who carries the world" (*P*, 258) and who runs toward the future. For if this book is a summing-up, if it celebrates and consecrates the simple realities of lives "which have reached a certain stage" (*P*, 318), it places its work in the context of an unknown futurity and imagines *l'or des grainées futures* ("the gold of future seeds") (*P*, 242). And we are given the sense in this poem of an effort to be carried on, of an enterprise which will blossom in unforeseeable ways, but, perhaps, at least, less painfully—as the poet, echoing Rimbaud's vision in his "Morning of Drunkenness," believes that "le fruit du premier arbre / A terminé sa journée dans les branches / De la douleur du monde" ("the fruit of the first tree / Has finished its moment in the branches / Of the world's sorrow") (*P*, 321), and as he envisions a new child born of sorrow transformed into light (*P*, 283). In this connection, Bonnefoy's constant evocation of the physical body will focus especially on "le sein / Qui est semblable à l'eau, une, infinie, / Gonflée d'argile rouge" ("the breast / Which is like water, one, infinite, / Bulging with red clay") (*P*, 296), although the shoulder and ankle play important roles as well.

Perhaps the most distinctive organizing device of the poem is the use of a series of litanies which serve to enforce the sense of an affirmative summing-up and to insure, in spite of the intellectual and meditative excursions to which the energy of the poem is largely devoted, an access

which Jackson has associated with the *oral* tradition.[3] These litanies take
the form of exhortations connected by repetition of the word *Heurte*
("Knock" or "Strike") in the second section of the book; they also take the
form of commemorations or "illuminations" connected by repetition of
the word *flamme* in the section entitled "La Terre." A tremendous credo
(one based, of course, on paradox and negation) is orchestrated, in the
final section, through the use of the repeated affirmations *Oui à* and *Je con-
sens*. These litanies contribute mightily to our impression that the poem
achieves its greatest power and intensity as *chant*. The "Dévotion" of 1959
was also a kind of affirmative summing-up, a credo in which were gathered
together the convictions of the spiritual and poetical research to that point.
Long passages from *Dans le leurre du seuil* (and especially the last section
of the book, "L'Épars, L'indivisible" ["The Scattered, the Indivisible"])
seem to answer the same need but more extensively and with a kind of
exalted certainty, as these affirmations are integrated into an overall poetic
scheme which allows them to emerge from the characteristic temptation
and mastery of alienation and flight.

The idea of "musical" organization has always been apparent in Bon-
nefoy's work. The four-part structures of *Hier régnant désert* and of *Pierre
écrite*, which announce a theme, develop it through opposition, and re-
solve the oppositions in acceptance, recall the symphonic form. The recog-
nition of contradiction as *la fatalité du réel* is based on Bonnefoy's convic-
tion that man is *une musique latente* (*R*, 152). *Dans le leurre du seuil* may
be viewed as the moment in which the struggles of the past, the tensions,
the oppositions begin to find expression in a kind of hymn or religious
chant. And it is true to say, I think, that there is an unmistakable feeling in
this book of a certain form of effort coming to an end, and of a future—
less tortured and rent—preparing itself in the form of a joyful child.

> *Oui, par l'enfant*
>
> *Et par ces quelques mots que j'ai sauvés*
> *Pour une bouche enfante. "Vois, le serpent*
> *Du fond de ce jardin ne quitte guère*
> *L'ombre fade du buis. Tous ses désirs*
> *Sont de silence et de sommeil parmi les pierres.*
> *La douleur de nommer parmi les choses*
> *Finira." C'est déjà musique dans l'épaule,*
> *Musique dans le bras qui la protège,*
> *Parole sur des lèvres reconciliées.*   (*P*, 323)

> Yes, by the child
>
> And by these few words I saved
> For a child's mouth. "Look, the serpent
> At the back of the garden hardly ever leaves

150

The lusterless shade of the boxtree. His only desire
Is for silence and for sleep among the stones.
The painfulness of naming among things
Will cease." There is already music in the shoulder,
Music in the arm that protects it,
Words on lips that have been reconciled.

Certain passages of *Dans le leurre du seuil* put one in mind of Carlyle's
notion of poetry as "musical thought," in spite of the fact that the poem is
often struggling in an atmosphere in which "a music has ceased," and in
which "Partout, dans ce qui est, / Le vent se lève et dénoue" ("Everywhere,
in what is, / The wind rises and unravels") (*P*, 276). "All deep things,"
Carlyle wrote, "are Song."

> It seems somehow the very central essence of us, Song; as if all the
> rest were but wrappages and hulls! The primal element of us; of
> us, and of all things. The Greeks fabled of Sphere-Harmonies; it
> was the feeling they had of the inner structure of Nature; that the
> soul of all her voices and utterances was perfect music. Poetry,
> therefore, we will call *musical Thought*. The Poet is he who *thinks*
> in that manner. At bottom, it turns still on power of intellect; it is
> a man's sincerity and depth of vision that makes him a Poet. See
> deep enough, and you see musically; the heart of Nature *being* ev-
> erywhere music, if you can only reach it.[4]

To see "musically": this apparent absurdity is nonetheless the deepest
aspiration of this book. "If you want to see, listen," writes Bonnefoy, citing
Saint Bernard.

> . . . and one should understand by this that the ear is freer than
> the eye from the trap of appearances, music freer than painting, or
> words, from the seduction of appearances which seeks to attach a
> work to language [*la langue*]. . . .[5] And it is not that music is
> more abstract; on the contrary, it makes time concrete, which al-
> lows it, in its understanding of existence and its notation of itself,
> to pass beyond everything that might become fixed or settled.[6] So
> that, breaking the seal of appearances, delivering eros from the
> spirit of possession, death from its negative quality, being art de-
> livered from itself, music sometimes reaches closer to presence
> than any poem. (*NR*, 263–64)

The opening imperative of *Leurre*—"Look! With all your might, look!"
(*P*, 232)—is an exhortation to participate in that kind of vision the musi-
cologist Boris de Schloezer experiences at the moment of death, in the act
of crossing the awesome threshold. He hears or seems to hear "a music /
Those close to him knew nothing about" (*P*, 234). And the fire of his life's
work reaches to a summit of *déliements, de retrouvailles, de joie* ("unbind-

ings, of reunions, of joy") (*P*, 235)—a transformation reminiscent of Leontes at the moment of recovery of the daughter he had thought lost, or again at the moment when the Hermione he has rendered lifeless through his possessiveness and doubt is reanimated.

> *Qu'avait-il aperçu, que comprenait-il,*
> *Qu'accepta-t-il?*   (*P*, 235)

> What had he seen, what was he coming to understand,
> What did he learn to accept?

The special, privileged perception, the momentary vision, is rendered as music: "Il écouta, longtemps" ("He listened, for a long time") (*P*, 235). Later, in the sixth section of the poem, "Les Nuées" ("The Clouds"), the poet will exclaim:

> . . . *Parles-tu, chantes-tu, enfant,*
> *Et je rêve aussitôt que toute la treille*
> *Terrestre s'illumine*. . . .   (*P*, 294)

> . . . When you speak, child, when you sing,
> All at once I dream that the entire earthly
> Trellis has grown bright. . . .

*   *   *

For all its "newness," however, *Dans le leurre du seuil* may be regarded as Bonnefoy's *Summa*: a recapitulation, in extended form, of the preoccupations of a lifetime. It might, in fact, be argued that the seven parts of the book retrace the progress of the preceding volumes, as the poem begins with a meditation on death, then summons moral resolve against the sense of futility, and then evokes the marriage place and the erotic experience which in turn leads to the exalted affirmation of the natural world and the merging of subjectivity with objective evidence. The passage from night into new dawning, and again through daylight to sunset, also reenacts former progressions, just as the affirmations continue the work of the earlier "Dévotion." And as I have said, concerns familiar to us from the previous collections—the significance of death, of dream, of the other—reappear for renewed consideration. Natural phenomena—the river, the earth, the clouds—are, as always, the metaphorical field for the idea of textuality and for the process of death and rebirth in language and meaning.

Furthermore, in spite of the sense of narrative continuity, the poem is still characterized by those moments of intense poetic vision and concentration which were an unmistakable element of the earlier work. Thus in the midst of the continuous flow and the musical sense of unity created by the litanies, the *principium individuationis* isolates the "flanc du corbeau, qui marque / De sa rouille la brume" ("flank of the crow that streaks / The mist with its rust") (*P*, 246), or "le cristal un peu jauni / De ces arbres" ("the slightly yellowed crystal / Of these trees") (*P*, 280).

Similarly, if place is rendered more specific than ever before, if the metonymic detail is espoused with a new freedom, the poetic vision continues here to be structured by archetypal images and by cultural and artistic mediations, such as Poussin's paintings on the "Finding of Moses" and Shakespeare's play *The Winter's Tale*. And the narrative line is so discrete in this poem that the reader has something of the impression felt (although in a very different way) while reading *Douve*—namely, that the "story" told is not only a series of specific events, but also the reenactment of a general and recurrent drama. That is, the time frame in *Leurre* will occasionally open to suggest what is perennial and timeless in experience, as the poem seeks to affirm and make manifest the notion of "yesterday reincarnated, this evening, tomorrow" (*P*, 327). Thus, the lovers awaken at the beginning of the section entitled "Les Nuées" not knowing how many summers they have slept. And the summer season of the "action" of the poem yields suddenly and without warning to the snow-covered dream scenes which doubtless are meant to suggest the poet's feeling of impasse and despair—a winter of the heart.

If the narrative line is discrete and elusive, it is nevertheless more clearly apparent than in Bonnefoy's other books of poetry. It is as though Bonnefoy had finally come to terms with the "story" he had from the beginning been seeking to tell. Philippe Jaccottet insists in particular on this dimension of the poem, arguing that it is "une sorte de *prose*."[7]

A mixture, then, of the new and of the familiar, *Dans le leurre du seuil* is clearly set in the context of a narrative sequence or diachronic ordering which it will be my purpose now to explore.[8] The "story" seems to recount the crisis and resolution of a single day, a roughly twenty-four-hour period which begins at night, moves toward dawn and then to afternoon, and finishes at evening time. Each of the first six sections occupies its "moment" in this sequence, just as each has its own particular tone and rhetorical emphasis. (The seventh and concluding section is reserved for the chanted affirmations which are experienced both as the fruit of the labors of the preceding sections and as the "devotions" of a life and poetic effort "which have reached a certain stage.") If I say that the poem "seems" to develop along these lines, it is by way of insisting that the narrative is extremely difficult to follow, that it is marked by abrupt shiftings and changes of perspective which the reader experiences without transition, something in the manner of a dream unfolding, and that it is, above all, characterized by a discretion, an elusiveness, and a polyvalence of signification which make any single interpretive reading virtually impossible.

The poem begins with an awakening in summer, that season in which "the incoherent / . . . assails our eyes" (*P*, 309). If the poet had hoped, as the final poem of *Pierre écrite* seemed to indicate, that self-mastery and peace had been achieved, here are the opening lines of the present poem to announce new departure, new anxiety and stirring—the wing of impossible aspiration opened once again. (And in this sense, the poem resembles *Hier régnant désert* and *Pierre écrite*, for as the former announces a despair and apathy to be mastered, the latter an exaltation to be tempered, so *Leurre* opens on a note of longing and interrogation which will eventually be converted into acceptance and affirmation.)

> *Mais non, toujours*
> *D'un déploiement de l'aile de l'impossible*
> *Tu t'éveilles, avec un cri,*
> *Du lieu, qui n'est qu'un rêve. Ta voix, soudain,*
> *Est rauque comme un torrent. Tout le sens, rassemblé,*
> *Y tombe, avec un bruit*
> *De sommeil jeté sur la pierre.*   (*P*, 231)

But no, always
With an unfolding of the wing of the impossible
You awake, with a cry,
From the place which is only a dream. Your voice, suddenly,
Has the raucous sound of a torrent. All meaning, brought
     together,
Is falling there, with the sound
Of sleep hurled against stone.

The passage juxtaposes the notion of place with the search for meaning and suggests that the quest for a new place in sense is eternally renewed. (A later passage will reiterate this notion with the assertion that "tout le visible infirme / Se désécrit, / Braise où passe l'appel / D'autres campagnes"— "the whole visible world, crippled, / Is unwritten, / Glowing embers traversed by the call of other lands" [*P*, 250].) The opening lines also suggest an awakening from a dream of place which confronts the "real" world with confusion. (Again, later passages will confirm this idea, evoking, for instance, "l'argile d'un éveil en rêve, trempée d'ombre"—"the clay, drenched with shadow, of an awakening in dream" [*P*, 289]). A passage from "Les Nuées" will maintain that ". . . nous ne sommes pas guéris du jardin, / De même que ne cesse pas, gonflé d'une eau / Noire, l'epanchement du rêve quand les yeux s'ouvrent"—". . . we are not cured of the garden, / Just as the outpouring of dream, heavy with a dark / Water, does not cease when we open our eyes" [*P*, 296].)

In this half-dreaming, half-wakeful condition, the *tu* goes to the window to contemplate the stillness of the night in which "the threshing-floor . . . seems painted on the void" (*P*, 232). He wonders if the scene before him is not perhaps the "reflection" of some other, and the question of images and reflections will continue to be a major and constant preoccupation of the book, as the issue is raised in a vast range of contexts. Looking at the stars, the *tu* thinks of meaning as having "coagulated on the flank of the Bear" (*P*, 232).

> *Blessure inguérissable qui divise*
> *Dans le fleuve de tout à travers tout*
> *De son caillot comme un chiffre de mort*
> *L'afflux étincelant des vies obscures.*   (*P*, 232)

> Incurable wound that breaks up
> With its clot like a cipher of death
> In the river of all and through all
> The dazzling flow of obscure lives.

He remembers his dream: it was of a boat loaded with dark earth pushing off from a shore, the boatsman leaning on a pole which fixes itself in the nameless depths of the river bottom. This dream evokes the memory of the painted image of a boatsman—doubtless from Poussin's pictures on the "finding of Moses" theme—and this representation ("in spite of the denial of being" [*P*, 233]) will structure much of the development of the poem.

Poussin did three paintings on this subject, and Bonnefoy devotes some discussion to two of them in his autobiographical work *L'Arrière-pays*. Bonnefoy sees the sort of charcoal which bathes the paintings as the dissipation of dream in the real. It is as though the dream has been put to the fire to allow a simple evidence to emerge. The ostensible subject of the paintings is of course the discovery and rescue of the infant Moses by the Pharoah's daughter and her servants. In the poem, these images suggest a world where "l'esprit avait . . . son souffle, égal . . ." (*P*, 234). The "even breath" is related, in turn, to the general notion of the "music of things" of which I spoke earlier. In Bonnefoy's view, some artists strive to welcome "rhythm, color, as they come to birth, as yet untroubled by the idea of the thing" and to which their own being responds "less by the sketching out of something represented than by their union, which is musical, with these colors and these rhythms: one might say that the world and the spirit are in perfect harmony, at these moments of harvested fields or tree branches" (*NR*, 362). The poet strives to recapture this world, to establish himself in this reality of calm accord in which there are no longer cries of alarm or feverish, clenched hands, but rather peace and smiling acceptance.

The principal figures in the Poussin painting—the boatsman, the Pharoah's daughter, the infant—will evoke a whole network of associations. The boatsman represents a voyaging consciousness. (Later, in the section "La Terre," the poet will identify himself with this figure: "I the ferryman,

Nicolas Poussin, *The Finding of Moses*. Courtesy of the Musée du Louvre, Paris.

/ I the bark of all and through all" [*P*, 287].) Symbol for the process of becoming, the boatsman pushing his bark across *le fleuve terrestre* is consciousness in the stream of life. His characteristic gesture, leaning on his pole, seeking the bottom of the river, is used to suggest the effort to find meaning, as well as to evoke the mysterious searchings of the seeds of life in the process of generation. In Poussin's painting of 1647,[9] now at the Louvre, Pharoah's daughter is dressed in the red robes Bonnefoy uses to evoke the feminine presence in poems from *Pierre écrite* onward. She has something of the look of the priestesslike figure in the second of the *Et in Arcadia Ego* pictures. It is the red color which blends with the "blue that takes on the green / Of the treetops" (*P*, 259) in that mingling of "two colors," that poetic suggestion of conception which constitutes the third section of the book. The Pharoah's daughter saves: she pulls from the water the menaced child. In the context of the poem, this will come to mean "the few words . . . saved for the mouth of a child"—"the gold of future seeds." This pure word is what remains after the fires and the chafing.

The image of the bark and the river bank also serves to suggest that moment when "le sens comme une barque à peine pressentie / Se dérobe de la couleur et de la forme" ("meaning like a boat barely imagined / Disappears from color and from form") (*P*, 233). The departure from the bank of the familiar toward unknown shores is the journey of becoming here initiated by the call from "somewhere else, near, far off" (*P*, 231). Rimbaud had insisted that "to survey the invisible and to hear the unheard of" were "something other than reverting to the spirit of what has died."[10] The bark comes to represent, then, a constantly renewed project, the "reopened book, red cloud" which appears in the West after the dissipation of dark and dying clouds (*P*, 293).

The notion that poetry and painting are related is an aesthetic commonplace which found a lasting formulation in Horace's notion of the *ut pictura poesis*. The Abbé Batteux reiterates the idea in his treatise of 1774, *Les Beaux Arts réduits à un seul principe*: "La Poésie étoit en tout une imitation, de même que la Peinture."[11] In neoclassical aesthetics, *imitation* is not simple mimesis but embellishment, ennoblement, and elevation. Thus, evocation of landscape becomes noble when painting collaborates with noble historical subject matter, that is, with literature. (Poussin, for instance, places his landscapes in the context of some literary subject, biblical, mythological, or historical, whereas Claude Lorrain tends to allow his landscapes to dominate. It is for this reason that Diderot, in his *Salon of 1765*, considers Lorrain inferior to Vernet, for instance. In his *Salon of 1767*, he said of Poussin's *Paysage au serpent*: "These are the scenes one must know how to imagine if one wants to be a landscape painter." It was not enough to simply evoke beautiful worlds. "Before devoting oneself to any genre of painting whatsoever," he wrote, "one should have read, reflected, thought deeply about things: . . . one should have practiced historical painting, which leads to everything.") [12] Similarly, after the publication of the translation of Thompson's *Seasons* in 1759, descriptive poetry becomes a new, if often criticized, genre. Poets defended their work as "paintings," and, in this way, neither landscape painting as such, nor descriptive poetry as such, could achieve complete respectability in the neoclassical aesthetic, without the support of either "literature," on the one hand, or "painting," on the other. It is partly for this reason that Lamartine would refer to neoclassical poets as *poètes anti-poétiques*. [13]

It is obvious, to be sure, that Bonnefoy is fundamentally poet. Nevertheless, all his work, particularly the later work, is characterized by the ability to write "pictures" of great vividness. Philippe Jaccottet, in fact, admires this ability above all others in *Dans le leurre du seuil* and reserves his greatest praise "for what is close to painting in the work." [14] The general problematics of representation and of images as "reflections" is, as I have said, a major preoccupation of the book. The painted image—"which is not appearance, which is not / Even murky dream" (*P*, 233)—structures and educates the poetic vision of *Dans le leurre du seuil*. By the same token, the status of the image is brought severely into question: "But always and distinctly I also see / The black smudge in the image . . ." (*P*, 295). At the same time, the image is what is able, in spite of the devastations of finitude, to "leave the form intact" (*P*, 297) which may be our "gift / Of at least the idea of meaning—to the light" (*P*, 306), and the poet will wonder if the relation between the image and the reality it reflects is not suggestive of the relation between our present situation in waking, daily life and some greater coherence and beauty on the threshold of which we seem to be hesitating or struggling.

In any case, it is the image of the boatsman which conjures up the memory of Boris de Schloezer's death, of his departure in the boat of the dead. His death, in turn, raises questions: What did he see on the threshold? If there is the certainty of departure in death, can there be hope in some unknown arrival, in a rescue by some unseen Pharoah's daughter? The waters burn with enigma. And the essential rhetorical posture of this opening section of the book is the question. Five problems are raised which ask questions about division, about the origin and loss of meaning, about the role of images in the life of consciousness, about death as a threshold experience. The use of such qualifiers as *peut-être*, *sembler*, *ignorer* also contributes to the sense of an evidence struggling to manifest itself through obscurity and enigma.

The images of the last part of the first section anticipate the second section, as we see "the pole that strikes the muddy waters," and a "chain that drags along the river bottom," while the poet scratches words upon a page and a poisoned dog paws at the bitter earth of night. These activities may all be grouped around the notion of the desire to penetrate obscurity, to dig into unfathomable depths. The second section of the book isolates clusters of just such impenetrable realities into which the poet urges himself to "strike." The rhetorical form of the second section, the *exhortation*, the summons to the will, thus follows and answers the line of interrogation and doubt of the first part.

The empty sentence, the wasteland of meaninglessness, our relation with others against the backdrop of emptiness and disappearance are isolated by the effort of the will to overcome futility—for the reflection of the distant star plays even on iron and mud, and the boatsman, though he has but one or two keys, struggles to unlock a future and joyful world. The poet hopes in recovery and salvation: he prays that his effort will be salvaged by a Pharoah's daughter, that in the separation of the chaff, some seeds will be found fruitful, that in the dark water, some image will suddenly reflect meaning.

But a negative voice now is raised to assure him that he will meet refusal everywhere, that what he seeks will be denied to him. It is worth noting that in this negative passage the refusals include a number of those very elements on which a future reconciliation will be based: the bread and wine are recovered in secular form on the kitchen table in the affirmations which end the book; the glass of lukewarm water will play an important role in the moments of revelation in the fourth section, "Deux Barques" ("Two Boats"); the child laughing on a sunny afternoon and for whose future the poet has struggled becomes the most positive force in the book.

There follows a long meditation on the problematics of writing and on the relation between textuality and movement. The poet ponders the nature of the relation of his critical intelligence to those voices which rise up in him, to the noise of which he feels himself a part. He wonders if some glimmering of meaning shines at the summit of the noise. He imagines the emergence of sense, reflected in water like a colored cloth and forming like the meaning which seemed to coagulate on the flank of Ursa Major at the beginning of the poem. Form, image, meaning, color, grain of wheat saved from the chaff—these are the means by which the poet evokes what is sought by the straining boatsman who searches the dark river bottom with his pole. And the work of the will, the sense it strives for, are like the light which burns in the night, that

> . . . *Ampoule*
> *Qui s'agenouille en silence*
> *Et brûle*
> *Déviée, secouée*
> *Par la nuit qui n'a pas de cime.* (*P*, 251–52)

. . . light bulb
Which kneels in silence
And burns,
Shaken, swept off course
By the night which has no limit.

Night, here, is associated with "le temps de la douleur / Avant l'image" ("the time of suffering / Before the birth of the image") (*P*, 252). The diachronic ordering of this part of the poem charts the struggle through night to the dawn of emerging meanings. The poet wonders which is more real, the image or things in themselves, form or disappearance. And the section ends with the evocation of a shoulder, then of a face forming on the "water" next to the reflection of the shoulder. Is this, as the third section, "Deux Couleurs" ("Two Colors"), seems to suggest, the moment of contact with another human being or, as the section suggests as clearly, the stirring toward the birth of the image?

The ambiguity resides in the fact that in this book Bonnefoy is considering the process of generation both from the sexual or biological point of view and from the point of view of artistic conception and the development of meaning. The fourth section, "Deux Barques," also pursues this ambiguity of "life born from dream" (*P*, 255).

In "Deux Couleurs," it is effort which causes birth. The two hands "dig," just as the ferryman searches the river bottom. On the level of the narrative, it would seem that the *je* has awakened the feminine "other" and that, "in the mounting breathing," some naked power rises in them that "wants a life" (*P*, 256). The thread of this narrative is maintained through the recurrence of the images. Here, the lover becomes the Moses figure touching the banks of an unknown Egypt, the beloved a rich and foreign land.

> *Je te touche des lèvres,*
> *Mon amie,*
> *Je tremble d'aborder, enfant, sommeil,*
> *A cette Egypte.*
> (*P*, 256)

> I touch you with my lips,
> Beloved,
> I tremble at reaching, child, sleep,
> This Egypt.

The awed lover drinks from the water of life, water being the dominant element in *Dans le leurre du seuil* and the element consistently evoked to suggest the continuity of being.

> *J'ai confiance, je bois,*
> *L'eau glisse de mes doigts,*
> *Non, elle brille.*

Terres, entr'aperçues,
Herbes d'avant le temps, pierres muries,
Couleurs autres, jamais
Rêvées si simples,
Je touche à vos épis, lourds, que courbe le flux
Dans la ténèbre.
Et notre cri, soudain,
Défait l'étreinte,
Mais quand tu te répands,
Aube, ce blé demeure.   (*P*, 257–58)

I trust, and so I drink,
The water slips through my fingers,
No, it glistens.
Lands, barely glimpsed at,
Grasses from before time, ripened stones,
Colors, different, never
Dreamt of so simple,
I touch your heavy ears of wheat, bent by the flow
In the darkness.
And our cry, sudden,
Breaks our embrace,
But when you are poured out,
Dawn, this wheat remains.

The child conceived from this exchange partakes of two essential colors which seem in Bonnefoy's vision to be associated with the aspiring masculine subject,

Un bleu qui prend au vert
Du faîte des arbres
Comme un feu se fait clair
Parmi des fruits   (*P*, 259)

A blue that takes on the green
Of the treetops
Like a fire growing bright
Amid fruit,

and the heavier, more grounded and peaceful feminine other:

Le rouge des lourdes
Étoffes peintes
Que lavait l'Egyptienne, l'irréveillée,
De nuit, dans l'eau du fleuve   (*P*, 259)

The red of the heavy
Painted cloth
That the Egyptian woman, the unawakened,
Washed in the river water at night.[15]

The next section, "Deux Barques," pursues the story which for the moment has been presented by the *je*. These sections are marked by a growing peacefulness.[16] The lovers are in the bed lit up by starlight. If water has been the means of suggesting the continuity of being, it is also repeatedly the reflecting surface. The poet remembers leaning over a cistern with the beloved.

> *Regarde comme ils se penchent, eux comme nous,*
> *Est-ce nous qu'ils écoutent, dont ils parlent,*
> *Souriant sous les feuilles du premier arbre*
> *Dans leur lumière heureuse un peu voilée?*
> *Et ne dirait-on pas qu'une lueur*
> *Autre, bouge dans cet accord de leurs visages*
> *Et, riante, les mêle? Vois, l'eau se trouble*
> *Mais les formes en sont plus pures, consumées.*
> *Quel est le vrai de ces deux mondes, peu importe.*
> *Invente-moi, redouble-moi peut-être*
> *Sur ces confins de fable déchirée.* (*P*, 262)

See how they are looking down, they like us,
Is it us they are listening to, speaking of,
Smiling under the leaves of the first tree
In their joyful, slightly veiled light?
And wouldn't one say that a glimmering
From elsewhere is stirring in this union of their faces,
And, laughing, mingles them? Look, the water is blurring
But these forms are the purer for it, consumed.
Which of these two worlds is the true one, it scarcely matters.
Invent me, make me twofold perhaps
On these confines of shattered myth.

Bonnefoy's questioning of the ontological status of the image is a constant element in his work. In *Douve*, as will be remembered, one of the early poems speaks of the apprehension of death as having placed the poet at a level of consciousness "where images no longer work" (*P*, 35). In *Hier régnant désert*, in the poem called "A San Francesco, le soir," the complexity of the question is pursued. The poem recounts a visit to the dark, abandoned chapel at night.

> *. . . Ainsi le sol était de marbre dans la salle*
> *Obscure, où te mena l'inguérissable espoir.*
> *On eût dit d'une eau calme où de doubles lumières*
> *Portaient au loin les voix des cierges et du soir.*
>
> *Et pourtant nul vaisseau n'y demandait rivage,*
> *Nul pas n'y troublait plus la quiétude de l'eau.*
> *Ainsi, te dis-je, ainsi de nos autres mirages,*
> *O fastes dans nos cœurs, ô durables flambeaux!* (*P*, 104)

.. . . And so the ground was made of marble in the darkened
Room, where you were led by incurable hope.
One might have said of calm waters on which twofold lights
Carried far off the voices of the candles and the twilight.

And yet, no vessel asked for shore there,
No step came to trouble the stillness of the water.
Thus, I tell you, thus shall it be with our other mirages,
O ceremonials in our hearts, O long lasting flames!

The poet imagines the marble floor of the chapel as a watery port reflecting
the candles and the lights of evening. As the church is abandoned, he es-
tablishes the connection between the "mirage" of waters without ships and
the fate of the more durable interior mirage: the dream of a plenitude and
a wholeness, forever missing here along our dark and mortal way. It is, of
course, this lack that leads the poet to the church in the first place, through
"incurable hope."

The notion of image as mirage is pursued in a more accepting way in
Pierre écrite, as lines I have already cited indicate: ". . . Oh, which is the
more real / Longing sorrow or painted image?" (*P*, 225). Here, the image
is seen as necessary for the expression of needs and emotions whose reality
is felt to "pierce the veil of the image." This alliance between image and
reality, between reflection and source—this merging of worlds so con-
stantly sought after throughout the entire span of Bonnefoy's career—
seems to reach a moment of great intensity and freedom in *Leurre*, as it is
this "marriage" that gives rise to the future child in whom these worlds are
joyfully reconciled. This "conception," as I have said, has its resonances on
both the biological and artistic levels. The passage from *Leurre* cited above
may be said to mark the distance from the earlier moment of solitude and
despair recorded in "A San Francesco, le soir." Here it is the *couple* that is
reflected in the water of the well, and this "mirage"—now fully accepted—
is seen as rich in truths for human existence. The "images" in the water
seem to conjure up some original possibility—lost, perhaps, but not for-
gotten. The mingling of the faces is a harbinger, of course, of the new life
made of two discrete colors. Sections 3 and 4 ("Deux Couleurs" and
"Deux Barques") stress the principle of contact with nameless otherness
(*P*, 261) as the origin of new beginnings, new life. The "glimmering /
From elsewhere" ("lueur / Autre") that contributes to the union of the
faces seems related to the "naked wandering power" of procreation and
reconciliation already evoked in the section "Deux Couleurs." Here, the
former distinctions between reality and image, between model and repre-
sentation, between original and reflection are breaking down, and the im-
age or the reflection which has been simplified, stripped of unnecessary
ornament and the extravagances of the imaginary, may be said now to no
longer pose a threat to being. The poet seems to have reconciled himself to

the idea of the interconnections of the worlds of image and reality, to the necessity of the "doubling," to the way in which ancient myths of origin and presence are recovered in daily experience, to the possibility of converting the old Narcissus and Creation stories.

The story proceeds as the lover gazes down on the beloved whom he imagines as the water "where our likeness is flowering" ("où fleurit notre ressemblance") (P, 263). It is water "that allows us to be, being not" ("qui fait que nous sommes, n'étant pas") (P, 262); it is water which the poet has purified of dreams and of that "evil desire for the infinite" (P, 264). It is as though Bonnefoy were insisting, like certain Zen-men[17] before him, that the material world around us, the world at hand, is not deficient in reality in comparison to some other ideal place, but rather is surcharged with reality, filled with a richness that "we cannot or will not see" (P, 263). Time seems to halt; the lover rises in the quiet to find in the shadowy darkness a half-filled glass of water. He has the beloved drink from it, then drinks from it himself. It is at this moment that the poet has a powerful experience of "light, changed" (P, 264), of illumination.

> Et quand je bois l'eau tiède où furent tes lèvres,
> C'est comme si le temps cessait sur les miennes
> Et que mes yeux s'ouvraient, à enfin le jour.   (P, 263–64)

And when I drink from the tepid water where your lips had
     been,
It is as though time were standing still on mine
And as though my eyes were opening, into daylight at last.

This kind of experience is vaguely reminiscent of what happens to the narrator of La Recherche when he tastes the madeleine which has been dipped in tea, except that it is not so much a question here of resurrecting the world of the past as it is of experiencing the world at hand as though for the first time. This experience is closer to the aspiration of the Zen Buddhist discipline—the so-called satori. D. T. Suzuki has written of the satori in the following way.

> Satori may be defined as an intuitive looking into the nature of things in contradistinction to the analytical or logical understanding of it. Practically, it means the unfolding of a new world hitherto unperceived in the confusion of a dualistically-trained mind. Or we may say that with satori our entire surroundings are viewed from quite an unexpected angle of perception. Whatever this is, the world for those who have gained a satori is no more the old world as it used to be; even with all its flowing streams and burning fires, it is never the same one again. . . . When poetically or figuratively expressed, satori is "the opening of the mind-flower," or "the removing of the bar," or "the brightening up of the mind-works."[18]

It is significant, given the work of the will which constitutes the second movement of this poem, that Suzuki will insist that "the intensity of feeling" in the satori experience "is proportional to the amount of effort the opener of satori has put into the achievement" (ibid., 97). And in terms of the direction the poem will now follow, it is worth noting that in this sort of experience "the mind is so completely possessed or identified with its object of thought that even the consciousness of identity is lost as when one mirror reflects another" and "the subject feels as if living in a crystal palace, all transparent, refreshing, buoyant, and royal" (ibid., 102).

> Another name for satori is "ken-sho" (*chien-hsing* in Chinese) meaning "to see essence or nature," which apparently proves that there is "seeing" or "perceiving" in satori. . . . the knowledge contained in satori is concerned with something universal and at the same time with the individual aspect of existence. . . . the knowledge realized by satori is final . . . no amount of logical argument can refute it. . . . Though the satori experience is sometimes expressed in negative terms, it is essentially an affirmative attitude towards all things that exist; it accepts them as they come along regardless of their moral values. . . . The individual shell in which [the] personality is so solidly encased explodes at the moment of satori. . . . individuality, . . . rigidly held together and definitely kept separate from other individual existences, becomes loosened somehow from its tightening grip and melts away into something indescribable, something which is of quite a different order. . . . The feeling that follows is that of a complete release or a complete rest—the feeling that one has finally arrived at the destination. "Coming home and quietly resting" is the expression generally used by Zen followers. The story of the prodigal son . . . points to the same feeling one has at the moment of a satori experience. (Ibid., 104–6)

I have dwelt at length on Suzuki's analysis of this kind of experience because so much of what he describes seems to parallel the general movement of the poem *Dans le leurre du seuil*. The simplest, most commonplace events of one's daily life may trigger the satori experience: "Someone takes hold of you, . . . or brings you a cup of tea, or makes some most commonplace remark . . . and when your mind is ripe for its outburst, you come at once to satori" (ibid., 107). Thus, drinking from the glass of lukewarm water initiates the experience or vision which will now dominate the general direction of the poem in which the restrictions normally imposed on individual consciousness are broken up and consciousness experiences a great sense of expansion and consent.

In the text of the poem, Bonnefoy uses a series of suspension points immediately after the words indicating that the eyes of the poet have been opened to a new experience, perhaps in order to indicate that there is much in such an experience that is "untellable," to borrow Plotinus's term, that such an experience is "not to be conveyed by any sound" or "known on any hearing but, if at all, by vision." [19] Nevertheless, there follow passages in the form of prayers, as the poet asks that "le bien de la source ne cesse pas / A l'instant où la source est retrouvée" ("the blessing of the water's source not cease / The moment the source is rediscovered") and that "les lointaines ne se separent pas / Une nouvelle fois du proche, sous la faux / De l'eau non plus tarie mais sans saveur" ("the distances not separate / Once again from what is close by, beneath the scythe / Of the water no longer dried up but without savor") (*P*, 264). These prayers for the conversion of excarnate desire are not incompatible with the desire to find the eternal center in fleeting experience, as the poet asks that "the rose of the water passing by" gather up all his experience "hollowing out here"— "then illuminate it / On the motionless hub of the wheel" (*P*, 265).

In the atmosphere of increasing peace ("one would say that the boat had stopped moving" [*P*, 266]), the poet leaves the house to wander in the vineyards, near the mountain of Vachères. He remembers that he has dreamed again: a woman servant with a lamp was walking far ahead of him in the snow, casting streams of red light down the folds of her dress and onto the snow. The figure in the dream, who is reminiscent of the force in the section "A Fire Goes Before Us" in *Pierre écrite*, anticipates the break up of the snow, the smiling power of affirmation of the last sections of *Leurre*. The poet contemplates the almond tree which shares obscurely in the same life force as the poet himself—"the water flowing / In a darker branch, of the same river" (*P*, 268). He addresses to the tree the exhortation which is applicable to all ephemeral forms:

> *Branche d'ici, brûlée d'absence, bois*
> *De tes fleurs d'un instant au ciel qui change.*   (*P*, 269)

Branch from here, burnt with absence, drink
With your momentary flowers from the changing sky.

At this moment before dawn, as night is breaking up (*P*, 265), the poet feels himself in another universe. He throws salt upon the snow. The image refers, on one level, to the dream, since the "action" of the poem is situated in summer. The image seems to refer back to *la servante* with her lamp. The gesture evokes the process of break up and evaporation associated with the "satori-experience" and anticipates the reanimation and new vision which are symbolized by Hermione's transformation at the end of *The Winter's Tale*.

The fifth section of the book is called "La Terre." It is the first movement of the vigorous acceptance and affirmative certainty which will characterize the last three sections of the poem. That this first movement should have for title "The Earth" is consistent with the nature of Bonnefoy's convictions to this point. Consciousness has now moved to the great outside. The poet is now guided by a smiling feminine power who is "in the certainty of the threshold" (*P*, 272). The direction of the section is toward that dawn, that world lit up by vision, already announced by the earlier prayer:

> . . . *et va se déchirer*
> *Notre éternelle nuit; va se pencher*
> *Souriante sur nous l'Égyptienne.* (*P*, 265)

> . . . and our eternal night
> Will soon shatter; the Egyptian girl
> Will soon bend over us, smiling.

In terms of the drama or story of the poem, this is the moment at which consciousness no longer identifies with a particular subject, but rather with "the undivided, the invisible," and consequently a process begins by means of which excarnate yearning is mastered and converted to the conviction that the real is forever reincarnated—"this evening, tomorrow, / Yes, here, there, somewhere else, here, over there once again" (*P*, 327).

> *Je crie, Regarde,*
> *Ta conscience n'est pas en toi,*
> *L'amont de ton regard*
> *N'est pas en toi*
> *Ta souffrance n'est pas en toi, ta joie moins encore.* (*P*, 275–76)

> I cry, Look,
> Your consciousness is not within you,
> The upstream of your gaze
> Is not within you
> Your suffering is not within you, your joy even less.

Consciousness seeks here to identify itself with an eternal process.

> *Et, vois, des mains*
> *De plus haut dans le ciel*
> *Prennent*
> *Comme passe une ondée, dans chaque fleur,*
> *La part impérissable de la vie.*

> *Elles divisent l'amande*
> *Avec paix. Elles touchent, elles prélèvent le germe.*

> *Elles l'emportent, grainée déjà*
> *D'autres mondes,*
> *Dans l'à jamais de la fleur éphémère.* (*P*, 272–73)

> And, look, hands
> From higher up in the sky
> Are taking

167

From each flower, like a passing rain,
The imperishable part of life.

They split the kernel
Peacefully. They touch, they lift out the seed.

They carry it off, already the beginnings
Of other worlds,
In the forever of the ephemeral flower.

And this process seems to involve not only biological continuity but also the persistence of the life of the spirit.

For a moment, the poet will see illuminated a number of realities he must affirm, from the bedroom in his house in the form of a ship to a simple glass in the kitchen and those stones on which the knife of dreams has labored. The "flame" of illumination here is associated with both celebration and sacrificial fire.

The poetic consciousness comes to affirm the present state of the artist when "entre l'œil qui s'accroît et le mot plus vrai / Se déchire la taie de l'achevable" ("between the growing eye and the truer word / The cover of what is finishable is torn apart") (*P*, 276). But illumination is seen to emerge from the embers of "dépossession" (*P*, 277) and imperfection (the dream of the perfect or finished "book" breaking down under the pressure of a wordless apprehension of immediate presences).

> *Est-ce deux combattants qui ont lâché prise,*
> *Deux amants qui retombent inapaisés?*
> *Non, la lumière joue avec la lumière*
> *Et le signe est la vie*
> *Dans l'arbre de la transparence de ce qui est.*   (*P*, 277–78)

Are these two fighters who have loosened their hold,
Two lovers who fall back unappeased?
No, the light plays with the light
And the sign is life
In the tree of the transparency of what is.

Here, place, life, and sign unite in a kind of transparent evidence. And the poet accepts the ephemeral nature of things and resigns himself to an "aesthetics" of movement and change: "la phrase de fumée un instant lisible / Avant de s'effacer dans l'air souverain" ("words of smoke legible for a moment / Before vanishing in the sovereign air") (*P*, 278). The section, like those which follow, elaborates litanies of affirmation and acceptance, in accordance with the notion of a poetry that places the simple on pillars of fire, a poetry "où rien ne reste / Que l'abondance comme telle, désignée" ("where nothing remains / But abundance as such, designated") (*P*, 279). This is the gold—that alchemical gold Baudelaire also knew, extracted from the "minutes" and the "mud"—which the poet says is "in us."

Or de ne pas durer, de ne pas avoir,
Or d'avoir consenti. . . .   (*P*, 280)

Gold of not lasting, of not having,
Gold of having consented. . . .

The existence of the alchemical vocabulary in Bonnefoy's work (the "creu-set" or crucible [*NR*, 280], the "alambic" or still [*P*, 280]) reminds us that his project has affinities with the alchemical ambitions of Rimbaud. The *or des grainées futures* of which he writes could be interpreted as the "grains of philosopher's gold" sought by the alchemist—the vision of God. Here, and as always, the God is an absent God, an "empty vase"—the God who works through the "evaporation" of the illusory self and whose face shines in the simple things whose value is augmented through finitude con-fronted and accepted: this is the God "who is not, but who saves the gift" (*P*, 281).

The poet emphasizes the notion that consciousness is not so much in the self as in what the self apprehends and consents to—here, through litanies of mystical identification.

> . . . *moi les pierres du soir* . . .
> . . . .
> *Moi la nuée*
> *Je consens. Moi l'étoile du soir*
> *Je consens.*
> . . . .
> *Moi le bruit de la fourgonnette* . . .
> . . . .
> *Moi la nuit d'août,*
> *Je fais le lit des bêtes dans l'étable.*
> . . . .
> . . . *Moi le passeur,*
> *Moi la barque de tout à travers tout,*
> *Moi le soleil,*
> *Je m'arrête au faîte du monde dans les pierres.*   (*P*, 286–87)

> . . . I the stones of evening . . .
> . . . .
> I the cloud
> I consent. I the evening star
> I consent.
> . . . .
> I the sound of the van . . .
> . . . .
> I the August night,
> I make the bed for the animals in the stable.
> . . . .
> . . . I the ferryman,
> I the bark of all and through all,

I the sun,
I halt at the summit of the world in the stones.

The last lines of the section seem to suggest, on one level, a return to the marriage bed after the experiences in the vineyards.

> *Perche*
> *De chimères, de paix,*
> *Qui trouve*
> *Et touche doucement, dans le flux qui va,*
>
> *A une épaule.*   (*P*, 288)

> Pole
> Of chimeras, of peace,
> That finds
> And gently touches, in the passing water's flow,
>
> Upon a shoulder.

(Section 2 also ends with the image of the ferryman's pole touching upon a shoulder. The section deals with the problematics of writing and the generation of the image. Section 3, which seems to deal with biological or physical generation, on the other hand, ends with the evocation of the ferryman's pole hitting upon "the word"—"in the mud of the image with its empty gaze." Bonnefoy seems to be suggesting that image making is grounded and authenticated in physical and material experience,[20] just as biological conception may be seen as a "word made flesh.") In any case, the next section, "Les Nuées," finds the lovers waking in the drowsy atmosphere of afternoon.

> *Nous avons donc dormi: je ne sais combien*
> *D'étés dans la lumière; et je ne sais*
> *Non plus dans quels espaces nos yeux s'ouvrent.*
> *J'écoute, rien ne vibre, rien ne finit.*   (*P*, 289)

> Thus we slept: I know not how many
> Summers in the light; nor do I know
> Into what spaces our eyes are opening.
> I listen, nothing stirs, nothing ends.

The section uses the image of the clouds for a sustained meditation on the problematics of textuality. The text is considered both from the point of view of dissipation ("a cloud was prowling darkly and the wind / Scattered in great flashings the futile phrase" [*P*, 290]) and from the point of view of renewed inspiration ("reopened book, red cloud" [*P*, 293]),[21] Bonnefoy having said, in his essay "Sur la fonction du poème," that "the self formed by a book is only one among many others which one might in turn wish for and drive out—clouds themselves—as soon as a new aspiration awakes in us" (*NR*, 276–77).[22] The section "Les Nuées" echoes many preoccupations from the second section of the poem.

> *Mais toujours et distinctement je vois aussi*
> *La tache noire dans l'image, j'entends le cri*
> *Qui perce la musique, je sais en moi*
> *La misère du sens. Non, ce n'est pas*
> *Aux transfigurations que peut prétendre*
> *Notre lieu, en son mal.* (*P*, 295)

> But always and distinctly I also see
> The black smudge in the image, I hear the cry
> That pierces the music, I know within me
> The misery of meaning. No, it is not
> To transfigurations that our place
> Can aspire, in its wounded state.

Nevertheless, the section strives for participation in that kind of vision Boris de Schloezer experiences on the threshold of death.

> *Tout n'est-il pas si cohérent, si prêt*
> *Bien que, certes, scellé?* (*P*, 294)

> Isn't everything so coherent, so ready
> Although, of course, still sealed?

Bonnefoy uses the model of Shakespeare's *The Winter's Tale* to develop this sense of new vision, this feeling the Buddhists describe as "coming home and quietly resting" and which has its echoes as well in the story of the prodigal son.

> *Quand chacun reconnaît chacun, quand on apprend*
> *De niveau en niveau dans la lumière*
> *Que ceux qu'avaient jetés l'orgueil, le doute*
> *De contrées en contrées dans le dire obscur*
> *Se retrouvent, se savent. Parole en cet instant*
> *Leur silence; et silence leurs quelques mots*
> *On ne sait si de joie ou de douleur*
> *"Bien qu'à coup sûr l'extrême de l'une ou l'autre."*
> *Ils semblent, dit encore*
> *Un témoin, méditant, et qui s'éloigne,*
> *Entendre la nouvelle*
> *D'un monde rédimé ou d'un monde mort.* (*P*, 291)

> When everyone recognizes everyone, when one learns
> From level to level in the light
> That those who had been cast by pride and doubt
> From land to land in dark utterance
> Have found and known each other once again. Their silence
> Becomes speech then; and their few words silence

171

Whether of joy or sorrow cannot be known
"But in the extremity of the one it must needs be."
They looked, adds
A witness, pondering all this, and who withdraws,
As they had heard of
A world ransomed, or one destroyed.

The last lines of the above passage reiterate the epigraph chosen for the entire poem. Bonnefoy's reading of Shakespeare's play is related to his deepest concerns: the relation of form to movement and becoming, the isolation of a possessive and controlling artistic temperament ("The artist [who] prefers the signs at his disposal to the referents that signs were made to recognize and [who] gives free play to signs, abandoning the idea of meaning" [*NR* 360]), the question of loss and recovery. The section evokes both the poet's attraction to the image in its capacity to create radiant, if ephemeral and unreal, worlds ("Je mens, à l'infini, mais je satisfais"—"I lie, endlessly, but I satisfy" [*P*, 296]) and the collapse of hope in the image (". . . it is not / To transfigurations that our place / Can aspire, in its wounded state" [*P*, 295]). The epigraph—"They look'd as they had heard of a world ransom'd, or one destroyed"—highlights a principal dynamic of the book, and indeed of Bonnefoy's entire poetic enterprise: the notion of finitude on the one hand, and of an unlimited plenitude on the other. The evocation of the enigmatic death of Boris de Schloezer that opens the poem suggests the necessity of basing vision on the acceptance of death. A major poem from *Hier régnant désert*, "À la voix de Kathleen Ferrier," had already celebrated the voice of "extreme joy and extreme sorrow" (*P*, 137), the apprehension and love of things which are present and loved because they pass. By the same token, the epigraph may be said to speak to the whole problematics of the image world. If the world is enriched through the image, it may also be destroyed or abandoned in its own being; similarly, the destruction or dissipation of the controlling mediation or image may redeem the stifled world, allow it to breathe at last.

Bonnefoy, echoing Rimbaud's prose poem "Being Beauteous," will see the statue Hermione as the *mère de la beauté, mère du sens* ("mother of beauty, mother of meaning") (*P*, 292). As such, she is "long motionless, / Her voice stifled century after century" (*P*, 292). She is what Bonnefoy has called, in another context, "the depths—wounded, ravaged—which nonetheless constantly make themselves heard" (*NR*, 351).[23]

> . . . *Foudre ses yeux*
> *Qui s'ouvrent dans le gouffre du safre clair,*
> *Mais foudre souriante commi si,*
> *Condamnée à suivre le rêve au flux stérile*
> *Mais découvrant de l'or dans le sable vierge,*
> *Elle avait médité et consenti.*
>
> (*P*, 292)

> . . . Lightning her eyes
> That open into the abyss of bright sandstone,
> But lightning that smiles as though,
> Condemned to follow the sterile flow of dream
> But finding gold in the virgin sand,
> She had thought deeply and consented.

She is the "night bright with stars / That is splayed, music" ("nuit étoilée / Qui s'ébrase, musique") (*P*, 292). Although she fades and is blown away—"black cloud"—the poet is reassured by the appearance of "a flat-bottomed boat, whose prow represents / A fire, a smoke . . . / Reopened book, red cloud . . ." (*P*, 293).

In this connection, the "negative voice" of the second section reemerges to warn that the book of which the poet dreams, that form which remains intact in spite of "the fire of time" that "catches on bodies, on cries, even on dreams" (*P*, 297) will forever be denied him, but that he will be forbidden as well to ever forget this dream of the book. The idea seems to be that God or "presence" is not accessible through the mediation of signs, but that to work through signs and images which will their own destruction is to elaborate a kind of negative approach to presence. The "God" who has died for Bonnefoy is above all, then, the objective reality of the "imaged God." He therefore places the image (as opposed to the situation) as an approach under radical suspicion. It is only through this *via negativa*—the suspicion and destruction of the image—that Bonnefoy sees the chance for construction and affirmation: "the imaginary has cleared up, we fall silent, we listen to the breathing of the meaning veiled by form" (*NR*, 362). The Zen-man would say that "those who have the Buddha, don't have him; those who don't have the Buddha, do have him."

If the poet is denied access to the Arcadian dream of innocence evoked in the next passages (passages I cited at the beginning of this chapter), it is in part because of the memory of the book ("I have not allowed you to forget the book" [*P*, 299]) and the "need for meaning" (*P*, 312). And it is significant that the passage on these "beautiful children" begins with the words "O dreams" (*P*, 299). Nevertheless, the poet must have felt some affinity with the "revolution" of the sixties, as some of his own quest is reflected in the effort of a younger generation to reach "the shores of the river earth" and to deliver "joy which is nothing, / From being sin" (*P*, 300). It would seem, however, that the complex orientation of this poet—an orientation which honors contradiction and paradox—will not allow him simply to "drink of the passing water and bathe / Beneath the arch where fruit not meaning ripens" (*P*, 299). Doubtless he knows that it is useless to dream of "curing ourselves of what we are" (*I*, 40).

The section then seems to pass outside: it is sunset and the lovers seem to be returning home from a walk. Light is reflected from afar on the window panes, although it disappears on approach. In this sense, the windows are a symbol of our experience with language: "illuminé / Au loin, pierreux ici" ("lit up / From afar, stony here") (*P*, 308).

> . . . *De près les vitres s'éteignent,*
> *Mais l'or se retirant à son autre rive*
> *A laissé à fleurir dans leur sable vierge*
> *Le rien, qui est la vigne.*   (*P*, 304)

> . . . Close up the windows grow dim,
> But the gold withdrawing to the other shore
> Has left nothingness to flourish in their virgin sand,
> Nothingness, which is the vine.

The smell of dry grass, the porosity of the light seem to satisfy the longings of the poet: "Tu accomplis le vœu puisque tu accueilles / La terre, qui excède le désir" ("You fulfill your wish since you welcome / The earth, which exceeds desire") (*P*, 305). The poet realizes that it is enough simply to trust (*P*, 305). The efforts of the will are here recompensed, and desire is transformed into love and acceptance. Still, the poet asks that his joy take form—"to make a gift / Of at least the idea of meaning—to the light" (*P*, 306).

The section ends as night falls. The lovers are now

> *Entre les colonnes des feux de l'été qui va prendre fin,*
> *Dans l'odeur de l'étoile et de la cendre.*   (*P*, 308)

> Between the parting summer's columns of fire,
> In the scent of the star and the ashes.

This crepuscular atmosphere, familiar to readers of Bonnefoy from a number of passages in previous collections (particularly from "A Fire Goes Before Us" in *Pierre écrite*), evokes that condition neither completely in the night of image desires nor in the day of sense making, but rather in some midway zone of aspiration and lucidity.

The book ends with a series of chanted affirmations which would perhaps seem shocking were we not aware of the pathway of negation and suspicion down which the poet had traveled to arrive at them. They are strung together, as though flowing from a single breath of inspired certainty, by a repeated *Oui* which seems to answer the *Mais non* with which the book began. The poet celebrates the ever frustrated "need for meaning." He affirms his dwelling—at once habitable and uninhabitable—yet drawing "d'un souffle égal / Aux réserves de songe de la terre" ("with an even breath / From the earth's store of dreams") (*P*, 317). The "even breath" of the atmosphere surrounding the house places the dwelling in the context of the Poussin paintings evoked in the opening pages of the poem—that world in which "l'esprit avait . . . son souffle, égal . . ." (*P*, 234). It is here that the poet will have his intuitions of the essential unity of being.

> *Et la guêpe qui heurte à la vitre a cousu*
> *Beaucoup déjà de la déchirure du monde.* (*P*, 321)

And the wasp that bumps against the window has sewn up
Already a great deal of the tear in the world.

Here, the poet feels himself closer, more at one, with the evident.

> *Et à ses vitres les feuillages sont plus proches*
> *Dans des arbres plus clairs.* (*P*, 322)

And at the windows the leaves are closer
In brighter trees.

The poet feels that his efforts with language may have for result that in certain signs the light burns more brightly. Nevertheless, in this atmosphere of convictions and conclusions, the poet renounces the dream of some perfected form.

> *(Et du livre rêvé, le feu*
> *A tourné les pages.*
> *Il les prit à la nuque et les alourdit*
> *De sa morsure.*
> *Elles ont disparu, selon*
> *Son axe courbe*
> *Qui les arqua, ainsi*
> *Le mystère d'amour.)* (*P*, 327)

(And the fire has turned the pages
Of the book we dreamt of
It took them by the neck and weighed them down
With its bite.
They have disappeared, along
Its curved axis
Which arched them, such is
The mystery of love.)

If the process which purges the dream of perfection is compared to love, it is because Bonnefoy feels that the artist who would build in the pride of empty forms lacks compassion and trust and fails to arrive at the simplest truths. This idea is expressed powerfully in the following passage.

> *Car celui qui ne sait*
> *Le droit d'un rêve simple, qui demande*
> *A relever le sens, à apaiser*
> *Le visage sanglant, à colorer*

175

La parole blessée d'une lumière,
Celui-là, serait-il
Presque un dieu à créer presque une terre,
Manque de compassion, n'accède pas
Au vrai, qui n'est qu'une confiance, ne sent pas
Dans son désir crispé sur sa différence
La dérive majeure de la nuée.
Il veut bâtir! Ne serait-ce, exténuée,
Qu'une trace de foudre, pour préserver
Dans l'orgueil le néant de quelque forme,
Et c'est rêver, cela encore, mais sans bonheur,
Sans avoir su atteindre à la terre brève.　　　　　　　(*P,* 324)

For he who does not know
The right of a simple dream, who seeks
To enhance meaning, to soothe
The bleeding face, to color
The wounded word with light,
This man, be he
Almost a god creating almost an earth,
Lacks compassion, does not attain to
The true, which is only a trusting, does not sense
In his desire clenched over his difference
The major drifting of the cloud.
He wants to build! Be it only a feeble
Trace of lightning, to preserve
In pride the emptiness of some form,
And this is dreaming too, but without joy,
Without having known how to reach the brief earth.

The poem ends with the closing up of the wing of the impossible aspiration which had opened in the first pages of the book. The poet accepts the notion of words "comme le ciel / Aujourd'hui / Quelque chose qui s'assemble, qui se disperse" ("like the sky / Today / Something that gathers together, that breaks apart") (*P,* 329), the idea that they are "infini / Mais tout entier soudain dans la flaque brève" ("infinite / But fully captured all at once in the brief pool") (*P,* 329). These lines, which are the last lines of the poem, are a recapitulation of the wisdom of Bonnefoy's poetic research: the eternal is reflected in the moment that passes, and vision is deepened in provisional expression.[24]

*　　*　　*

Dans le leurre du seuil is the last book of Bonnefoy's poetry to have appeared.[25] Ten years separated its publication from that of *Pierre écrite,* prompting some to have feared real impasse; or, as Richard Vernier put it in his review of *Leurre*, "on a pu avoir un moment l'impression que l'œuvre d'Yves Bonnefoy allait, telle Douve-rivière, se perdre dans les sables" ("one got the feeling for a moment that Yves Bonnefoy's work was going to vanish in the sands, like the river Douve").[26] Many passages in *Leurre*, of course, speak about the difficulties of ordering and constructing.

> *Aujourd'hui la distance entre les mailles*
> *Existe plus que les mailles,*
> *Nous jetons un filet qui ne retient pas.*
> *Achever, ordonner,*
> *Nous ne le savons plus.*   (P, 276)

> Today the space between the meshes
> Exists more than the meshes themselves,
> We throw out a net that cannot hold.
> We no longer know how
> To finish or organize.

The notion of a crumbling habitation merges with the idea of a disintegrating project of "a single book [of poetry] in at least four parts."[27]

> *Regarde,*
> *Le quatrième mur s'est descellé,*
> *Entre lui et la pile du côté nord*
> *Il y a place pour la ronce*
> *Et les bêtes furtives de chaque nuit.*
> *Le quatrième mur et le premier*
> *Ont dérivé sur la chaîne,*
> *Le sceau de la présence a éclaté*
> *Sous la poussée rocheuse.*
> *J'entre donc par la brèche au cri rapide.*   (P, 277)

> Look,
> The fourth wall has come unsealed,
> Between it and the pile on the north side
> There is room for the brambles
> And the furtive animals of every night.
> The fourth wall and the first
> Have shifted on the chain,
> The seal of presence has burst
> Beneath the rocky thrust.
> So I pass through the breach with a rapid cry.

It is difficult not to read this passage as speaking about what is happening to Bonnefoy while working on *Leurre*—which would be the last of the four walls of the house of poetry he had dreamed ("mais par mirage peut-être")[28] of constructing. Certainly what we have in this last book is a very new and different Bonnefoy in many respects. Gone, most visibly, are the emblematic references to the sacred: the Phoenix, the sword, the salamander. A plain pointing to evidence is now the poet's deepest desire. This is not to say, of course, that the book now dispenses entirely with the mediations and allusions which characterized much of the former work. But the Poussin paintings and Shakespeare's *The Winter's Tale* are evoked as "mediations" that speak about the need to abandon mediations, that urge us to loosen a too rigorous hold on those shaping forces—on those *images*—which can imprison or stifle the world. In this sense, Bonnefoy evokes these works as "reflections" of the deepest and most important concerns of the poem.

Philippe Jaccottet sees *Leurre* as marking the point at which Bonnefoy has "for the first time set foot in the concrete, namable reality of a particular place, of a period that can be given a date—the step toward 'the love of mortal things' that for so long was merely wished for, has been taken."[29] Bonnefoy is striving here for a fuller recognition that "the sign is life / In the tree of the transparency of what is" (*P*, 278). There is, of course, a danger here which Jaccottet has expressed very well.

> But in the real, in the immediate, isn't there something that can lead our knowledge astray, that can confuse the all too beautiful, the all too clear paths we were following—at the risk, it is true, of reducing us to silence? The being stalked by a certain poetry is like a wild animal that dies when captured. But can one cease being this avid hunter?[30]

The future for Bonnefoy? I have already said that *Dans le leurre du seuil* is characterized by a special attention to the question of the future—to that "child / Who carries the world" (*P*, 258), who "runs ahead of us joyfully / Toward his unknown life" (*P*, 308) and in whom the poet imagines the reconciliation of former oppositions.

> *Désir se fit Amour par ses voies nocturnes*
> *Dans le chagrin des siècles; et par beauté*
> *Comprise, par limite acceptée, par mémoire*
> *Amour, le temps, porte l'enfant, qui est le signe.*   (*P*, 306)

> Desire turned to Love by its noctural paths
> In the sorrow of the centuries; and by beauty
> Understood, by limit accepted, by memory
> Love, time, bears the child who is the sign.

Speaking of the "poet of the time to come" in a recent (1976) essay on Rimbaud, Bonnefoy has said that this poet tries to establish contact with origin where it "empties itself of what denies it": "His act of memory is already a projection forward, across the present darkness of history"

(*NR*, 216). It is in this sense that Bonnefoy will evoke "God the child and still to be born" ("Dieu enfant et à naître encore") (*P*, 281). And the child-sign bears witness to the pure incarnation, is the simple designation of life—forever reuttered—which has been the object of the poet's quest, the reason for his effort at self-mastery.

Friedhelm Kemp has written of the child in Bonnefoy's work in a particularly moving way.

> In Bonnefoy's work, for the first time in a very long while, the child is restored to his proper place: *the child who is the sign*; and in such a way that, each day, the world is organized anew around him, acquires, thanks to him, and for him, a purer meaning, and the ever renewed search for such a meaning thus appears an inescapable duty. I think that it would not be impossible to show what is missing in art and literature wherever the child "has lost his right of expression" (Konrad Weiss); how many ignominies, not only in art and literature, are linked to the loss of respect for the child; respect that we owe him and that it should seem almost impossible to refuse him consciously.[31]

Claudel, too, in that elliptical recounting of the moment of his conversion in Notre Dame, that moment which, as he says, came to "dominate his entire life," mentions, above all, an intuition into the essential *innocence* of God: "I had had suddenly a heartrending sense of the innocence, of the eternal child in God—an ineffable revelation."[32] Bonnefoy's future development will no doubt show a continued concern for this child.

When the poet writes in *Leurre* that "the seal of presence has burst," he may be thought of as indicating that things will now speak for themselves. The first four books of poetry may be seen as a theater of self-knowing, as the struggle toward self-mastery. One has the unmistakable feeling that this process has come, naturally and of itself, to an end. Doubtless Yves Bonnefoy is of those to whom "the simple acceptance of oneself (powers as much as limitations)" (*AP*, 127) is granted only after struggle and resistance—one for whom, therefore, the "radiance beyond the image" (*NR*, 362) is achieved only with difficulty, rejoined only through "a dialectic . . . of representation and presence" (*NR*, 362). *Dans le leurre du seuil* may perhaps be viewed, however, as the indication of a stronger, more assured acceptance. And Yves Bonnefoy perhaps is closer now to the "musical union," to that state when "the world and the spirit are in harmony" (*NR*, 362). One looks forward to his future work with curiosity, it is true, but also with confidence.

Notes

CHAPTER 1

1. Bonnefoy, *Du mouvement et de l'immobilité de Douve,* suivi de *Hier régnant désert* (Paris: Gallimard, Collection Poésie, 1970), 222.

2. Bonnefoy, *L'Improbable* (Paris: Mercure de France, 1980), 20.

3. John E. Jackson, *Yves Bonnefoy* (Paris: Seghers, 1976), 178.

4. Richard Vernier, "Prosodie et silence dans un recueil d'Yves Bonnefoy," *Studia Neophilologica* 45 (1973):290.

5. Paul Claudel speaks of the Alexandrine as "something barbarous, at once childish and old-fashioned, pawnlike and mechanical, invented to rob the deepest vibrations of the soul, the sonorous experiments of the Psyche of their most innocent accents, of their most delicate flower." "Réflexions sur le vers français" in *Positions et propositions* (Paris: Gallimard, 1928), 59.

6. Vernier, 292.

7. See F. C. St. Aubyn, "Yves Bonnefoy: First Existential Poet," *Chicago Review* 27 (1964):118–29.

8. See Plotinus, *The Enneads,* trans. Stephen MacKenna (London: Faber and Faber, 1956), xxvi.

9. Bonnefoy, "Entretien avec John E. Jackson," *L'Arc* 66 (October 1976):88.

10. Bonnefoy, "Readiness, Ripeness: Hamlet, Lear," Preface to William Shakespeare, *Hamlet, Le Roi Lear,* trans. Yves Bonnefoy (Paris: Gallimard, Collection Folio, 1978), 14.

11. Martin Heidegger, *Being and Time,* trans. John MacQuarrie and Edward Robinson (New York: Harper and Row, 1962), 262.

12. See note 1 above.

13. See Jackson, *Yves Bonnefoy,* 179.

14. See *Popol Vuh, The Sacred Book of the Ancient Quiche Maya,* English Version by Delia Goetz and Sylvanus G. Morley from the Translation of Adrián Recinos (Norman: University of Oklahoma Press, 1950), 3–76.

15. See Jackson, *Yves Bonnefoy,* 179.

16. *Popol Vuh,* 87.

17. "Entretien avec John E. Jackson," 89.

18. "Readiness, Ripeness: Hamlet, Lear," 23.

19. Claudel, "Préface aux Oeuvres d'Arthur Rimbaud," in *Positions et propositions,* 133.

20. Paul Claudel, *Oeuvre poétique,* new ed., ed Jacques Petit (Paris: Bibliothèque de la Pléiade, 1967), 684.

21. See "Entretien avec John E. Jackson," 88.

22. Lev Shestov, *Potestas Clavium,* trans. with intro. by Bernard Martin (Athens: Ohio University Press, 1968), 18.

23. Jackson, *Yves Bonnefoy,* 180.

24. For Bonnefoy's reservations about Piero, for a discussion of what the poet considers the abolition of existential time in the painter's work, see "Le Temps et l'intemporel dans la peinture du Quattrocento," in *I,* 81–82.

25. "Here there might be torment, but not death," *Purgatorio*, XXVII, 21.

26. Bonnefoy, "On the Translation of Form in Poetry," in *World Literature Today* 53, no. 3 (summer 1979):379.

27. Bonnefoy, "Shakespeare and the French Poet," *Encounter* 105 (June 1962):41.

28. Graham Dunstan Martin, "Bonnefoy's Shakespeare Translations," in *World Literature Today* 53, no. 3 (summer 1979):470.

29. "Shakespeare and the French Poet," 43.

30. Ibid., 43.

31. Roland Barthes, *Camera Lucida. Reflections on Photography*, trans. Richard Howard (New York: Hill and Wang, 1981), 109. In another place Barthes writes: "The *studium* is ultimately always coded, the *punctum* is not. . . . What I can name cannot really prick me" (51).

32. "Shakespeare and the French Poet," 43.

33. Bonnefoy, "Gilbert Lely" (*tiré à part* through courtesy of the author) (Paris: Thierry Bouchard, 1979), 5.

34. Ibid., 8.

35. Paul Claudel–Jacques Rivière, *Correspondance 1907–1914* (Paris: Librairie Plon, 1926), 156.

CHAPTER 2

1. Fyodor Dostoevsky, *The Brothers Karamazov*, trans. Constance Garnett (New York: Macmillan Company, 1926), 265.

2. See *The New Oxford Annotated Bible with Apocrypha*, ed. Herbert G. May and Bruce M. Metzger (New York: Oxford University Press, 1973), 1174.

3. *The Brothers Karamazov*, 265.

4. See *la Sainte Bible, traduite en français sous la direction de l'École Biblique de Jerusalem* (Paris: Les Éditions du Cerf, 1961), 1293.

5. See *The Jerome Biblical Commentary* (Englewood Cliffs, N.J.: Prentice-Hall, Inc., 1968).

6. Bonnefoy, "Entretien avec John E. Jackson," 89.

7. See Martin E. Marty, *A Short History of Christianity* (New York: William Collins and World Publishing Co., Fontana Books, 1959), 77–94. See also J. W. C. Ward, *A History of the Early Church to A.D. 500* (London: Methuen and Co., 1937). See also Hans Jonas, *The Gnostic Religion: The Message of the Alien God and the Beginnings of Christianity*, 2d., enlarged (Boston: Beacon Press, 1963). For more recent discussions of the question in light of the discoveries at Nag Hammadi, see Elaine Pagels, *The Gnostic Gospels* (New York: Random House, 1979; Vintage Books, 1981) and *The Nag Hammadi Library*, ed. James M. Robinson (San Francisco: Harper and Row, Publishers, 1981).

8. Poussin's painting *Paysage au serpent* (*Landscape with a Man Killed by a Snake*) is an excellent example of what I mean. No artist typifies the moral evaluation of art by the artist more for Bonnefoy than Nicolas Poussin. For Bonnefoy, the art of Poussin is "determined by preoccupations that are more moral than religious, or in any case, Christian . . ." (*Rome 1630*, 110). In the *Landscape with a Man Killed by a Snake* of 1648 a rational ordering creates a series of logically coordinated steps from the tranquil and dreamily removed landsape in the background to the scene of horror and strangulation in the foreground. The serenity of the background exists on three levels: noble, majestic mountains in the distance; perfected structures and buildings beneath the mountains; the reflection of these structures in the limpid water toward the middle ground of the painting, on which may be seen fishermen in a boat. A group of travelers, oblivious to the tragedy, is resting, barely visible, in the left middle ground of the picture, but a woman with a basket of linen has thrown up her arms in reaction to a man who is closer still to the cruel fact and who has begun to flee in terror, the reflection of his moving legs caught in a pool of water or marsh. In the left foreground lies a figure completely wrapped up by a giant black snake.

Diderot, who admired this painting greatly and considered it *le pendant* of the *Et in Arcadia Ego* pictures, speaks particularly of "the immense expanse" of the work: "from the peaceful travelers in the background all the way to this ultimate spectacle of terror, what an immense expanse, and along this expanse, what a series of different emotions, all the way to you who are the last object, the completion of the picture! The whole thing is beautiful! It all holds together wonderfully! A single and unique idea gave birth to the picture. . . . These are the scenes one must know how to imagine if one wants to be a landscape painter." See Denis Diderot, *Salons III, 1767*, ed. Jean Seznec and Jean Adhémar (London: Oxford University Press, 1963), p. 268. Diderot's "reading" of the Poussin painting, expressed more than two centuries earlier, is very close to Bonnefoy's critique of the imaginary, his ontological evaluation of "the background of dream." Those who are "the most exposed to the danger," wrote Diderot, "are the ones who are the furthest from it." "They do not realize what is happening; they are untroubled" (see Diderot, *Salons III, 1767*, 268).

9. T. S. Eliot, "Baudelaire," from *Selected Prose of T. S. Eliot*, edited with an introduction by Frank Kermode (New York: Harcourt Brace, 1975), 236.

10. Stephane Mallarmé, "Hamlet," in *Igitur, Divagations, Un Coup de dés*, Préface d'Yves Bonnefoy (Paris: Gallimard, Collection Poésie, 1976), 189.

11. Bonnefoy, "Entretien avec John E. Jackson," 90.

12. Charles Baudelaire, "Exposition Universelle de 1855," in *Œuvres complètes*, ed. and anno. Y.-G. Le Dantec (Paris: Bibliothèque de la Pléiade, 1963), 972.

13. Yves Bonnefoy, "The Feeling of Transcendency," in *Yale French Studies* 31 (May 1964):137.

14. Bonnefoy, "Entretien avec John E. Jackson," 85.

15. "The Feeling of Transcendency," 137.

16. André Breton, *Manifestes du surréalisme* (Paris: Jacques Pauvert [n.d.]), 42.

17. "The Feeling of Transcendency," 135.

18. Breton, *Manifestes*, 42.

19. Bonnefoy, "Entretien avec John E. Jackson," 90.

20. Yves Bonnefoy, *Rue traversière* (Paris: Mercure de France, 1977), 63.

21. Bonnefoy, "Entretien avec John E. Jackson," 91.

22. "The Feeling of Transcendency," 136.

23. The peacock is the symbol of immortality in Fra Angelico's *Adoration of the Magi*. For Bonnefoy, Fra Angelico "was a doctrinaire, a propagandist, a man of action, as it were, attached to the service of the Church" (*I*, 142). Incarnations, for this poet, are always realized in our situation of finitude.

24. Bonnefoy, "Entretien avec John E. Jackson," 91.

25. Jean Starobinski, "On Yves Bonnefoy: Poetry between Two Worlds," trans. Mary Ann Caws in *World Literature Today* 53, no. 3 (summer 1979):391–99.

26. Frost's "The Mending Wall," Eliot's "Journey of the Magi," Eberhart's "The Ground Hog," Shapiro's "The Auto-Wreck" are examples among countless others. Bonnefoy's distinction certainly seems less valid for more recent Anglo-American poetry.

27. T. S. Eliot, "Tradition and the Individual Talent," in *The Sacred Wood: Essays on Poetry and Criticism* (London: Methuen & Co., 1920), 58.

28. Two chapters of *L'Ordalie* were published in 1975 by Maeght with illustrations by Claude Garache.

29. Yves Bonnefoy, *L'Ordalie* (Paris: Maeght, 1975), 40.

30. Bonnefoy, "Entretien avec John E. Jackson," 91.

31. Pierre-Jean Jouve, "Inconscient, spiritualité et catastrophe," in *Noces*, suivi de *Sueur de sang* (Paris: Gallimard, Collection Poésie, 1966), 142.

32. Bonnefoy, "Entretien avec John E. Jackson," 92.

33. Ibid., 86.

34. It is tempting to cite, apropos of this anonymity, some memorable lines from *Dans le*

leurre du seuil, although I am, of course, removing them from a rather different context. (See chap. 6 of the present study.)

> *Fais que je n'aie pas de visage, pas de nom*
> *Pour qu'étant le voleur je te donne plus*
> *Et l'étranger l'exil, en toi, en moi*
> *Se fasse l'origine . . .*
>
> <div align="right">(<i>P</i>, 261–62)</div>

> Make me be faceless, nameless
> So that being the thief I might give you more
> And being the stranger, the exile, in you, in me
> Might become the starting point . . .

CHAPTER 3

1. Jean Grosjean, "Yves Bonnefoy: *Du mouvement et de l'immobilité de Douve*," in *La Nouvelle Revue Française* 21 (September 1954):511.

2. Edgar Allan Poe, "The Philosophy of Composition," in *Selected Writings of Edgar Allan Poe*, ed. Edward H. Davidson (Cambridge, Mass.: Riverside Press, Houghton Mifflin Company, 1956), 458.

3. Bonnefoy has written that "the truth of *parole* exists beyond every formula. It is the life of the spirit, and no longer merely described, but in action. Original, issuing from the dwelling of the soul, distinct from the meaning of words and stronger than words" (*I*, 29).

4. Bonnefoy seems to be using these terms in a rather personal way, while taking as a general point of departure Saussure's distinction (and here I am citing Fredric Jameson's version of this distinction) between *la langue*, which is "the ensemble of linguistic possibilities or potentialities at any given moment," and *la parole*, which is "the individual act of speech, the individual and partial actualization of some of those potentialities." See Fredric Jameson, *The Prison-House of Language: A Critical Account of Structuralism and Russian Formalism* (Princeton, N.J.: Princeton University Press, 1972), 22. Bonnefoy consistently repudiates the "passivity" associated with the *langue*. Roland Barthes's *Writing Degree Zero*, published the same year as *Douve*, locates the moral resolve and choice making of writers in an area Barthes calls "writing," as opposed to "language" and "style." It is the "mode of writing" which, in Barthes's terms, makes of Form a value.

> Within any literary form, there is a general choice of tone, of ethos, if you like, and this is precisely where the writer shows himself clearly as an individual because this is where he commits himself. A language and a style are data prior to all problematics of language, they are the natural product of Time and of the person as a biological entity; but the formal identity of the writer is truly established only outside the permanence of grammatical norms and stylistic constants, where the written continuum, first collected and enclosed within a perfectly innocent linguistic nature, at last becomes a total sign, the choice of a human attitude, the affirmation of a certain Good. It thus commits the writer to manifest and communicate a state of happiness or malaise, and links the form of his utterance, which is at once normal and singular, to the vast History of the Others. A language and a style are blind forces; a mode of writing is an act of historical solidarity.

See Roland Barthes, *Writing Degree Zero*, trans. Annette Lavers and Colin Smith (New York: Hill and Wang, 1968), 13–14. An extended discussion of the terms *langue* and *parole* appears in Bonnefoy's essay on Jouve (*NR*, 251–52).

5. See Richard Ellmann, *James Joyce* (New York: Oxford University Press, 1965), 87.

6. Bonnefoy clearly shares Nathalie Sarraute's "suspicion" of the traditional "character." Her book *L'Ere du soupçon*, which would appear just three years after the publication of *Douve*, indicts *personnages-poupées* ("doll-like characters"), that is, characters "such as the old novel conceived of them (and all the old machinery used to show them off)". For Sarraute,

traditional characters "no longer manage to contain the current psychological realities." See Nathalie Sarraute, *L'Ere du soupçon* (Paris: Gallimard, 1956), 87.

7. Alex L. Gordon, "Things Dying, Things New Born: The Poetry of Yves Bonnefoy," *Mosaic* 6, no. 2 (1973):55–70.

8. Yves Bonnefoy, "Anti-Platon," in *La Révolution la Nuit* 2 (1947):15.

9. Philippe Jaccottet, "Une Lumière plus mûre," in *L'Arc* 66 (October 1976):24.

10. Yves Bonnefoy, "Entretien avec John E. Jackson," 86.

11. Alex L. Gordon, "From *Anti-Platon* to *Pierre écrite*: Bonnefoy's 'Indispensable' Death," in *World Literature Today* 53, no. 3 (summer 1979):435.

12. *Inferno*, XIX, 46–47.

13. *Inferno*, XXXIV, 104, 90, 63.

14. *Inferno*, XXXIV, 101. (Plato's Timaeus gives expression to the notion that "it is to the heavens, whence the soul first came to birth, that the divine part attaches the head or root of us and keeps the whole body upright." See *Plato's Cosmology: The "Timaeus" of Plato*, trans., with commentary, by F. M. Cornford [Indianapolis: Bobbs-Merrill Company, 1975], 353.)

15. Pierre-Jean Jouve, "Incarnation," in *Sueur de sang*, in *Noces* suivi de *Sueur de sang* (Paris: Gallimard, Poésie), 196.

16. Georges Bataille, *Œuvres complètes* 9 (Paris: Gallimard, 1979):174.

17. Georges Bataille, *L'Erotisme* (Paris: Editions de Minuit, 1957), 49.

18. *Purgatorio*, XXXI, 1, 97.

19. The mythic presentation of the poems is supported on occasion by concrete or specific "moments" of experience. The poem on the Brancacci Chapel (like the poem "Lieu de la salamandre" about which I will say more in a later place) gives a suddenly concrete and vivid sense to the abstract notion of place. It functions, here, as a metonymic or "syntagmatic" precision in a largely metaphoric or "systematic" order (in which associations by substitution predominate). (For a short discussion of these distinctions, see Roland Barthes, *Elements of Semiology*, trans. Annette Lavers and Colin Smith [New York: Hill and Wang, 1968], 58–88.) The poem "tells a story" and provides for the major concerns of the book a kind of *exemplum* through the specific tableau evoked. The light burning in the cold night represents an unflagging spiritual vigilance and obstination before the evidence of that mortality which renders "vain" the approach of the visitor.

20. Bonnefoy, *L'Ordalie*, 42.

21. See Gaëtan Picon, *L'Usage de la lecture* (Paris: Mercure de France, 1961), 199–207.

22. Bonnefoy, *L'Ordalie*, 43. See also Barthes's discussion of the differences between classical and modern poetry in "Is There Any Poetic Writing," in *Writing Degree Zero*, 41–52. For Barthes, the classical poet follows the "order of an ancient ritual"; his language is "immediately social"; his thought is "devoid of duration."

23. Lev Shestov, *Potestas Clavium*, 58.

24. *Inferno*, XVII, 112–14.

25. *Purgatorio*, XXVII, 25.

26. Soren Kierkegaard, *Concluding Unscientific Postscript*, trans. David F. Swenson and Walter Lowrie (Princeton, N.J.: Princeton University Press, 1941), 74.

27. See Shestov: "May not this man who contradicts himself be in communion with some mysterious reality? May not this confusion, this mass of inextricable contradictions hide in themselves that precisely which is indispensable, most significant, and most meaningful for us? Will it not then occur to us that the pride of the conqueror is less desirable than the humility of the conquered?" *Potestas Clavium*, 46.

28. *Purgatorio*, XXVII, 24.

29. In her book on Rimbaud, Enid Starkie has an extended discussion of color symbolism in the alchemical process. "There are seven stages, or processes," she writes, "in the production of the gold: calcination, putrefaction, solution, distillation, sublimation, conjunction and finally fixation. They produce, during the processes, and in their correct progression, the

various colours which are proof that the experiment is proceeding satisfactorily. There are three main colours. First the black—the indication of dissolution and putrefaction—and when it appears it is a sign that the experiment is going well, that the calcination has had its proper effect of breaking down the various substances. Next comes the white, the colour of purification; and the third is the red, the colour of complete success." Enid Starkie, *Arthur Rimbaud* (London: Faber and Faber, 1961), 162–63.

30. John E. Jackson, *Yves Bonnefoy* (Paris: Seghers, 1976), 179.

31. Marcel Jousse, *L'Anthropologie du Geste* (Paris: Gallimard, 1974), 35.

32. See Antonin Artaud, *Œuvres complètes* 4 (Paris: Gallimard, 1964); 51. Many other notions developed by Artaud may be applied to Bonnefoy's "theater," particularly the idea that gesture, mime, and dance ("everything that . . . appeals first of all to the senses instead of appealing primarily to the mind as does the language of words") serve to create a kind of "poetry in space . . . which will be resolved in precisely the domain of what does not belong strictly to words" (ibid., 46–47). Like Bonnefoy, Artaud felt that "we have lost all contact with true theater since we limit it to the area of what everyday thinking can reach, to the familiar or unfamiliar area of consciousness;—and if we try through theater to deal with the unconscious, it is merely to take from it what it has been able to accumulate (or conceal) of accessible, everyday experience" (ibid., 57).

Mary Ann Caws has a discussion of Artaud and of Bonnefoy in her book *The Inner Theater of Recent French Poetry* (Princeton, N.J.: Princeton University Press, 1972).

33. Artaud, 51.

34. Heidegger, *Being and Time*, trans. MacQuarrie and Robinson, 311.

CHAPTER 4

1. In fact, there are three versions of *Hier régnant désert* that I know of: the first version of 1958; a new version, substantially revised "in an effort to understand it" for the Gallimard edition of 1970; a final version, largely but not completely like the first version, for the complete *Poèmes* of 1978. It is beyond the range of the present discussion to analyze in detail the extent and significance of these changes. The Gallimard edition has only three sections, omitting the section entitled "Le Visage mortel," and placing the poems of this section in various places throughout the remaining three sections. The changes in the versions all appear interesting to me and merit an attention I will not be able to give here. Clearly, however, *Hier régnant désert* is a problematical work for Bonnefoy. On the occasion of its revision for the Gallimard edition, he wrote of it that it was "unclear and, at some points, almost foreign."

2. See Barthes: "The disintegration of language can only lead to the silence of writing." *Writing Degree Zero*, 75.

3. Arthur Rimbaud, *Oeuvres*, ed. Suzanne Bernard (Paris: Éditions Garnier Frères, 1960), 241.

4. See Dante Alighieri, *La Divina Commedia*, ed. and annot. C. H. Grandgent, rev. Charles S. Singleton (Cambridge, Mass.: Harvard University Press, 1972), 464.

5. See *Purgatorio*, XVIII.

6. Dante Alighieri, *Purgatory*, trans., with commentaries, by Dorothy L. Sayers (Baltimore, Md.: Penguin Books, 1955), 209.

7. Bonnefoy, *L'Ordalie*, 45.

8. Again see Barthes: "The word, dissociated from the husk of habitual clichés, and from the technical reflexes of the writer, is . . . freed from responsibility in relation to all possible context; it appears in one brief act, which, being devoid of reflections, declares its solitude, and therefore its innocence. This art has the very structure of suicide." *Writing Degree Zero*, 75.

9. Bonnefoy, *L'Ordalie*, 42. (In his analysis of Mallarmé's "Toast funèbre," Wallace Fowlie writes: "The dream about reality constitutes for the poetic temperament the temptation and the trap of indolence. Poetry is the subjugation of the dream to words." Fowlie, *Mallarmé* [Chicago: University of Chicago Press, 1953; Phoenix Books, 1962], 180.)

10. Barthes, *Writing Degree Zero*, 75.

11. In this connection, see Jean-Pierre Attal, "Nuit et Jour," *Critique* 161 (October 1960):870–78.

12. A piece from *Rue traversière* (1977) called "Rentrer, le soir" provides an example of this other type of memory. One has the impression here that Bonnefoy is no longer trying to formulate or reconstruct but, rather, is submitting, as in a dream, to the images which present themselves to him. Gone, in this prose-poem, are the elements of nightmare and fear. They are replaced by an atmosphere of mystery and awe. The poem is presented in simple, almost colloquial language, and the syntax, while somewhat hesitating and searching, is freer and less constrained than in the highly restrained and carefully controlled poems of *Hier*.

RENTRER, LE SOIR

Une allée de jardin botanique, avec beaucoup de ciel
rouge au-dessus des arbres humides. Et un père, une mère
des aciéries qui y ont mené leur petit enfant.
    Puis, du côté du soir, les toits sont une main qui tend
à une autre main une pierre.
    Et c'est soudain un quartier de boutiques basses et
sombres, et la nuit qui nous a suivis pas à pas a un souffle
court, qui cesse parfois; et la mère est immense près du
garçon qui grandit.

GOING HOME, IN THE EVENING

A walkway in the botanical gardens, with a lot of red
sky above the damp trees. And a father, a mother from the
steelworks who have brought their little child there.
    Then, in the direction of evening, the roofs are a hand
that offers a stone to another hand.
    And all of a sudden it's a neighborhood of humble and
somber shops, and the night which has followed us step by step
is short-winded, sometimes completely out of breath; and the
mother is enormous next to the boy's lengthening shadow.

13. Eugenio Donato, "The Ruins of Memory: Archeological Fragments and Textual Artifacts," *Modern Language Notes* 93 (1978):585.

14. See the interesting variants of this poem in the other versions of *Hier*. For instance: "Le Sphinx qui se tait demeure / Dans le sable de l'Idée. / Le Sphinx qui parle se déforme / A l'informe Oedipe livré" (Gallimard Edition, 174).

15. Charles Baudelaire, "La Beauté," in *Les Fleurs du mal*, ed. A. Adam (Paris: Editions Garnier Frères, 1961), 24.

16. See first version, as well as the Gallimard edition.

17. In his *L'Arrière-pays*, Bonnefoy speaks in this fashion of a certain tree he studies on a hillside during the funeral of one of his grandparents: "Isolated between the earth and the heavens, intense, well-defined figure—sign, deprived of meaning—I could recognize in it an individual like me, who knew henceforth that human reality has its roots in finitude" (*AP*, 106).

18. Perhaps it would be more appropriate, given Bonnefoy's tendency to look beyond specific theologies, to evoke the sword of *Hier* (a locus, as well, of contradiction)—that sword on which "un signe fut gravé / Sur la garde, au point d'espérance et de lumière" ("a sign was engraved / On the guard at the point of hope and of light") (*P*, 136).

19. That Bonnefoy is aware of the mystic literature—and of St. John of the Cross in particular—is evident from the numerous references to this literature in his essays. See, for instance, *NR*, 239; *I*, 155, 299. Bonnefoy's reservations about the approach of a St. John of the

Cross are developed in the essay on Pierre-Jean Jouve (*NR*, 235–65). In Bonnefoy's view, mystics are apt to be *trop abyssale*: "Their mystical overcoming of pain, far from being the perfect incarnation is doubtless only the absolute scandal: spirits once again dualistic having consumed more than assumed the level of the tears, the sweating of blood, the dust of Good Friday, having withdrawn from everything 'para venir a serlo todo,' in order to attain to being the all" (*NR*, 265).

By the time he came to write his piece on Jouve (1972), Bonnefoy seems to have become convinced that it was not in "la flamme d'inexister" that "l'incarnation est possible" (*NR*, 264–65).

20. *The Collected Works of St. John of the Cross*, trans. Kieran Kavanaugh, O.C.D., and Otilio Rodriguez, O.C.D., with intro. by Kieran Kavanaugh, O.C.D. (Garden City, N.Y.: Doubleday and Company, 1964), 302.

21. Ibid., 345.

22. Paul Claudel, *Mémoires improvisés* (Paris: Editions Gallimard, 1969), 117.

23. Grosjean, "Yves Bonnefoy: *Du mouvement et de l'immobilité de Douve*," 510.

24. Bonnefoy, "Readiness, Ripeness: Hamlet, Lear," 12.

25. On one level, of course, the insistence on the color grey may be seen as part of the effort to deflate writing ("nulle beauté nulle couleur ne la retiennent"—"no beauty no color can hold it" [*P*, 111]) and to reconnect with the stony real and with the limitations imposed by finitude. Thus the poet will say, "I celebrate the voice that is mingled with the color grey" (*P*, 137). On the other hand, the relative absence of color in these poems may be interpreted as the bleak landscape of loss, as the world of the Stranger, as the fate of the artist lost in his own schemes. (In "Le Bel Été," the poet tells of living in a wounded time—"greyer with each new dawn" [*P*, 105].) The feminine voice which rises at the end of the book—"verte, / Sourire calciné d'anciennes plantes sur la terre" ("green, / Charred smile of plants that once were on the earth")—promises renewal in the garden of presences, thus announcing the opening scenes of *Pierre écrite*.

26. Both Claudel and Barthes will characterize Mallarmé as "the Hamlet of writing." See Barthes, *Writing Degree Zero*, 75. Mallarmé represents, for Barthes, the "precarious moment of History in which literary language persists only the better to sing the necessity of its death" (ibid., 75). For Claudel, the "Hamlet phase" is "sympathy with the Night, complacency in suffering, the bitter communion between the darkness and the misfortune of being a man." Paul Claudel, "La Catastrophe d'Igitur," in *Positions et Propositions*, 198. Bonnefoy himself, in a poem from *Pierre écrite* which reads very much like a critique of this phase of his own work, will speak of wanting his poetic inspiration "au chevet de ma fièvre d'inexister" ("at the bedside of my fever not to live") (*P*, 176).

27. Bonnefoy, "Readiness, Ripeness: Hamlet, Lear," 24.

CHAPTER 5

1. In his essay on Sylvia Beach, published in 1963, Bonnefoy describes a dream in which he finds himself in a house which gives onto a garden "where the green of the leaves mingles with the moving blotches of orange from the ripened fruit." He wakes from this dream "into the dense singing of the birds." See *I*, 202–3.

2. The phrase leaps out at the reader with an astonishing conviction from page 126 of Bonnefoy's *Rome, 1630: L'horizon du premier Baroque* (Paris: Flammarion, 1970).

3. John E. Jackson, *Yves Bonnefoy*, 181.

4. "La main pure dormait près de la main soucieuse" ("The pure hand slept next to the careworn hand"). See Bonnefoy's essay on Pierre-Jean Jouve where the word *souci* ("care" or "worry") is defined as "ce qui peut hanter sans trouver formule" ("what haunts us without finding expression") (*NR*, 255).

5. A similar device is used in *Hier régnant désert*. The poem "A San Francesco, Le soir" (*P*, 104) begins with suspension points perhaps suggesting the "road that does not want to

end," the "torture that seizes on nothing" (*P*, 125), perhaps insisting on the continuity be-tween the more abstract evocations of despair and the specific tableau presented in the chapel—"to which you were led by incurable hope."

6. The hint of menstruation, too, is unmistakable—as such a reality not only imposes itself disruptively on the idealizing mind, but also reinstates an awareness of passing time and mor-tality. Bonnefoy consciously incorporates suggestions of menstruation into his poetry, from the early *Anti-Platon* with its insistence on the corrective *pays des robes tachées* ("land of stained dresses") (*P*, 11) to the recent *Dans le leurre du seuil* which evokes "Les lèvres dési-rant / Même quand le sang coule . . ." ("Lips that desire / Even when blood is flowing . . .") (*P*, 240).

7. The reference to the "shoulder" in a line such as this one seems to suggest that Bonnefoy may be thinking of the four figures—Night, Day, Dawn, and Twilight—Michelangelo sculp-ted for the New Sacristy of San Lorenzo. The chapel, one of the most sublime of Michelan-gelo's labors, presents "the continuous coincidence and coexistence of opposites." The fig-ures, of course, have been variously interpreted as "the emblem of the continuous change of earthly things and the brevity of human life, its tragic quality, the personification of the ele-ments of the earth and the various temperaments of man" and so forth. Night and Dawn are feminine figures, while Day and Twilight are masculine. The feminine Night figure is often seen as a "symbol of fecundity." The only statue to have attributes, Night is depicted with a diadem. A mask is at her side. (See Bonnefoy on Jouve: "And the night which has obliterated appearances, and with them aesthetic concerns as well as the desire for possession, signifies, in growing 'darker,' that the masks fall, that speech begins, and a reality in it, from within" [*NR*, 261].) And an owl is seen beneath the arch of the bent leg of Night. (Bonnefoy also places an owl in his night, as a voice says, "Je t'avais converti aux sommeils sans alarmes, / Aux pas sans lendemains, aux jours sans devenir, / A l'effraie aux buissons quand la nuit claire tombe, / Tournant vers nous ses yeux de terre sans retour"—"I had converted you to sleep without fear, / To steps without tomorrows, to days without movement, / To the owl in the bushes when the bright night comes, / Turning toward us its eyes filled with endless earth" [*P*, 209].) *Pierre écrite* deals very specifically with the four times of day, and often the abstract notion is given explicit bodily attributes. See, for instance, "Ton épaule soit l'aube" ("May your shoulder be the dawn" (*P*, 200) and "Mais l'Un se déchirant contre la jambe obscure" ("But the One tearing apart against the dark leg") (*P*, 205). See Umberto Baldini, "Sculp-ture," in *The Complete Work of Michelangelo* (New York: Reynal and Company, An Artabras Book, [n.d.]), 121–36.

8. See C. J. Jung: "From ancient times any relationship to the stars has always symbolized eternity. The soul 'comes from the stars' and returns to the stellar regions." "The Psychologi-cal Aspects of the Kore," in *The Archetypes and the Collective Unconscious*, vol. 9, part 1 of *The Collected Works of C. J. Jung*, Bollingen Series 20, trans. R. F. C. Hull (Princeton, N.J.: Princeton University Press, 1959), 196.

9. At least Bonnefoy sees this fracturing in this way. Most commentators of Plotinus's thought insist, however, that the One may not be spoken of in these terms. One of them, John N. Deck, writes of the One: "It is called the Good—the Good in the sense that all things, primarily the Nous, desire it, act toward it, act because of it (III, 8, 11, 8–10; VI, 8, 7, 3–6)—are what they are because of it (cf. VI, 7, 23, 18–24) and know by a desire to know it (V, 6, 5, 5–10). It is the good for all things. But does this mean that it is the good for itself? Obviously not, since "good for itself" involves a duality: the Good has no good, since there is nothing beyond it." John N. Deck, *Nature, Contemplation, and the One: A Study in the Philosophy of Plotinus* (Toronto: University of Toronto Press, 1967), 9.

Arthur O. Lovejoy in his book *The Great Chain of Being*, discusses the problematics of the relation of multiplicity to Oneness at great length. "The concept of Self-Sufficing Perfection, by a bold logical inversion, was—without losing any of its original implications—converted into the concept of a Self-Transcending Fecundity. A timeless and incorporeal One became the logical ground as well as the dynamic source of the existence of a temporal and material and extremely multiple and variegated universe." From this "reversal" was introduced "into European philosophy and theology the combination of ideas that for centuries was to give rise to many of the most characteristic internal conflicts, the logically and emotionally opposing strains, which mark its history—the conception of (at least) Two-Gods-in-One, of a divine completion which was yet *not* complete in itself, since it could not be itself without the existence of beings other than itself and inherently incomplete; of an Immutability which required, and expressed itself in, Change; of an Absolute which was nevertheless not truly absolute because it was related, at least by way of implication and causation, to entities whose nature was not *its* nature and whose existence and perpetual passage were antithetic to its immutable subsistence." Arthur O. Lovejoy, *The Great Chain of Being: A Study of the History of an Idea* (New York: Harper and Row, Harper Torchbooks, 1960), 49–50.

10. See John E. Jackson, *La Question du Moi, un aspect de la modernité poétique européenne* (Neuchâtel: Editions de la Baconnière, 1978), 289.

11. See Walter Friedlaender, *Nicolas Poussin: A New Approach* (New York: Harry N. Abrams), 116. See also Anthony Blunt, *Nicolas Poussin: The A. W. Mellon Lectures in the Fine Arts, 1958* (New York: Bollingen Foundation, Pantheon Books, 1967), 114.

12. The spirit of this figure may be said to pervade the book and may be thought of, in this sense, as having replaced the frenzied Maenad of *Douve*.

13. "La felicità soggetta alla morte" ("Happiness subjected to, or subdued by, death"). See Friedlaender, 150. See Blunt, 304.

14. In fact, much of the composition of the section "Pierre écrite" precedes the elaboration of the rest of the book. An edition illustrated by Raoul Ubac appeared in 1959.

15. *Rome, 1630*, 110.

16. In the work of Ubac exposed in 1966, Bonnefoy seemed to see "springing from the plowed up earth . . . those dead, lying parallel, crowded together even, already intermingled, those dead, band upon band, faceless for a long time—or more precisely, not quite yet faceless . . . so durable that they become limitless and one never ceases being close to them when one walks in the deserted countryside" (*I*, 311).

17. Ovid, *Metamorphoses*, bk. 5, lines 383–463, trans. Rolfe Humphries (Bloomington: Indiana University Press, 1955), 119–21. All citations from the *Metamorphoses* will be from this translation of the text.

18. See *The Oxford Companion to Classical Literature*, ed. Sir Paul Harvey (Oxford: The Clarendon Press, 1937); *Illustrated Encyclopaedia of the Classical World*, ed. Michael Avi Yonah and Israel Shatzman (New York: Harper and Row, 1976); *Who's Who in the Ancient World: A Handbook to the Survivors of the Greek and Roman Classics*, selected with intro. by Betty Radice (Middlesex, England: Penguin Books, 1971); *The New Century Classical Handbook*, ed. Catherine B. Avery (New York: Appleton-Century-Crofts, 1962).

Again see Jung: "It seems clear enough that the man's anima found occasion for projection in the Demeter cult. The Kore doomed to her subterranean fate, the two-faced mother, and the theriomorphic aspects of both afforded the anima ample opportunity to reflect herself, shimmering and equivocal, in the Eleusinian cult, or rather to experience herself there and fill the celebrants with her unearthly essence, to their lasting gain. For a man, anima experiences are always of immense and abiding significance." C. G. Jung, "The Psychological Aspects of the Kore," 203.

19. In fact, Keith Andrews, in a recent study (1977) of Elsheimer, argues that the painting in the Prado is a copy: "The version in the Prado, though once in Rubens's collection, cannot possibly be from Elsheimer's own hand, as it is far too superficially painted." See Keith Andrews, *Adam Elsheimer: Paintings, Drawings, Prints* (Oxford: Phaidon, 1977), 34.

20. Even in *Pierre écrite*, the category *night* is never used in any one sense. One poem, for instance, will speak of "tout mon obscur déchirement de nuit" ("all my dark night-rending") (*P*, 200).

21. "L'Humour, les ombres portées," in *I*, 192.

22. See also, for instance, the poem beginning "J'imagine souvent, au-dessus de moi," for the line, "Les lèvres et les yeux sont *souriants*" ("the lips and the eyes are *smiling*") (*P*, 219; italics mine).

23. See Plotinus, *The Enneads* (trans. MacKenna), 5.5: "Both the thing that comes to be and Being itself are carriers of a copy, since they are outflows from the power of The Primal One" (p. 407).

24. In an essay on Georges Duthuit, Bonnefoy said of Byzantine art that "it tends to produce a *place*, that is to say, to arch, to color, to embellish a room" (*NR*, 137–38). For Bonnefoy, the verb *voûter* characterizes the elaboration of meaning, the quest for centrality, and suggests as well the "hearth" or "place" of sense evoked both by him and by Plotinus.

25. See Plotinus, *The Enneads*, 4.4.11: "Diversity is simplex still; that multiple is one; for it is a Reason-Principle, which is to say a unity in variety: all Being is one; the differing being is still included in Being; the differentiation is within Being, obviously not within non-Being. Being is bound up with the unity which is never apart from it; *wheresoever Being appears, there appears its unity*" (p. 528; italics mine). Susanna Lang has translated *l'impartageable amour* by "the one love"—a bold, but highly interesting interpretation since it evokes the relation of love to unity, the way to "the One" through adherence to specific mortal beings. See *Words in Stone/Pierre écrite*, trans. Susanna Lang (Amherst: University of Massachusetts Press, 1976), 33.

26. Marcel Raymond, *Mémorial* (Paris: José Corti, 1971), 13.

27. In his book *The Four Loves* (London: Collins, Fontana Books, 1960), 89, C. S. Lewis remarks that "without Eros sexual desire, like every other desire, is a fact about ourselves. Within Eros it is rather about the Beloved. It becomes almost a mode of perception, entirely a mode of expression. It feels objective; something outside us, in the real world. That is why Eros, though the king of pleasures, always (at his height) has the air of regarding pleasure as a by-product."

28. An interesting comparison might be made between these statements and the poem on the salamander in *Douve*.

29. *Enneads*, 408.

30. In his "Dévotion"—the short litany of affirmations (which anticipates the affirmations of *Dans le leurre du seuil*) published in 1959—Bonnefoy celebrates the "patient and saving words" ("mots patients et sauveurs") (*P*, 157). Of the project of *the* book, Bonnefoy, doubtless thinking of Mallarmé, has written: "The person who has dreamed of 'another world' where certain of the aspects of this world can take on new meaning as he wishes according to another order, in itself considered 'truer' or 'more real'—this person will select rare words or even rarer feelings, and will seek the formula by means of which this secret order may be revealed to the mind. His idea of the *logos* is that it will be able to be condensed into speech at once utterable and definitive, stronger than the chance which rules the sorrowful world down here. We know about these dreams of *Books*. They are only one of the ways of searching for presence by means of appearance, which is, however, the salt that separates it" (*I*, 252–53).

31. The color appears once in *Hier régnant désert*: "—L'huile brisant aux ports de la mer cendreuse / Va-t-elle s'empourprer d'un dernier jour . . ." ("—Will the oil breaking at the ports of the ashy sea / Redden with a final day . . .") (*P*, 110).

32. Nothing is new under the sun: see Victor Hugo's "Puisque mai tout en fleurs . . ."

> *Viens! ne te lasse pas de mêler à ton âme*
> *La campagne, les bois, les ombrages charmants . . .*

> Come! never weary of blending your soul
> With the countryside, the woods, the charming shades . . .

CHAPTER 6

1. Sarah Lawall, speaking of the differences in *Leurre* on the basis of her examination of the only two sections of the poem which had appeared at the time, mentions that *Leurre* "extends and fragments syntactic patterns," that it "questions the whole idea of passing to an absolute presence," and that it "develops a far-reaching, more fluid system of images than the somewhat static, miraculous glimpses given in previous poems." Sarah Lawall and Mary Ann Caws, "A Style of Silence: Two Readings of Yves Bonnefoy's Poetry," *Contemporary Literature* 16 (spring 1975):199.

2. Edgar Allan Poe, "The Poetic Principle," in *Selected Writings of Edgar Allan Poe*, ed. Edward H. Davidson (Cambridge, Mass.: Riverside Press, Houghton Mifflin Company, 1956), 464. David Mus's response to first encounters with *Leurre* is a case in point. "The élan with which I enter the experience," he wrote in his review article in *Poetry*, "is broken page by page." *Poetry*, June 1976, 163. Mus's impatient article makes for extremely interesting reading, as his frustration leads him to raise provocative critical issues which his impatience prevents him from fully resolving.

3. John E. Jackson, *La Question du Moi*, 322.

4. Thomas Carlyle, *On Heroes, Hero-Worship, and the Heroic in History* (New York: E. P. Dutton and Company, 1908), 316–17.

5. Nietzsche says much the same thing in his *The Birth of Tragedy*. "The poems of the lyrist can express nothing that did not already lie hidden in that vast universality and absoluteness in the music that compelled him to figurative speech. Language can never adequately render the cosmic symbolism of music, because music stands in symbolic relation to the primordial contradiction and primordial pain in the heart of the primal unity, and therefore symbolizes a sphere which is beyond and prior to all phenomena. Rather, all phenomena, compared with it, are merely symbols: hence *language*, as the organ and symbol of phenomena, can never by any means disclose the innermost heart of music; language, in its attempt to imitate it, can only be in superficial contact with music; while all the eloquence of lyric poetry cannot bring the deepest significance of the latter one step nearer to us." Friedrich Nietzsche, *The Birth of Tragedy*, trans., commentary, by Walter Kaufmann (New York: Random House, Vintage Books, 1967), 55–56.

6. Again see Nietzsche: "Music . . . gives the inmost kernel which precedes all forms, or the heart of things" (*Birth of Tragedy*, 102). Music is "the immediate idea" of "the eternal life beyond all phenomena, and despite all annihilation" (104).

7. Philippe Jaccottet, "Une Lumière plus mûre," *L'Arc* 66 (October 1976):25. In his *Introduction à l'Histoire Universelle*, Michelet speaks of prose as "'the ultimate form of thought, what is furthest removed from vague and inactive reverie, what is closest to action.'" The passage from poetry to prose marks for Michelet the progress toward equality and "'intellectual levelling.'" Quoted by Enid Starkie in *Arthur Rimbaud*, 212.

8. I realize that I am setting off along the path of the so-called "paraphrase heresy," but it does seem worthwhile to try to establish this sequence.

9. This is the date given by Anthony Blunt in his *Nicolas Poussin*. See vol. 2, plate 169.

10. Arthur Rimbaud to Paul Demeny, 15 May 1871, in *Rimbaud: Complete Works, Selected Letters*, trans., with intro. and notes by Wallace Fowlie (Chicago: University of Chicago Press, 1966), 310.

11. As quoted by Mary Ellen Birkett in her essay "*Pictura, Poesis* and Landscape," *Stanford French Review*, spring 1978, 235–46. I am greatly indebted to Ms. Birkett for the viewpoint expressed in this paragraph, which summarizes the main lines of her article.

12. Diderot, *Salons III, 1767*, ed. Seznec and Adhémar, 268.

13. See also Lee W. Rensselaer, *Ut Pictura Poesis: The Humanistic Theory of Painting* (New York: Norton, 1967).

14. Jaccottet, "Une Lumière plus mûre," 26.

15. Bonnefoy's analysis of "Le Nuage rouge" of Piet Mondrian is extremely interesting in this regard. "This blue shimmering in green. . . . It is as though earth and sky were still

mingled a little, after their creation or some flood. . . . And . . . the cloud, which, in its blazing without visible origin, has an extraordinary intensity, and a highly remarkable form as well—this cloud is a letter from an unknown alphabet, but with something breathing, if not sexual, crimson mass that has thrown out its seed—, the cloud grows even more intense, offering itself as a *sign*, in the way that the sudden flight of a bird or an unusual looking rock were so often signs for the archaic mind" (*NR*, 116). Bonnefoy refers to the picture as "eminently musical" (*NR*, 116) and, in another passage, speaks of the three principal colors of "Le Nuage rouge" as "the three fundamental tones of our condition that is trying to break through its limits." These colors are the "blue of the Virgin's mantle, the emerald green of alchemy, the red with which Delacroix bloodied the Ideal" (*NR*, 117).

16. See Marcel Raymond's *Mémorial* (26) for a remarkable passage on *l'amour charnel*: "Carnal love is a highly mysterious gift that in all likelihood has its place in the unconscious. Through it, the lovers are flooded with the certainty that they are in touch for a moment with the power that engenders and advances worlds. In their eyes, everything glistens as though it were coming forth from a fountain of youth—the water, the sky, the verdure, the flowers; the slightest sensation provokes a myriad of echoes; a depth, undreamed of, opens up behind things. . . . The most moving of all, perhaps, is the incomparable tenderness revealed during the moments and the hours following love; peace is recovered in harmonies of an astonishing fullness which multiply with the humming of the blood in the arteries; sometimes there is sadness, but more frequently wonder, gratitude. 'The feeling of life immeasurably increased' (Baudelaire)—this is what carnal love can give us, better than any drug."

17. Thomas Merton, in his book *Zen and the Birds of Appetite*, insists on the distinction between Zen and Buddhism. "To regard Zen *merely* and *exclusively* as Zen Buddhism is to falsify it and, no doubt, to betray the fact that one has no understanding of it whatever. Yet this does not mean that there cannot be 'Zen Buddhists,' but these surely will realize (precisely because they are Zen-men) the difference between their Buddhism and their Zen—even while admitting that for them their Zen is in fact the purest expression of Buddhism." In Merton's analysis, what fits into social, religious, and cultural system is "Buddhist rather than Zen." See Thomas Merton, *Zen and the Birds of Appetite* (New York: New Directions Books, 1968), 1–14.

18. D. T. Suzuki, "Satori, or Enlightenment," in *Zen Buddhism: Selected Writings of D. T. Suzuki*, ed. William Barrett (Garden City, N.Y.: Doubleday Anchor Books, Doubleday and Company, 1956), 84–85.

19. Plotinus, *The Enneads*, trans. MacKenna, 408. Just how deeply indebted Bonnefoy is to the philosophy of Plotinus remains somewhat problematical. The insistence in Plotinus that the soul must learn to "take no pleasure in the things of earth" (ibid., 625), that it must take "another life as it draws nearer and nearer to God . . . all the earthly environment done away" (623), seems to contradict the most fundamental convictions of this poet of the earth. ("Whatever may have been my doubts and my contradictions," he wrote in his essay on Jouve, "I have never called into question the evidence of earth; to me, it seems to carry what is true, and I see nothing reprehensible in its incitements, in its occurrences, or in its ends" [*NR*, 241].) Plotinus is doubtless referring particularly to earthly "distractions," to "fleshly embraces" (*Enneads*, 623), and Bonnefoy's quest seems clearly to align itself with the movement in Plotinus toward "a going forth from the self, a simplifying, a renunciation, a reach toward contact and at the same time a repose" (624). And although Plotinus seems to emphasize a disdain for matter, an intellectual unity with *invisible* and perfect transcendence, his insistence on simplicity, on oneness, on the disappearance of the "craving" self finds its echoes in Bonnefoy's poetics. At the moment of illumination, of unity with God, there is, says Plotinus, "nothing within . . . or without inducing diversity; no movement . . . no passion, no outlooking desire . . . images [are left] behind" (624). "No doubt we should not speak of seeing; but we cannot help talking in dualities, seen and seer, instead of, boldly, the achievement of unity. In this seeing, we neither hold an object nor trace distinction; there is no two.

The man is changed, no longer himself nor self-belonging; he is merged with the Supreme, sunken into it, one with it: center coincides with center, for centers of circles, even here below, are one when they unite, and two when they separate; and it is in this sense that we now (after the vision) speak of the Supreme as separate. This is why the vision baffles telling; we cannot detach the Supreme to state it; if we have seen something thus detached we have failed of the Supreme which is to be known only as one with ourselves" (624).

20. See, for instance, the essay "Terre Seconde": "The experience of the One, what I call meaning, demands an attention of the body as much as of the intellect, a breathing, a balance one lives" (*NR*, 355).

21. Again see Bonnefoy's analysis of "Le Nuage rouge" of Mondrian. "A sign, that event in the sky? On condition that one not forget that it will be absolute for only a moment, that it will disappear into figures, into iridescences that are already less astonishing; and that these in turn will be transformed, endlessly, or dispelled, telling of 'change' which is always there, and no longer of a seal stamped on the world" (*NR*, 117).

22. Or, put another way: "One must struggle against the destruction of lived experience begun by all writing; one should therefore and at every moment abandon one's work as much as accomplish it: and know that it is a cloud, it too, a mass of beauties that are always questionable, of aspirations that can be surpassed, of dizzying heights, of rendings sometimes too, of sudden brightnesses" (*NR*, 122).

23. See Polixenes' speech in act 4 of *The Winter's Tale*:

> Yet Nature is made better by no mean,
> But Nature makes that mean: so over that Art,
> (Which you say adds to Nature) is an Art
> That Nature makes. . . .
> . . . .
> The Art itself, is Nature. (4.4.89–97)

24. See also Bonnefoy's essay on Pierre-Jean Jouve: "Writing is an enclosure, it's true, but mainly for the person who is absorbed there in the 'work' which is infinite" (*NR*, 265).

25. Unless, of course, one excepts the "prose-poems," which separate the narratives of *Rue traversière*.

26. Richard Vernier, "Dans la certitude du seuil: Yves Bonnefoy, aujourd'hui," *Stanford French Review*, spring 1978, 139.

27. Bonnefoy, *Du mouvement et de l'immobilité de Douve*, suivi de *Hier régnant désert*, 222.

28. Ibid.

29. Jaccottet, "Une Lumière plus mûre," 25.

30. Ibid., 26.

31. Friedhelm Kemp, "'Dans le leurre du seuil,'" in *L'Arc* 66 (October 1976):40.

32. Paul Claudel, "Ma Conversion," in *Contacts et circonstances*, in *Œuvres en prose*, ed. and anno. Jacques Petit and Charles Galpérine (Paris: Gallimard, Bibliothèque de la Pléiade, 1965), 1010.

Temperamentally and philosophically, of course, Claudel and Bonnefoy are very far apart. See, for instance, Bonnefoy's remark about Claudel "locked up in orthodoxy with the list of things" in his essay "L'Acte et le lieu de la poésie" (*I*, 118).

Select Bibliography

WORKS BY YVES BONNEFOY

1946. "Traité du pianiste." Paris: *La Révolution la Nuit.*
1947. "Anti-Platon." *La Révolution la Nuit,* second cahier, 14–15.
      "Un Barrage d'oiseaux." *Les Quatre Vents* 8:102–5.
      "Donner à vivre." *Le Surréalisme en 1947.* Paris: Maeght. 66–68.
      "L'Eclairage objectif." *Deux Sœurs,* no. 5.
1953. *Du mouvement et de l'immobilité de Douve.* Paris: Mercure de France.
1954. *Peintures murales de la France gothique. Les Fresques du XIIIe au XVe siècle.*
      Paris: Hartmann.
1958. "Critics—English and French / And the Distance between Them." *En-counter* 58 (July):39–45.
      Hier régnant désert. Paris: Mercure de France.
1959. "La Critique anglo-saxonne et la critique française." *Preuves* 95 (January):68–73.
      L'Improbable. Paris: Mercure de France.
      Pierre écrite. Ardoises taillées par Raoul Ubac. Paris: Maeght.
      "Shakespeare et le poète français." *Preuves* 100 (June):42–48.
1960. "La Décision de Rimbaud." *Preuves* 107 (January):3–16.
1961. *Rimbaud par lui-même.* Paris: Éditions du Seuil.
1962. "La Poésie d'André du Bouchet." *Critique* 179 (April):291–98.
      "La Religion de Chagall." *Derrière le Miroir,* no. 132.
      "Une Idée de la traduction." In Shakespeare, *Hamlet,* trans. Yves Bonnefoy. Paris: Mercure de France.
      "Shakespeare and the French Poet." *Encounter* 105 (June):38–43.
      "Transposer ou traduire *Hamlet.*" *Preuves* 134 (April):31–34.
1964. "Comment traduire Shakespeare." *Études Anglaises* 17 (October–November):341–51.
      "The Feeling of Transcendency." *Yale French Studies* 31 (May):135–37.
      Miró. Paris: La Bibliothèque des Arts.
      "Transpose or Translate?" *Yale French Studies* 33 (December):120–26.
      "Ubac." *Derrière le Miroir,* no. 142.
1965. *Pierre écrite.* Paris: Mercure de France.
      "Les Romans Arthuriens et la légende du Graal." *La Quête du Graal.* Ed. Albert Béguin and Yves Bonnefoy. Paris: Seuil.
1967. *Un rêve fait à Mantoue.* Paris: Mercure de France.
1968. "L'Art et le sacré. Baudelaire parlant à Mallarmé." in *L'Art dans la Société*

195

d'Aujourd'hui. Textes des conférences et entretiens organisés par les rencontres internationales de Genève, 1967. Neuchâtel: Editions de la Baconnière. 75–94.

"La Traduction de Shakespeare." *Revue d'Esthétique* 21:94–96.

1969.   "Dans le leurre du seuil." *L'Ephemère* 11:344–57.

1970.   *Du mouvement et de l'immobilité de Douve* suivi de *Hier régnant désert* et accompagné d'*Anti-Platon* et de deux essais. Paris: Gallimard, Collection Poésie.

Rome 1630: L'Horizon du premier Baroque. Paris: Flammarion.

1972.   *L'Arrière-pays.* Geneva: Éditions d'Art Albert Skira.

1973.   "Dans le leurre du seuil (autres fragments)." *L'Ephémère* 19–20 (winter–spring) 293–307.

"Hommage à Philippe Jaccottet." *Revue de Belles-Lettres*, nos. 3–4, 107–11.

"In the Threshold's Lure." Translation by Yves Bonnefoy of his *Dans le leurre du seuil* (fragments). In *Modern Poetry in Translation*. Special French Issue. 12–13.

1975.   *Dans le leurre du seuil.* Paris: Mercure de France.

"L'Egypte et quelques poèmes." *Argile* 7 (summer):5–17.

L'Ordalie. Paris: Maeght.

"Peinture, poésie; vertige, paix." *Derrière le Miroir* 213 (March):1–10. Issue on Claude Garache.

Introduction to *Tout l'Œuvre peint de Giovanni Bellini*. Anno. Terisio Pignatti. Paris: Flammarion.

1976.   "Entretien avec John E. Jackson." *L'Arc* 66 (October):85–92.

"La Poétique de Mallarmé." Preface to Mallarmé's *Igitur, Divigations, Un Coup de dés.* Paris: Gallimard. 7–40.

"La Traduction de la poésie. Une Conférence à l'ATLF." *Bulletin des Traducteurs Littéraires de France* 7 (January).

1977.   "Georges Henein." *La Quinzaine Littéraire* 253 (1–15 April).

Le Nuage rouge. Paris: Mercure de France.

"Poésie et critique." Presented to the A.I.E.F., Collège de France. July. Printed in *Les Cahiers.*

"Poésie et pensée analogique." Contribution to colloquium "Langage poétique et pensée analogique," Loches, 19–24 July. Printed in *Bulletin.*

Rue traversière. Paris: Mercure de France.

Trois Remarques sur la couleur, avec cinq gravures de Bram Van Velde. Dijon: Thierry Bouchard.

"Trois Souvenirs d'un voyage." *La Nouvelle Critique, Ecrire*, special issue, June–July.

1978.   "Miklos Bokor." Illustrated catalog for a show at Ratilly.

"Du Haiku." Introduction to *Haiku* by Roger Munier. Paris: Fayard.

"Un Héritier de Rimbaud." *Derrière le Miroir*, no. 229 (May). Issue on Palazuelo.

Mantegna. Paris: Flammarion.

Poèmes. Paris: Mercure de France.

"Readiness, Ripeness: Hamlet, Lear." Preface to William Shakespeare, *Hamlet, Le Roi Lear*, trans. Yves Bonnefoy. Paris: Gallimard, Collection Folio.

"Rimbaud: 'Les Reparties de Nina.'" *Le Lieu et la Formule*. Neuchâtel: La Baconnière, 1978.

1979. "Deux Soirées au théâtre." *World Literature Today* 53, no. 3 (summer): 370–74.

Gilbert Lely. Paris: Thierry Bouchard.

"On the Translation of Form in Poetry." *World Literature Today* 53, no. 3 (summer):374–79.

1980. *L'Improbable* suivi de *Un Rêve fait à Mantoue*, rev. ed., enlarged. Paris: Mercure de France.

1981. *Entretiens sur la poesie*. Neuchâtel, Switzerland: Editions de la Baconnière.

1983. *Presence et Image*. Paris: Mercure de France.

WORKS ON YVES BONNEFOY

Abe, Yoshio. "La Tentation de l'Intelligible." *L'Arc* 66 (October 1976):71–82.

Agosti, Stephano. "Violence de l'oubli." *L'Arc* 66 (October 1976):42–48.

Albert, Walter. "Yves Bonnefoy and the Architecture of Poetry." *MLN* 82 (December 1967):590–603.

———. "Yves Bonnefoy. *Un Rêve fait à Mantoue*." Rev., *French Review* 65 (March 1969):629–30.

Attal, Jean-Pierre. "Nuit et jour." *Critique* 161 (October 1960):870–78.

———. "La Quête d'Yves Bonnefoy." *Critique* 217 (June 1965):535–40.

Blanchot, Maurice. "Comment découvrir l'obscur?" *La Nouvelle Revue Française* 83 (November 1959):867–79.

———. "Le Grand Refus." *La Nouvelle Revue Française* 82 (October 1959):678–89.

———. "Rimbaud et l'œuvre finale." *La Nouvelle Revue Française* 18 (1961): 293–303.

Blot, Jean. "Le Progrès d'Yves Bonnefoy." *La Nouvelle Revue Française*, 282 (June 1976):71–74.

Bosquet, Alain. "Yves Bonnefoy ou la fuite devant le signifiant." In *Verbe et vertige. Situations de la poésie*. Paris: Hachette, 1961. 165–73.

Breunig, Leroy C. "Bonnefoy's Hamlet." *World Literature Today* 53, no. 3 (summer 1979):461–65.

Caws, Mary Ann. *The Inner Theater of Recent French Poetry*. Princeton, N.J.: Princeton University Press, 1972.

———. "Reading, the Cast Shadows: A Reflection." *World Literature Today* 53, no. 3 (summer 1979):450–56.

———, and Sarah N. Lawall. "A Style of Silence: Two Readings of Yves Bonnefoy's Poetry." *Contemporary Literature* 16 (spring 1975):193–217.

Clancier, Georges-Emmanuel. "Yves Bonnefoy. *Hier régnant désert*." Rev., *Mercure de France* 334 (October 1958):293–98.

Deloffre, Frédéric. "Versification traditionnelle et versification libérée d'après un recueil d'Yves Bonnefoy." In *Le Vers français au 20ᵉ siècle*: Colloque organisé par le Centre de philologie et de littérature romanes de l'Université de Strasbourg du 3 mai au 6 mai 1966. Published by Monique Parent. Paris: Librarie C. Klincksieck, 1967. 43–64.

Diéguez, Manuel de. "Yves Bonnefoy et la critique du style." *Esprit* 12 (December 1960):2120–28.

Duits, Charles. "L'Énigme poétique d'Yves Bonnefoy." *Critique* 137 (October 1958):832–37.

Esteban, Claude. "L'Écho d'une demeure." *La Nouvelle Revue Française* 225 (September 1971):19–34.

Frank, Joseph. "Yves Bonnefoy: Notes of an Admirer." *World Literature Today* 53, no. 3 (summer 1979):399–405.

Glissant, Edouard. "Note sur Bonnefoy et le chemin de la vérité." *Les Lettres Nouvelles* 65 (November 1958):583–87.

Gordon, Alex L. "From *Anti-Platon* to *Pierre écrite*: Bonnefoy's 'Indispensable' Death." *World Literature Today* 53, no. 3 (summer 1979):430–40.

———. "Things Dying, Things New Born: The Poetry of Yves Bonnefoy." *Mosaic* 6 (winter 1973):55–70.

Greene, Robert W. "Bonnefoy and Art Criticism: A Preliminary Study." *World Literature Today* 53, no. 3 (summer 1979):447–50.

Grosjean, Jean. "Yves Bonnefoy: *Du mouvement et de l'immobilité de Douve*." *La Nouvelle Revue Française* 21 (September 1954):510–11.

Hofstadter, Marc. "The Search for Transcendence in Yves Bonnefoy's 'Un feu va devant nous.'" *Romance Notes* 19, no. 1 (1978):1–6.

An Homage to French Poet Yves Bonnefoy. World Literature Today, vol. 53, no. 3 (summer 1979).

Jaccottet, Philippe. "Une Lumière plus mûre." *L'Arc* 66 (October 1976):24–27.

———. "Pierre écrite." Rev., *La Nouvelle Revue Française* 149 (May 1965):919–21.

———. "Vers le 'Vrai Lieu.'" *L'Entretien des Muses. Chronique de poésie.* Paris: Gallimard, 1968. 251–57.

Jackson, John E. "En personne." *L'Arc* 66 (October 1976):82–85.

———. *La Question du Moi, un aspect de la modernité poétique européenne.* Neuchâtel: Éditions de la Baconnière, 1978.

———. "Rilke, Eliot and Bonnefoy as Readers of Baudelaire." *World Literature Today* 53, no. 3 (summer 1979):456–61.

———. *Yves Bonnefoy.* Paris: Seghers, 1976.

Jourdain, L. "Rimbaud par un autre." *Tel Quel* 6 (summer 1961):47–52.

Jourdan, Pierre-Albert. "L'Écriture comme nuée." *L'Arc* 66 (October 1976):67–71.

Kanes, Martin. "Bonnefoy, Architect." *World Literature Today* 53, no. 3 (summer 1979):440–47.

Kemp, Friedhelm. "Dans le leurre du Seuil." *L'Arc* 66 (October 1976):37–41.

Lang, Susanna. "The Word and the Place Between." *World Literature Today* 53, no. 3 (summer 1979):417–21.

Lawall, Sarah N. Introduction to Yves Bonnefoy, *Pierre écrite/Words in Stone*, trans. Susanna Lang. Amherst: University of Massachusetts Press, 1976.

———. "Poetry, Taking Place." *World Literature Today* 53, no. 3 (summer 1979):411–17.

————, and Mary Ann Caws. "A Style of Silence: Two Readings of Yves Bonnefoy's Poetry." *Contemporary Literature* 16 (spring 1975):193–217.

————. "Yves Bonnefoy and Denis Roche. Art and the Art of Poetry." In Mary Ann Caws, ed., *About French Poetry from Dada to "Tel Quel." Text and Theory.* Detroit: Wayne State University Press, 1974. 69–81, 91–92.

Lawler, James R. "Celebrating the Obscure." *World Literature Today* 53, no. 3 (summer 1979):405–11.

Madeleine-Perdrillat, Alain. "L'Arrière-pays et la patrie inconnue de Vinteuil." *L'Arc* 66 (October 1976):48–56.

Magny, Olivier de. "*L'Improbable* d'Yves Bonnefoy." Rev., *Les Lettres Nouvelles* 16 (17 June 1959):12–14.

————. "Yves Bonnefoy." In Bernard Pingaud, ed., *Écrivains d'aujourd'hui, 1940– 1960. Dictionnaire anthologique et critique.* Paris: Bernard Grasset, 1960. 127–36.

Martin, Graham Dunstan. "Bonnefoy's Shakespeare Translations." *World Literature Today* 53, no. 3 (summer 1979):465–70.

————. "Yves Bonnefoy and the Temptation of Plato." *Forum for Modern Language Studies* 2 (April 1974):95–108.

Maurin, Mario. "On Bonnefoy's Poetry." *Yale French Studies* 21 (1958):16–22.

Munier, Roger. "Le Cri." *L'Arc* 66 (October 1976):16–24.

————. "Le Pays. Yves Bonnefoy—*Un Rêve fait à Mantoue. Pierre écrite. L'Arrière-pays.*" *Critique* 325 (June 1974):515–28.

Mus, David. "Stances on Love." *Poetry*, June 1976, 163–77.

Picon, Gaëtan. "S'il est aujourd'hui une poésie . . ." *L'Arc* 66 (October 1976):41–42.

————. *L'Usage de la lecture*, vol. 2. Paris: Mercure de France, 1961. 195–209.

Piroué, Georges. "Bonnefoy ou l'acte de dégager la présence dans l'absence." *Mercure de France* 333 (June 1958):365–68.

————. "Bonnefoy, Shakespeare et la tragédie." *Mercure de France* 340 (December 1960):732–36.

Pons, Christian. "Transposition et traduction. A propos du *Hamlet* d'Yves Bonnefoy." *Études Anglaises* 17 (October-December 1964):536–48.

Poulet, Georges. "Un Idéalisme renversé." *L'Arc* 66 (October 1976):58–67.

Prothin, Annie. "The Substantive Language of Yves Bonnefoy." *Sub-Stance* 20 (1978):45–58.

————. "Yves Bonnefoy: A Bibliography." *Bulletin of Bibliography* 36, no. 3 (1979):128–43.

Raillard, Georges. "Yves Bonnefoy par sa poésie et ses essais sur les peintres livre passage à un ailleurs." *La Quinzaine Littéraire* 253 (1–5 April 1977):4–5.

Richard, Jean-Pierre. "Yves Bonnefoy, entre le nombre et la nuit." *Critique* 168 (May 1961):387–411.

Roudant, Jean. "Les Arrière-livres." *L'Arc* 66 (October 1976):56–58.

————. "Le Lit de la poésie." *Critique* 254 (July 1968):635–47.

Saillet, Maurice. "Du mouvement et de l'immobilité de Douve." *Les Lettres Nouvelles* 9 (November 1953):1, 166–72.

————. *Sur la route de Narcisse.* Paris: Mercure de France, 1958.

St. Aubyn, F. C. "Yves Bonnefoy: First Existential Poet." *Chicago Review* 27 (1964):118–29.

Schneider, Pierre. "La Poésie d'Yves Bonnefoy." *Critique* 83 (April 1954):293–302.

Schwab, Raymond. "*Du mouvement et de l'immobilité de Douve.*" Rev., *Mercure de France* 319 (December 1953):682–87.

Stamelman, Richard. "The Allegory of Loss and Exile in the Poetry of Yves Bonnefoy." *World Literature Today* 53, no. 3 (summer 1979):421–30.

———. "Landscape and Loss in Yves Bonnefoy and Philippe Jaccottet." *French Forum* 5 (January 1980):30–47.

Starobinski, Jean. "On Yves Bonnefoy: Poetry, between Two Worlds." Trans. Mary Ann Caws. *World Literature Today* 53, no. 3 (summer 1979):391–99.

———. "La Prose du voyage." *L'Arc* 66 (October 1976):3–9.

Vernier, Richard. "Dans la certitude du seuil: Yves Bonnefoy aujourd'hui." *Stanford French Review*, spring 1978, 139–47.

———. "Locus Patriae." *L'Arc* 66 (October 1976):9–16.

———. "Prosodie et silence dans un recueil d'Yves Bonnefoy." *Studia Neophilologica* 45 (1973):288–97.

———. "Un Récit d'Yves Bonnefoy." *Romanic Review* 63 (February 1972):34–41.

———. "Words like the Sky: The Accomplishment of Yves Bonnefoy." *World Literature Today* 53, no. 3 (summer 1979):384–91.

Vigée, Claude. "L'Enfant qui porte le monde." *L'Arc* 66 (October 1976):27–37.

———. *Révolte et louanges: Essais sur la poésie moderne.* Paris: José Corti, 1962. 126–27.

Wevill, David. "Death's Dream Kingdom." *Delos* 4 (1970):235–41.

York, R. A. "Bonnefoy and Mallarmé: Aspects of Intertextuality." *Romanic Review* 71, no. 3 (May 1980):307–18.

Yves Bonnefoy. L'Arc, vol. 66 (October 1976).

OTHER WORKS CONSULTED

Alighieri, Dante. *La Divina Commedia.* Ed. and anno. C. H. Grandgent. Rev. Charles S. Singleton. Cambridge, Mass.: Harvard University Press, 1972.

———. *The Divine Comedy.* 6 vols. Trans., with Commentary, by Charles S. Singleton. Princeton, N.J.: Princeton University Press, Bollingen Series 50, 1970 (*Inferno*); 1973 (*Purgatorio*); 1975 (*Paradiso*).

———. *Hell.* Trans. Dorothy L. Sayers. Baltimore: Penguin Books, 1949.

———. *Paradise.* Trans. Dorothy L. Sayers and Barbara Reynolds. Baltimore: Penguin Books, 1962.

———. *Purgatory.* Trans. Dorothy L. Sayers. Baltimore: Penguin Books, 1955.

Andrews, Keith. *Adam Elsheimer: Paintings, Drawings, Prints.* Oxford: Phaidon, 1977.

Artaud, Antonin. *Le Théâtre et son double*, in *Oeuvres complètes*, vol. 4. Paris: Gallimard, 1964.

Bachelard, Gaston. *On Poetic Imagination and Reverie.* Selections from the Works of Gaston Bachelard. Trans., with Intro., by Colette Gaudin. New York: Bobbs-Merrill Co., The Library of Liberal Arts, 1971.

———. *La Poétique de l'espace*. 3d ed. Paris: Presses Universitaires de France, 1961.

Baldini, Umberto, et al. *The Complete Work of Michelangelo*. New York: Reynal and Company, An Artabras Book, [n.d.].

Barthes, Roland. *Camera Lucida. Reflections on Photography*, trans. Richard Howard. New York: Hill and Wang, 1981.

———. *Elements of Semiology*. Trans. Annette Lavers and Colin Smith. New York: Hill and Wang, 1968.

———. *Writing Degree Zero*. Trans. Annette Lavers and Colin Smith. New York: Hill and Wang, 1968.

Bataille, Georges. *L'Erotisme*. Paris: Éditions de Minuit, 1957.

———. *Œuvres complètes*, vol. 9. Paris: Gallimard, 1979.

Baudelaire, Charles. *Les Fleurs du mal*. Edition de A. Adam. Paris: Garnier Frères, 1961.

———. *Œuvres complètes*. Ed. and anno. Y.-G. LeDantec. Rev. Claude Pichois. Paris: Gallimard, Bibliothèque de la Pléiade, 1961.

Bazin, Germain. *The Avant-Garde in Painting*. Trans. Simon Watson Taylor. New York: Simon and Schuster, 1969.

Birkett, Mary Ellen. "*Pictura, Poesis* and Landscape." *Stanford French Review*, spring 1978, 235–46.

Blunt, Anthony. *Nicolas Poussin*. New York: Bollingen Foundation, Pantheon Books, 1967.

Breton, André. *Manifestes du Surréalisme*. Paris: Jacques Pauvert [n.d.].

———. *Nadja*. Paris: Gallimard, Folio, 1964.

Brown, Norman O. *Life Against Death: The Psychoanalytical Meaning of History*. Middletown, Conn.: Wesleyan University Press, 1959.

———. *Love's Body*. New York: Random House, Vintage Books, 1966.

Bruns, Gerald L. *Modern Poetry and the Idea of Language*. New Haven: Yale University Press, 1974.

Bultmann, Rudolf, et al. *Kerygma and Myth*. Ed. Hans Werner Bartsch. Rev. Reginald H. Fuller. New York: Harper and Row, Harper Torchbooks, The Cloister Library, 1961.

Carlyle, Thomas. *On Heroes, Hero-Worship, and the Heroic in History*. New York: E. P. Dutton and Company, 1908.

Chatain, Jacques. *Georges Bataille*. Paris: Seghers, 1973.

Clark, Kenneth. *Piero della Francesca*. London: Phaidon, 1969.

———. *Landscape into Art*. Boston: Beacon Press, 1961.

Claudel, Paul. *Mémoires improvisés. Quarante et un entretiens avec Jean Amrouche*. Ed. Louis Fourner. Paris: Gallimard, Collection Idées, 1969.

———. *Œuvre poétique*. Intro. Stanislas Fumet. Paris: Gallimard, Bibliothèque de la Pléiade, 1962.

———. *Œuvres en prose*. Preface by Gaëtan Picon. Texts ed. and anno. Jacques Petit and Charles Galpérine. Paris: Gallimard, Bibliothèque de la Pléiade, 1965.

———. *Positions et propositions*. Paris: Gallimard, 1928.

———. *Théâtre*. 2 vols. Intro. Jacques Madaule. Paris: Gallimard, Bibliothèque de la Pléiade, 1947–48.

Claudel, Paul, and Jacques Rivière. *Correspondence 1907–1914*. Paris: Plon, 1926.

Cohn, Robert Greer. *Mallarmé's "Un Coup de dés": An Exegesis*. New Haven: Yale French Studies, 1949.

———. *The Poetry of Rimbaud*. Princeton, N.J.: Princeton University Press, 1973.

———. *Toward the Poems of Mallarmé*. Expanded ed. Berkeley: University of California Press, 1980.

Contemporary French Poetry: Fourteen Witnesses of Man's Fate. Ed. Alexander Aspel and Donald Justice. Intro. Alexander Aspel. Postface by Paul Engle. Ann Arbor: University of Michigan Press, 1965.

Deck, John N. *Nature, Contemplation, and the One: A Study in the Philosophy of Plotinus*. Toronto: University of Toronto Press, 1967.

Diderot, Denis. *Salons III, 1767*. Ed. Jean Seznec and Jean Adhémar. London: Oxford University Press, 1963.

Donato, Eugenio. "The Ruins of Memory: Archeological Fragments and Textual Artifacts." *MLN* 93 (1978):575–96.

Dostoevsky, Fyodor. *The Brothers Karamazov*. Trans. Constance Garnett. New York: Macmillan Company, 1926.

Duthuit, Georges. *Représentation et présence*. Intro. Yves Bonnefoy. Paris: Flammarion, 1974.

Egyptian Book of the Dead: The Papyrus of Ani in the British Museum. Trans. E. A. Wallis Budge. New York: Dover Publications, 1967.

Eliot, T. S. *The Complete Poems and Plays 1909–1950*. New York: Harcourt Brace and World, 1952.

———. *Four Quartets*. London: Faber and Faber, 1959.

———. *The Sacred Wood: Essays on Poetry and Criticism*. London: Methuen and Co., 1920.

———. *Selected Prose of T. S. Eliot*. Ed. with Intro. by Frank Kermode. New York: Harcourt Brace, 1975.

Ellmann, Richard. *James Joyce*. New York: Oxford University Press, 1965.

Encyclopaedia Britannica. 11th ed. New York: Encyclopaedia Britannica, 1910–11.

European Literary Theory and Practice from Existential Phenomenology to Structuralism. Ed. with Intro. by Vernon W. Gras. New York: Dell Publishing Co., A Delta Book, 1973.

Fowlie, Wallace. *Mallarmé*. Chicago: University of Chicago Press, 1953; Phoenix Books, 1962.

Friedlaender, Walter. *Nicolas Poussin: A New Approach*. New York: Harry N. Abrams [n.d.].

Greene, Robert W. *Six French Poets of Our Time: A Critical and Historical Study*. Princeton, N.J.: Princeton University Press, 1979.

Heidegger, Martin. *Being and Time*. Trans. John MacQuarrie and Edward Robinson. New York: Harper and Row, 1962.

Higgins, John J., S.J. *Thomas Merton on Prayer*. Garden City, N.Y.: Doubleday and Co., Image Books, 1975.

Illustrated Encyclopaedia of the Classical World. Ed. Michael Avi Yonah and Israel Shatzman. New York: Harper and Row, 1976.

An Introduction to Haiku, An Anthology of Poems and Poets from Bashō to Shiki. With Translations and Commentary by Harold G. Henderson. Garden City, N.Y.: Doubleday and Company, Doubleday Anchor Books, 1958.

Jaccottet, Philippe. *L'Entretien des Muses. Chroniques de poésie*. Paris: Gallimard, 1968.

———. *Poésie 1946–1967*. Preface by Jean Starobinski. Paris: Gallimard, Collection Poésie, 1971.

———. *Rilke par lui-même*. Paris: Seuil, 1970.

———. *La Semaison*. Paris: Gallimard, 1971.

Jameson, Fredric. *The Prison-House of Language: A Critical Account of Structuralism and Russian Formalism*. Princeton, N.J.: Princeton University Press, 1972.

The Jerome Biblical Commentary. Englewood Cliffs, N.J.: Prentice-Hall, 1968.

Jonas, Hans. *The Gnostic Religion:.The Message of the Alien God and the Beginnings of Christianity*. 2d ed. enlarged. Boston: Beacon Press, 1963.

Jousse, Marcel. *L'Anthropologie du geste*. Paris: Gallimard, 1974.

Jouve, Pierre-Jean. "Inconscient, spiritualité et catastrophe." In *Noces*, suivi de *Sueur de sang*. Paris: Gallimard, Collection Poésie, 1966.

———. *Noces*, suivi de *Sueur de sang*. Paris: Gallimard, Collection Poésie, 1966.

Jung, C. G. *Answer to Job*. Trans. R. F. C. Hull. Bollingen Series 20. Princeton, N.J.: Princeton University Press, Bollingen Paperback Edition, 1971.

———. *Four Archetypes*. Trans. R. F. C. Hull. Bollingen Series 20. Princeton, N.J.: Princeton University Press, Bollingen Paperback Edition, 1970.

———. *The Portable Jung*. Trans. R. F. C. Hull. Ed. with Intro. by Joseph Campbell. New York: Viking Press, Penguin Books, 1971.

———. "The Psychological Aspects of the Kore." In *The Archetypes and the Collective Unconscious*, vol. 9, pt. 1 of *The Collected Works of C. G. Jung*. Trans. R. F. C. Hull. Bollingen Series 20. Princeton, N.J.: Princeton University Press, 1959.

———. *Psychology and Religion*. New Haven: Yale University Press, 1938.

———. *The Spirit in Man, Art, and Literature*. Vol. 15 of *The Collected Works of C. G. Jung*. Trans. R. F. C. Hull. Bollingen Series 20. Princeton, N.J.: Princeton University Press, 1966.

Kierkegaard, Soren. *Concluding Unscientific Postscript*. Trans. David F. Swenson and Walter Lowrie. Princeton, N.J.: Princeton University Press, 1941.

———. *A Kierkegaard Anthology*. Ed. Robert Bretall. New York: The Modern Library, 1946.

Lawler, James R. *The Language of French Symbolism*. Princeton, N.J.: Princeton University Press, 1969.

Lewis, C. S. *The Four Loves*. London: Collins, Fontana Books, 1960.

Lovejoy, Arthur O. *The Great Chain of Being, A Study of the History of an Idea*. New York: Harper and Row, The Academy Library, 1936; Harper Torchbooks, 1960.

Mallarmé, Stéphane. *Correspondance 1862–1871*. Ed. and anno. Henri Mondor. Paris: Gallimard, 1959.

———. *Igitur. Divagations. Un Coup de dés*. Preface by Yves Bonnefoy. Paris: Gallimard, Collection Poésie, 1976.

———. *Œuvres complètes*. Ed. and anno. Henri Mondor et G. Jean-Aubry. Paris: Gallimard, Bibliothèque de la Pléiade, 1945.

————. *Poésies*. Preface by Jean-Paul Sartre. Paris: Gallimard, Collection Poésie, 1978.

Mansuy, Michel. *Gaston Bachelard et les éléments*. Paris: José Corti, 1967.

Marty, Martin E. *A Short History of Christianity*. New York: William Collins and World Publishing Co., Fontana Books, 1959.

Merton, Thomas. *Zen and the Birds of Appetite*. New York: New Directions, 1968.

Morisot, Jean-Claude. *Claudel et Rimbaud: Étude de transformations*. Paris: Minard, 1976.

Nadeau, Maurice. *Histoire du Surréalisme*. Paris: Seuil, 1964.

The Nag Hammadi Library. Ed. James M. Robinson. San Francisco: Harper and Row Publishers, 1981.

New Catholic Encyclopedia. New York: McGraw-Hill Book Co., 1967.

The New Century Classical Handbook. Ed. Catherine B. Avery. New York: Appleton-Century-Crofts, 1962.

The New Oxford Annotated Bible with Apocrypha. Ed. Herbert G. May and Bruce M. Metzger. New York: Oxford University Press, 1973.

Nietzsche, Friedrich. *Beyond Good and Evil: Prelude to a Philosophy of the Future*. Trans., with commentary, by Walter Kaufmann. New York: Random House, Vintage Books, 1966.

————. *The Birth of Tragedy* and *The Case of Wagner*. Trans., with commentary, by Walter Kaufmann. New York: Random House, Vintage Books, 1967.

Nygren, Anders. *Agape and Eros*. Authorized trans. by Philip S. Watson. London: Society for Promoting Christian Knowledge, 1953.

Outka, Gene. *Agape: An Ethical Analysis*. New Haven: Yale University Press, 1972.

Ovid. *Metamorphoses*. Trans. Rolfe Humphreis. Bloomington: Indiana University Press, 1955.

The Oxford Companion to Classical Literature. Comp. and ed. Sir Paul Harvey. Oxford: The Clarendon Press, 1937.

Pagels, Elaine. *The Gnostic Gospels*. New York: Random House, 1979; Vintage Books, 1981.

Plato. *Plato's Cosmology: The "Timaeus" of Plato*. Trans., with commentary, by F. M. Cornford. Indianapolis: Bobbs-Merrill Co., 1975.

Plotinus. *The Enneads*. 3d ed., rev. B. S. Page. Trans. Stephen MacKenna. Foreword by E. R. Dodds and Intro. by Paul Henry, S.J. London: Faber and Faber, 1956.

Poe, Edgar Allan. *Selected Writings of Edgar Allan Poe*. Ed. Edward H. Davidson. Cambridge, Mass.: Houghton Mifflin Company, Riverside Press, 1956.

Poems and Texts. An Anthology of French Poems, Translations and Interviews with Ponge, Follain, Guillevic, Frénaud, Bonnefoy, Du Bouchet, Roche, and Pleynet. Ed. Serge Gavronsky. New York: October House, 1969.

La Poésie contemporaine de la langue française depuis 1945. Ed. Serge Brindeau. Paris: Editions Saint-Germain-des-Prés, 1973.

Ponge, Francis. *Le Parti pris des choses*, précédé de *Douze Petits Écrits* et suivi de *Proêmes*. Paris: Gallimard, Collection Poésie, 1979.

Popol Vuh. The Sacred Book of the Ancient Quiche Maya. English Version by Delia Goetz and Sylvanus G. Morley from the translation of Adrián Recinos. Norman: University of Oklahoma Press, 1950.

Proust, Marcel. *À la recherche du temps perdu.* 3 vols. Texte établi et présenté par Pierre Clarac et André Ferré. Paris: Gallimard, Bibliothèque de la Pléiade, 1954.

Quillet, Pierre. *Bachelard.* Présentation, choix de textes, bibliographie. Paris: Seghers, 1964.

Raymond, Marcel. *De Baudelaire au Surréalisme.* Paris: José Corti, 1940.

————. *Mémorial.* Paris: José Corti, 1971.

Renssalaer, Lee W. *"Ut Pictura Poesis": The Humanistic Theory of Painting.* New York: Norton, 1967.

Richard, Jean-Pierre. *Onze Études sur la poésie moderne.* Paris: Seuil, 1964.

Rimbaud, Arthur. *Œuvres.* Édition de Suzanne Bernard. Paris: Garnier Frères, 1960.

————. *Rimbaud: Complete Works, Selected Letters.* Trans., Intro., and Notes by Wallace Fowlie. Chicago: University of Chicago Press, 1966.

Robbe-Grillet, Alain. *Pour un nouveau roman.* Paris: Les Éditions de Minuit, Collection "Critique," 1963.

Rougemont, Denis de. *L'Amour et l'Occident.* Paris: Plon, 1946.

St. John of the Cross. *Aphorismes de Saint Jean de la Croix.* Texte établi et traduit d'après le manuscrit autographe d'Andújar et précédé d'une introduction par Jean Baruzi. Bordeaux: Feret et Fils, 1924.

————. *The Collected Works of St. John of the Cross.* Trans. Kieran Kavanaugh, O.C.D., and Otilio Rodriguez, O.C.D., with Intros. by Kieran Kavanaugh, O.C.D. Garden City, N.Y.: Doubleday and Co., 1964.

La Sainte Bible, traduite en français sous la direction de l'École Biblique de Jerusalem. Paris: Les Éditions du Cerf, 1961.

Sarraute, Nathalie. *L'Ere du soupçon.* Paris: Gallimard, 1956.

Shakespeare, William. *The Complete Plays and Poems of William Shakespeare.* The New Cambridge Edition. Ed. and anno. William Allan Neilson and Charles Jarvis Hill. Cambridge: Houghton Mifflin Co., The Riverside Press, 1942.

————. *The Riverside Shakespeare.* Boston: Houghton Mifflin Co., 1974.

————. *The Winter's Tale.* Ed. Frank Kermode. New York: New American Library, Signet Classics, 1963.

Shestov, Lev. *Athens and Jerusalem.* Trans. Bernard Martin. Athens: Ohio University Press, 1966.

————. *Potestas Clavium.* Trans. with Intro. by Bernard Martin. Athens: Ohio University Press, 1968.

————. *A Shestov Anthology.* Ed. with Intro. by Bernard Martin. Athens: Ohio University Press, 1970.

Spivak, Gayatri Chakravorty. "Translator's Preface" to Jacques Derrida, *Of Grammatology.* Baltimore: Johns Hopkins University Press, 1976.

Starkie, Enid. *Arthur Rimbaud.* London: Faber and Faber, 1961.

————. *Baudelaire.* Norfolk, Conn.: New Directions, 1958.

Steiner, George. *After Babel: Aspects of Language and Translation.* London: Oxford University Press, 1975.

Suzuki, D. T. *An Introduction to Zen Buddhism.* Foreword by C. G. Jung. New York: Grove Press, An Evergreen Black Cat Book, 1964.

———. *What Is Zen?* Two Unpublished Essays and a Reprint of the First Edition of *The Essence of Buddhism.* New York: Harper and Row, Perennial Library, 1972.

———. *Zen Buddhism. Selected Writings of D. T. Suzuki.* Ed. William Barrett. Garden City, N.Y.: Doubleday and Co., Doubleday Anchor Books, 1956.

Valéry, Paul. *Œuvres.* Vol. 1. Ed. and anno. Jean Hytier. Paris: Gallimard, Bibliothèque de la Pléiade, 1957.

———. *Paul Valéry: An Anthology.* Selected, with Intro., by James R. Lawler from *The Collected Works of Paul Valéry,* ed. Jackson Mathews. Princeton, N.J.: Princeton University Press, 1976.

Ward, J. W. C. *A History of the Early Church to A.D. 500.* London: Methuen and Co., 1937.

Who's Who in the Ancient World: A Handbook to the Survivors of the Greek and Roman Classics. Selected, with Intro., by Betty Radice. Middlesex, England: Penguin Books, 1971.

Wilson, Edmund. *Axel's Castle.* New York: Charles Scribner's Sons, 1936.

Yeats, W. B. *The Collected Poems of W. B. Yeats.* Definitive Edition, with the Author's Final Revisions. New York: Macmillan Publishing Co., 1956.

———. "Poems." Trans. Yves Bonnefoy. *Argile* 1 (winter 1973):65–93.

Index